ARIZONA WATER POLICY

Management Innovations
in an Urbanizing, Arid Region

ARIZONA WATER POLICY

Management Innovations in an Urbanizing, Arid Region

EDITED BY
BONNIE G. COLBY
AND KATHARINE L. JACOBS

RFF PRESS
RESOURCES FOR THE FUTURE

New York • London

An RFF Press book

For a full list of publications please contact:
Earthscan
2 Park Square, Milton Park, Abingdon, Oxon OX14 4RN
711 Third Avenue, New York, NY 10017

Earthscan is an imprint of the Taylor & Francis Group, an informa business

Library of Congress Cataloging-in-Publication Data

    Arizona water policy : management innovations in an urbanizing, arid region / edited by Bonnie G. Colby and Katharine L. Jacobs. — 1st ed.
      p. cm.
    Includes bibliographical references and index.
    ISBN 1-933115-34-3 (hardcover : alk. paper) 1.
    Water-supply—Government policy—Arizona. 2.
    Water-supply—Arizona—Management. I. Colby, Bonnie G. II. Jacobs, Katharine L.
    TD224.A6A75 2006
    363.6'109791—dc22   2006024718

The paper in this book meets the guidelines for permanence and durability of the Committee on Production Guidelines for Book Longevity of the Council on Library Resources. This book was typeset by Peter Lindeman. It was copyedited by Paula Berard. The cover was designed by Maggie Powell.

Cover photos, left to right, provided by Nancy Bannister, iStockphoto, and Paul N. Wilson.

ISBN 1-933115-34-3 (cloth)

About Resources for the Future *and* RFF Press

RESOURCES FOR THE FUTURE (RFF) improves environmental and natural resource policymaking worldwide through independent social science research of the highest caliber. Founded in 1952, RFF pioneered the application of economics as a tool for developing more effective policy about the use and conservation of natural resources. Its scholars continue to employ social science methods to analyze critical issues concerning pollution control, energy policy, land and water use, hazardous waste, climate change, biodiversity, and the environmental challenges of developing countries.

RFF PRESS supports the mission of RFF by publishing book-length works that present a broad range of approaches to the study of natural resources and the environment. Its authors and editors include RFF staff, researchers from the larger academic and policy communities, and journalists. Audiences for publications by RFF Press include all of the participants in the policymaking process—scholars, the media, advocacy groups, NGOs, professionals in business and government, and the public.

Resources for the Future

ISSUES IN WATER RESOURCE POLICY

Ariel Dinar, World Bank, Series Editor

Books in the *Issues in Water Resource Policy* series are intended to be accessible to a broad range of scholars, practitioners, policymakers, and general readers. Each book focuses on critical issues in water policy at a specific subnational, national, or regional level, with the mission to draw upon and integrate the best scholarly and professional expertise concerning the physical, ecological, economic, institutional, political, legal, and social dimensions of water use. The interdisciplinary approach of the series, along with an emphasis on real world situations and on problems and challenges that recur globally, are intended to enhance our ability to apply the full body of knowledge that we have about water resources—at local, country, and international levels.

For comments and editorial inquiries about the series, please contact *waterpolicy@rff.org*.

For information about other titles in the series, please visit *www.Rffpress.org/water*.

The *Issues in Water Resource Policy* series is dedicated to the memory of Guy LeMoigne, a founding member of the Advisory Committee.

Dedication

We dedicate this volume to our families and all who have had confidence in us. Your support has brought us to where we are today. Also, to the resource managers who take personal risks to make the tough long-term choices and are willing to bear the consequences. Finally, to our current and former students. The future depends on your foresight and leadership.

Contents

Figures and Tables

Foreword

In February 2006, Phoenix, Arizona, already in the grips of a prolonged drought, broke its own record for consecutive days without rain. By the time this dry spell ended, Phoenix had experienced 143 consecutive days without rainfall. This drought attracted considerable attention in the media as it served to highlight the acute scarcity of water that is characteristic of Arizona and the southwestern United States. Indeed, to those from moister climes, Arizona and some of its sister states appear to suffer from permanent drought. However, in spite of the severe constraints on the availability of water, Arizona has experienced explosive population growth over the past 50 years, and Phoenix, where average annual rainfall is only 7 inches, has become the fourth largest city in the nation. How did this happen? And can the explosive growth, which is expected to continue, be sustained with the meagerest of indigenous water supplies?

This is a book about water in Arizona, and its contributors are among the most distinguished of students of water resources in Arizona. In the pages that follow, they describe the water resources of the state; outline the historical, economic, and social contexts in which water policy has been made for Arizona; and characterize the unique institutions that Arizona has devised to allow available water supplies to be stretched far beyond what was thought possible in previous eras. The essence of the story is that Arizona has been able to circumvent the constraints imposed by its accustomed aridity through the development and importation of supplemental water supplies and through significant groundwater overdraft. Though the development of imported supplies was originally conceived without particular reference to groundwater overdraft, the two water routes have become inextricably linked because imported supplies are now seen as the primary remedy for overdraft and a crucial element in the quest for a sustainable water supply.

Arizona's apparent success in managing limited water supplies could not have occurred without the development of a host of institutions that govern and manage water. As chronicled in this volume, these institutions were created ad seriatim first in response to acute water scarcity, and second, to address the threat posed by continuation of unsustainable groundwater extractions and threats to water quality. One of the most important lessons to emerge from the history related here is the ultimate importance of institutions and institutional arrangements in managing water resources. In fact, the effectiveness of institutions outweighs in importance technological innovations in managing water scarcity. Thus, the failure to design institutions that formally acknowledge the crucial hydrological linkages between groundwater and surface water may foretell future levels of use and exploitation that are not sustainable. Also, despite a stunningly effective groundwater quality protection program, the failure to link water quality and quantity through institutions could lead to a future of shrinking supplies of water of appropriate quality.

There are other important lessons and issues that emerge from this story. They include the need to:

1. integrate land use and water resource planning and management;
2. reflect the scarcity value of water in virtually all decisions;
3. practice flexibility and adaptiveness in the management of water in the face of global change;
4. define the concept of sustainability in a useful and operational way; and
5. accommodate changing social values and to address the plight of indigenous peoples, who are often denied access to the simplest of water supply and sanitation services.

As the chapters in this volume show, Arizona's past success in addressing its water problems in no way ensures that it will be similarly successful in confronting the daunting array of problems that loom in the future.

The story that the contributors and editors of this book relate is not a parochial story about some parochial corner of North America. The conditions and circumstances in Arizona mirror those found throughout the world. Consider a land where a growing population and a growing economy press hard on available water supplies; past progress has been fueled in part on groundwater overdraft; supplemental surface supplies to offset overdraft and support growth are no longer available; agriculture accounts for between two-thirds and four-fifths of the consumptive use; prices, the conventional signals of scarcity, are largely absent with water; environmental uses of water are now also a strong competitor for supplies; and indigenous peoples, long cut off from traditional sources of water, are demanding equitable treatment. Such a land could be Arizona, Australia, India, the Middle East, northern China, or North Africa. And these characteristics are not just those of the arid and semiarid lands of the world. They apply equally to many of the humid regions, especially those where precipitation is seasonal. Water scarcity is becoming every bit as much of a problem in southeast Asia and other humid regions as it is in the world's arid and semiarid regions.

The world stands on the threshold of facing the serious consequences of failing to husband and manage its water resources carefully and responsibly. As we seek to address the multitude of water problems that will emerge in the coming decades, we will often be forced to approach them through trial and error. To a large extent, our experience in managing water scarcity in places like Arizona can help to guide us. We are indebted to the authors and editors of this volume for organizing and analyzing an important body of experience in one of the most arid corners of the globe. The lessons of success and failure from Arizona stand to benefit us all.

Henry Vaux, Jr.
Berkeley, California

Contributors

MARK T. ANDERSON is currently the director of the South Dakota Water Science Center of the U.S. Geological Survey (USGS), in Rapid City, South Dakota. Before 2006, he was associate director of the U.S. Geological Survey's Arizona Water Science Center in Tucson. Among many other projects, Anderson leads and directs the work of USGS scientists and, while in Arizona, he was responsible for developing and overseeing hydrologic investigations on groundwater, surface water, and water quality problems. From 1999 through 2001, Anderson was a senior policy analyst at the Office of Science and Technology Policy (OSTP) in the executive office of the president, including portions of the Clinton and George W. Bush administrations.

JACK L. AUGUST, JR. serves as the executive director of the Arizona Historical Foundation at Arizona State University, where he teaches graduate courses in water policy and management. He has taught at the University of Houston, University of Northern British Columbia, Prescott College, and Northern Arizona University, where his courses focused on the history of the American West and environmental history. August is a former Fulbright Scholar, National Endowment for the Humanities Research Fellow, and Pulitzer Prize nominee in history for his volume *Vision in the Desert: Carl Hayden and Hydropolitics in the American Southwest.* He has served as a historian and expert witness in the Natural Resources Section of the Arizona Attorney General's Office, where his work focused on Indian versus non-Indian water rights issues and state trust lands. He has also worked in that capacity for Arizona State University, the cities of Tempe, Buckeye, and Tucson in Arizona, and private law firms.

BONNIE G. COLBY is a professor of agricultural and resource economics at the University of Arizona. Colby's expertise is in the economics of interjurisdictional water disputes, water rights valuation, water transactions, and water policy. She has written more than 100 journal articles and 5 books, including the books *Braving the Currents: Resolving Conflicts over the River Basins of the West; Water Markets in Theory and Practice;* and *Negotiating Tribal Water Rights.* In addition to her teaching and research, Colby advises public- and private-sector organizations throughout the western United States on drought preparedness, water acquisitions, and water pricing. She has provided invited testimony to state legislatures, city and tribal councils, federal and state court officials, and the U.S. Congress. She served on the National Academy of Science Committee on Western Water Management, the Committee on Glen Canyon Dam, and the Committee on Upper Mississippi River Management.

MICHAEL A. CRIMMINS is on the faculty of the Department of Soil, Water, and Environmental Science at the University of Arizona and is an extension specialist in climate science for Arizona's Cooperative Extension. He worked as a private-sector environmental scientist, focusing on hydroclimatology, urban and agricultural nonpoint source runoff modeling, remote sensing, and geographic information systems applications for watershed management. Crimmins now works with local, state, and federal land managers across Arizona to access and use climate information for natural resource management decisionmaking. He conducts research in the areas of wildfire climatology, drought impacts monitoring, and the development of climate science applications for resource managers.

GEORGE B. FRISVOLD joined the faculty at the University of Arizona in 1997. He has been a visiting scholar at the National Institute of Rural Development in Hyderabad, India, a lecturer at Johns Hopkins University, and chief of the Resource and Environmental Policy Branch of USDA's Economic Research Service. His research interests include domestic and international environmental policy, as well as the causes and consequences of technological change in agriculture. In 1995 and 1996, Frisvold served on the senior staff of the President's Council of Economic Advisors, with responsibility for agricultural, natural resource, and international trade issues.

GRADY GAMMAGE, JR. is an attorney specializing in land use planning and real estate law, an adjunct professor at the Arizona State University College of Architecture and Environmental Design and the College of Law, and a senior fellow at ASU's Morrison Institute for Public Policy. He teaches classes on land use regulation, property rights, and historic preservation planning. Gammage graduated from Stanford Law School and founded the Gammage and Burnham law firm in 1983. He formerly served as chairman of the board of the Central

Arizona Project. He also served on the Governor's Water Management Commission and the Arizona Water Banking Authority.

GREGG GARFIN is the project manager for the Climate Assessment for the Southwest (CLIMAS), a NOAA-funded regional center designed to identify and evaluate climate impacts and climate services useful in coping with climate-related risks. His research interests include climate variability, drought, and the effects of climate on society. Garfin is cochair of the Arizona Drought Monitoring Technical Committee and has been instrumental in the design and implementation of Arizona's drought plan. He is a member of the team for the development of a National Integrated Drought Information System. He is trained as a climatologist, dendroclimatologist, and geographer.

ROBERT GLENNON is the Morris K. Udall Professor of Law and Public Policy in the Rogers College of Law at the University of Arizona. He has more than 30 years of professional experience and specializes in constitutional law, American legal history, and water law. Glennon is the recipient of the Mortar Board Citation Award from the University of Arizona Mortar Board Honor Society, the Leslie F. and Patricia Bell Faculty Award from the Rogers College of Law, and two National Science Foundation grants. He has served as a water policy adviser to Pima County, Arizona, and as a commentator and analyst for television and radio programs. Glennon is author of *Water Follies: Groundwater Pumping and the Fate of America's Fresh Waters.*

CHARLES G. GRAF served as the deputy director of the Water Quality Division at the Arizona Department of Environmental Quality from 1998 until his retirement in 2006. Currently, he represents the department in his role as associate director of the Arizona Water Institute. He received a B.S.E. degree in engineering science from Arizona State University and is a registered geologist in Arizona. He has worked in engineering, hydrological, and water resources positions with the U.S. Forest Service, Arizona Department of Water Resources, and Arizona Department of Environmental Quality. Before starting to work for the Department of Environmental Quality in 1984, Graf managed a regional water resources office as a hydrogeological consultant in the Sultanate of Oman.

PATRICK J. GRAHAM is the executive director of the Nature Conservancy of Arizona, overseeing the extensive work of the conservancy in this arid state. He joined the Nature Conservancy's team as the state director in Arizona in July 2001. Previously, he served in a variety of leadership positions during 25 years with the Montana Department of Fish, Wildlife and Parks and was appointed director of the department in 1993 by the governor of Montana, in which position he served for 8 years. The Nature Conservancy of Arizona is responsible for conserving land and water in one of the most biologically rich states in the nation.

JAMES M. HOLWAY is the associate director of the Global Institute of Sustainability at Arizona State University. He is also a professor of practice in civil and environmental engineering, a senior research fellow with the Morrison Institute for Public Policy, and the ASU coordinator for the Arizona Water Institute. Holway previously served as assistant director of the Arizona Department of Water Resources. His responsibilities included overseeing the Water Management Division and its five regional active management area offices as well as the state's conservation, assured water supply, recharge, well permitting, and groundwater and surface-water rights programs. Before his 12 years with the Arizona Department of Water Resources, he coordinated environmental programs for the Regional Council of Governments in Baltimore, Maryland. Holway earned both Ph.D. and master's degrees in regional planning from the University of North Carolina.

KATHARINE L. JACOBS is the executive director of the Arizona Water Institute, a consortium of the three Arizona state universities focusing on water-related research, technical assistance, education, and technology transfer related to water supply sustainability. She is also the deputy director of the National Science Foundation's Center for Sustainability of Arid Region Hydrology and Riparian Areas at the University of Arizona and has been a professor and specialist at the Department of Soil, Water and Environmental Science and Water Resources Research Center. She has more than 20 years of experience as a water manager for the Arizona Department of Water Resources, including 14 years as director of the Tucson Active Management Area. Her research interests include water policy, connecting science and decisionmaking, stakeholder engagement, use of climate information for water management applications, rural water issues, and drought planning.

STANLEY A. LEAKE is the project chief of the Lower Colorado Region Water Availability Study in the Tucson office of the Arizona Water Science Center of the U.S. Geological Survey. He recently completed a five-year study of groundwater and surface-water interactions and their effects on the availability and sustainability of groundwater supplies in the Southwest. The project included regional synthesis of information on the interaction of groundwater and surface water, development of improved methods of quantifying inflow to groundwater systems and application of these recharge methods in the Southwest, assessments of the effects of groundwater development on riparian systems, and assessments of the effects of climate variations on recharge to and discharge from groundwater systems.

SHARON B. MEGDAL is the director of the Water Resources Research Center and a professor of agricultural and resource economics at the University of Arizona. Her work focuses on state and regional water resource management and policy and includes teaching a graduate course on Arizona water policy. She previously served on the economics faculty at the University of Arizona and at Northern Arizona University. From 1985 until 1987, she was a member of the Arizona Corporation Commission. She was executive director of the Santa Cruz Valley Water District and has also served on the Water Quality Appeals Board, the Arizona State Transportation Board, the Governor's Water Management Commission, and the Arizona Medical Board.

ROBERT NEEDHAM was raised on a corn farm in central Nebraska. He received his bachelor's degree in agriculture and business from the University of Nebraska in 1999. Following his undergraduate program, Needham farmed for two years and worked for the U.S. Department of Agriculture for another two years. He earned his master of science degree in agriculture and resource economics from the University of Arizona in 2005. He is currently a self-employed consultant in agriculture, natural resources, and economic development issues.

MICHAEL J. PEARCE is an attorney with the law firm of Fennemore Craig, P.C., in Phoenix, Arizona, specializing in water-related land development issues, interstate stream disputes, the federal Endangered Species Act, the National Environmental Policy Act, Clean Water Act compliance, and Colorado River matters. He served as the chief counsel of the Arizona Department of Water Resources for more than 7 years, representing Arizona in connection with interstate and international stream issues, Native American water rights settlements, the Central Arizona Project, groundwater management, surface-water rights administration, and dam safety enforcement. He is the editor of the American Bar Association Section of Environment, Energy, and Resources' *Trends* publication and chair of the Arizona State Bar Environment and Natural Resources Law Section.

KATHERINE PITTENGER recently completed her master's degree in agricultural and resource economics at the University of Arizona, working with Bonnie Colby on economic strategies to enhance dry-year water supply reliability. She is pursuing her doctoral degree at the University of California, Davis.

DONALD R. POOL is a hydrologist for the U.S. Geological Survey's Water Science Center in Tucson, Arizona. He received a master of science degree in hydrology from the University of Arizona in 1986. His expertise is in the hydrogeology of Arizona basins, geophysical methods in groundwater investigations, and groundwater flow modeling. He has written many reports describing the hydrogeology of regions in Arizona. He has also written or cowritten journal articles describing applications of temporal gravity methods to monitoring groundwater storage change and climate and recharge relations in southeast Arizona.

DANA R. SMITH received a law degree in May 2006 from the University of Arizona's James E. Rogers College of Law. While in law school, she was an articles editor for the *Arizona Journal of International and Comparative Law* and a research assistant for Bonnie Colby. Currently, she works as an attorney for the Southern Nevada Water Authority.

KAREN L. SMITH is the deputy director of the Arizona Department of Water Resources. Before this, she served as the water quality director for the Arizona Department of Environmental Quality for 7 years and also worked for the Salt River Project for 16 years in a variety of positions, including water resources management. She holds a Ph.D. in history from the University of California, Santa Barbara, specializing in the history of technology, and has written several works on water resources, including *The Magnificent Experiment: Building the Salt River Reclamation Project*. Smith is currently an adjunct professor at Arizona State University. She has served as president of the Association of State and Interstate Water Pollution Control Administrators, and on the board of directors of the Arizona Center for Disability Law.

LINDA S. STITZER is a program manager in the Office of Statewide Planning at the Arizona Department of Water Resources, where she has worked since 1986. Before her current position, she was the planning supervisor and acting director of the Tucson Active Management Area office. She is the Arizona representative to the Border Governors' Conference Water Committee and is project manager of the Arizona Water Atlas, a compilation of water-related information for the state.

PAUL N. WILSON has been a professor of agricultural and resource economics at the University of Arizona since 1994. His teaching and research programs focus on the economic dimensions of agribusiness organization and management, irrigated agriculture, environmental management, and global hunger. Wilson has worked in the private and public sectors, including long-term professional activities overseas in Costa Rica, the Dominican Republic, Mexico, and Nicaragua. The U.S. Department of Agriculture, Bureau of Reclamation, Office of the Governor of Arizona, Arizona Department of Water Resources, and the Mexican Foundation for Rural Development have funded Professor Wilson's research. He has published more than 150 professional articles and papers.

Acknowledgments

The editors wish to express sincere gratitude to Dana Smith for her skillful and dedicated work in bringing together this volume. Without her excellent knowledge of Arizona water policy, her careful eye for detail, and her thoroughness in communicating among the various contributors, this book project would have been a great burden instead of an enjoyable collaboration. Nancy Bannister provided invaluable support with her expertise on graphics, maps, figures, and photos. We also thank Sharon Megdal, Director of the Arizona Water Resources Research Center, and Jim Shuttleworth, Director of the University of Arizona Center for Sustainability of Semi-Arid Hydrology and Riparian Areas (SAHRA), for their financial support and personal encouragement for this project.

We appreciate the hard work of Dr. Ariel Dinar, World Bank, in bringing this book series together and inviting us to contribute an Arizona volume. We enjoyed working with Don Reisman and the staff at RFF Press and thank them for their efforts in the publication process. Finally, we sincerely appreciate the participation of our chapter authors and their substantial intellectual and collegial contributions to this book project.

This work was supported by the University of Arizona, the Technology and Research Initiative Fund, the Water Sustainability Program through the Water Resources Research Center, and SAHRA under the STC Program of the National Science Foundation, Agreement No. EAR–9876800.

1

Water Management Challenges in an Arid Region

Key Policy Issues

Katharine L. Jacobs and Bonnie G. Colby

The central water management challenge for Arizona, as for many other arid and semiarid regions throughout the world, is sustainability of water supplies in the context of intense population growth pressures and increasing competition for water. The state has burgeoning urban areas, large agricultural regions, water-dependent habitats for endangered fish and wildlife, and a growing demand for water-based recreation. A multiyear drought and the consequences of climate-related water supply variability complicate the already intense competition for water. Arizona's water management system is unique, in part because of the "hydropolitics" of multiple water-related incidents in Arizona's history, and in part because of the unusual framework of the 1980 Groundwater Management Act. Arizona's complex body of water law illustrates the important and sometimes conflicting roles that federal, tribal, state, and municipal jurisdictions play in water management and the delicate balance between the judicial, legislative, and administrative branches of government. This book explores Arizona's water management context and its innovations to extract important themes that have applicability more broadly in arid and semiarid areas around the globe.

As Chapters 2 and 3 relate, the competition to have favored water uses protected has shaped the development of the state of Arizona and its institutions. The unique qualities of water as both a public and private good and an evolving commodity have been played out in Arizona's history of shaping a harsh arid environment into a place habitable for large numbers of people. Early in Arizona's history, water management policies were directed at promoting irrigated agriculture. However, as the nature of the state's economy and population has changed, the focus of Arizona's hydropolitics has moved to accommodating explosive urban growth. Arizona's water politics illustrate the "us and them" nature of water in modern societies. Those with whom we readily share water are "us," and those who seek to take our water are "them," the enemy. Currently, Arizona is known for its unique groundwater management act, for its innovative underground storage and water banking programs, and for having the largest number of congressionally approved tribal water rights settlements of any state in the United States.

The backdrop for our discussion of Arizona's water management policies and institutions is the state's physical and hydrogeologic conditions, which are discussed in Chapter 4. Arizona's natural water supply consists of surface water and groundwater contained in vast underground aquifers in groundwater basins throughout the state. The state's renewable surface-water supply is largely developed, and few opportunities remain for further enhancement or augmentation of the supply through dam or reservoir building (Figure 1-1).

Because water flows in Arizona streams and rivers are variable and essentially fully allocated to existing water users, much of Arizona relies on groundwater pumping. However, the rates of water storage and aquifer depletion vary across the state and its three water resource provinces, depending on the physical properties of the groundwater aquifer. Though surface-water resources are monitored by stream gages, monitoring the recharge, storage, and depletion conditions for groundwater is more difficult. Consistent long-term monitoring of aquifer conditions is critical to sustainable management of aquifers. This measurement challenge is a component of the complexity involved in meeting the goals of the 1980 Groundwater Management Act, which is designed to bring excessive groundwater pumping in specified areas within the state to a safe-yield level.

Much has been learned about how Arizona's climate varied in the past, including evidence of droughts that exceed, in length and severity alike, any droughts recorded in the instrumental record of the past 100 years. However, there are still major challenges in integrating this new knowledge into the water management system. As Chapter 5 explains, the uncertainty of future water management conditions is exacerbated by the issue of global warming because although today's global circulation models yield strong evidence that Arizona's climate is warming and is likely to continue to do so, the evidence about whether the future will bring more or less precipitation is inconclusive. As in many other parts of the world, in Arizona there is a tendency to study such problems rather than making decisions that are likely to reduce future risks, despite relatively obvious evidence that water supplies are being managed in an unsustainable manner in some regions. When the political stakes are high, there is commonly a call for more studies rather than for action. However, as Chapter 6 suggests, water transactions and transfers between agricultural and urban water users can be a key management technique in times of drought.

Though the focus of many Arizona water management techniques is on protecting water supplies for farming or human use, the state also faces critical issues related to environmental uses. As Chapter 7 relates, there is a dichotomy between the high value the average Arizonan places on scenic

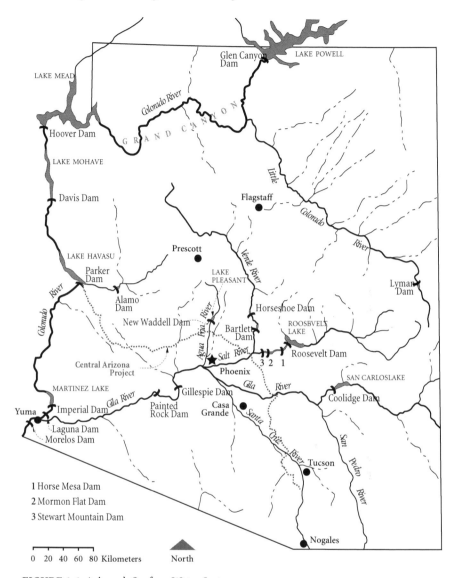

FIGURE 1-1. Arizona's Surface-Water Systems

beauty, recreation, and habitat protection and the virtual lack of protection of such areas in the legal arena. The limited amount of protection afforded to environmental water uses in the Arizona water rights system is in part due to the strong historic focus on adequacy of water supplies for human consumptive uses, with virtually no state laws in place to address the protection of riparian areas. At this time, the only statute that has a significant impact in these areas is the Endangered Species Act of 1973. Chapter 8 explores how Arizona's bifurcated legal system—which manages surface water and groundwater through separate statutes—essentially prevents meaningful protection of surface-water flows and riparian habitats in areas where groundwater base flow provides a significant contribution to these habitats. Whereas Chapters 7 and 8 focus on the need for water to fulfill environmental demands, Chapter 9 explores Arizona's water quality programs, which benefit both environmental and human needs.

A major current concern for water managers throughout the state involves water supplies for population growth, but as Chapter 10 discusses, agricultural water use continues to be by far the largest consumptive water use in the state. There are state-level programs that are intended to limit agricultural water use (or at least increase the efficiency of farming operations) within the active management areas (AMAs). However, federal subsidies and economic conditions appear to have greater influence on total agricultural water use than do the state conservation programs. A related issue is that Arizona's water laws are quite limiting in the context of providing the flexibility that might be desirable for leasing of agricultural water rights in a manner that facilitates municipal drought responses, though they have been successful at protecting the agricultural economy.

But Arizona has multiple innovative institutions that are designed to ensure long-term water supplies, many of these do not have broad applicability across the state. Rather, they are focused primarily within areas that historically had the most significant water supply issues, the five AMAs that are located in the central and southern parts of the state (Figure 1-2). As described in Chapter 11, even within the AMAs, it is likely that the mechanisms currently in place are inadequate to ensure renewable water supply availability in the long term for some categories of municipal users. An area of particular concern that is mentioned in Chapter 13 and several other chapters in this book is the Central Arizona Groundwater Replenishment District, which is designed exclusively to replenish overdrafted groundwater associated with new housing subdivisions in the AMAs.

As discussed in Chapter 12, additional statewide and local water management challenges include inadequate access to data, limited public agency funding, and uncertainties in the climate regime. Although in multiple areas of the state water supply and water quality information are well developed, in other areas little is known, particularly about groundwater conditions and the quantities of water available for extraction on a sustainable basis. In addition, even in areas for which there are relatively rich data, such as the AMAs, the San Pedro River basin, and the Verde River basin, data are stored in multiple agencies and are not easily retrievable in a meaningful and useful format.

Difficulties in funding and providing technical support for effective long-range planning, drought planning, and water conservation programs are ongoing issues and are keenly felt in the rural areas of the state. The key state agencies for water management, the Arizona Department of Water Resources and the Arizona Department of Environmental Quality, have been seriously

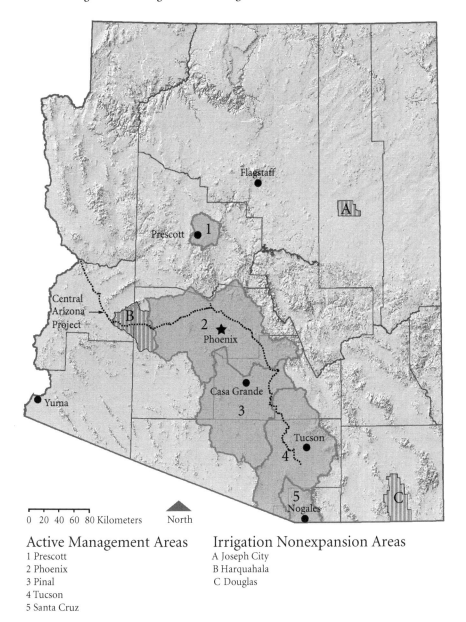

Active Management Areas
1 Prescott
2 Phoenix
3 Pinal
4 Tucson
5 Santa Cruz

Irrigation Nonexpansion Areas
A Joseph City
B Harquahala
C Douglas

FIGURE 1-2. Arizona's Active Management and Irrigation Nonexpansion Areas

constrained in funding and staffing for many years, and, in some cases, have also been constrained by limited authority. As described in Chapter 12, in rural parts of the state inadequate resources limit the ability to ensure adequate water supplies while also promoting appropriate stewardship of watersheds and long-term planning in the face of uncertainties such as climate change and variability. Funding for infrastructure improvements for water supply and water quality management is particularly critical in many rural parts of Arizona, including the Native American reservations. An economic issue of major proportions throughout the state is the ability of the often rural smaller water providers to meet the new Environmental Protection Agency maximum contaminant level for arsenic.

Chapter 14 covers the challenges that Arizona also faces relating to the resolution of tribal water rights and other interjurisdictional water management conflicts. Arizona has led the nation in resolution of tribal water rights, yet of the 20 tribes that have reservations within the state, only 6 have resolved their water rights through settlement. The largest settlement in the history of the United States, the Gila River Indian Community Settlement, has been approved at the federal level but has not been fully implemented as of the date of this publication. Several major Native American water rights claims are outstanding, including the Navajo, Hopi, and San Carlos Apache water claims.

Arizona faces several transboundary water challenges, as there are multiple aquifers and river systems that are shared with Mexico. The challenges relate to both water quality and water quantity, with particular concerns about untreated wastewater flowing north across the border, the potential for contaminated groundwater to enter the United States, and the obligation of the United States to provide Colorado River water with acceptable salinity levels to Mexico. There are also multiple international, federal–state, and interstate conflicts related to management of the Colorado River; not the least of these is how to manage water deliveries during drought. These conflicts are similar to those on the Rio Grande and multiple other locations throughout the world where rivers and lakes cross national boundaries. As indicated in Chapter 7, recent international participatory discussions regarding options for running the Yuma Desalting Plant in Arizona while still protecting the Cienega de Santa Clara in Mexico may be a prototype for suggested solutions elsewhere around the globe.

Cross-Cutting Issues

Issues that cut across several areas of concern addressed in this book include the following:

- growing demand and finite supplies;
- changing social values;
- safe yield vs. sustainability;
- connecting land use and water supply planning;
- connecting water's value and users' costs;
- climate change and supply variability; and
- framing issues and making choices.

Growing Demand and Finite Supplies

The historical approach to limited water supplies was an engineering solution: building more infrastructure to enhance water availability by moving water from one location to another, with or without storage features. Although there are still areas of the world where building dams and new infrastructure is commonplace, opportunities for water supply augmentation in Arizona are more limited than they have been in the past. Furthermore, the federal dollars that previously subsidized water projects in the western United States are now much harder to acquire. The easy solutions of the past are generally no longer available, meaning that we are in an era of limits relative to the total water supply. This limitation means that the role of both regulation and economics will become more important. Water is more likely to move from lower to higher economic uses, which means that water leasing, water banking, and water transfers will become more common. It also means that the role of federal subsidies in agriculture will become more contentious. There will likely be more conflict, as well as a need for collaborative and innovative solutions to water supply problems.

Changing Social Values

Native American water rights settlements, Endangered Species Act requirements, and recreational needs for in-stream flows are examples of relatively new demands on the overallocated water systems of the western United States. To the extent that such new demands cannot be accommodated without affecting existing water rights, regulatory or economic incentives for some users to give up their water rights are inevitable. However, economic and political dislocations are likely to happen, resulting in increased need for clear articulation of values, as well as the costs and benefits of alternative policy decisions. New water quality regulations also have significant impacts, creating tensions between economic considerations and public and environmental health.

Safe Yield vs. Sustainability

Although safe yield is the management goal within four of the five AMAs, there is increasing awareness that this goal is likely to be insufficient if flowing surface-water and riparian water uses are to be protected. Safe yield focuses exclusively on the long-term water balance within groundwater aquifers, without acknowledging changes that may result in surface flows when groundwater pumping occurs. For the remaining free-flowing rivers of the state, it is clear that safe yield is an inadequate management construct. However, so long as groundwater withdrawals cannot be managed conjunctively with surface water, it is unlikely that even a sustainability management goal would be sufficient actually to protect riparian habitat.

Connecting Land Use and Water Supply Planning

A critical issue throughout the world is the need to connect land use decisions to water supply availability. In general, the issue is not the total quantity of water available relative to the total demand, it is where the demand is located relative to the sources of supply. Arizona has addressed this issue more successfully than virtually any other state, in the context of the assured water supply program within AMAs. This program requires that no new subdivisions can be approved unless there is a 100-year supply of renewable water that is of sufficient quality for the intended uses. The importation of new sources of water through the Central Arizona Project is critical to the success of this approach. Although there are some loopholes in this system, much can be learned from Arizona's experience with this program.

Connecting Water's Value and Users' Costs

Our cheapest source of water in the state is also our most valuable source: groundwater. To the extent that groundwater is generally of higher quality than surface water, requires less treatment before delivery, is virtually always available (unless overdrafted), is stored for free in the aquifer, and has few of the reliability issues associated with surface water, groundwater is often of higher value as a water supply than surface water. Yet, many of the renewable supplies that are critical to achieving our management goals, such as the Central Arizona Project and effluent, are more expensive than groundwater. This inverse relationship between the value of water and its cost is likely one of the primary reasons that the Arizona Groundwater Management Act has such a strong regulatory approach. It is also a reason why the implications and impacts of the subsidies associated with agricultural water use need to be well understood.

Climate Change and Supply Variability

Although the specific implications of climate change on water management in the future are subject to some debate, there is no question that climate variability is already a major challenge. There is also a general consensus that the pace of global change is increasing, whether the issue is land use change, changes in climate conditions, or changes in social conditions. Significant uncertainties exist about future water supply availability, and there is substantial focus on attempts to reduce uncertainty and to understand the sources of uncertainty. A general consensus has emerged that global warming will increase the severity of droughts in the southwestern United States, even in the context of the potential for more intense precipitation events. Snowpack-dependent river systems, such as the Colorado River, have been projected to have significant reductions in average flows, due in part to higher temperatures leading to more rain and less snow, earlier snowmelt, a higher evapotranspiration rate, and lower soil moisture. The combination of a faster rate of change with significant uncertainties requires improved observations and faster integration of scientific information into the water management process.

Framing Issues and Making Choices

The changing conditions described above require close scrutiny of the ability of water management institutions to adapt and innovate. Decisionmaking processes need to become more receptive to changing situations because of improved scientific understanding and changes in public perceptions and values. Water management institutions at all levels will need to become more proactive and strategic to prepare for a future that is inevitably different from the past. Although Arizona has proven to be quite adept and strategic in responding to hydrologic and political imperatives in the past, the pace of innovation will likely need to increase.

This book will outline many of the innovative policy approaches to reconciling competing water needs in a desert environment that the arid state of Arizona has implemented. The state contains rapidly growing cities and towns, large agricultural regions, water-dependent habitat for endangered fish and wildlife, and a burgeoning demand for water-based recreation. Moreover, the entire region is in the grip of a multiyear drought, which poses many challenges to water management institutions. Solving the region's water supply issues requires interstate, tribal, federal, and urban–rural cooperation. This collection of essays by well-known water experts from over a dozen fields of expertise contains important lessons for all arid regions facing competing water demands.

References

Endangered Species Act of 1973. U.S. Code. Vol. 16, sec. 1531 et seq.
Groundwater Management Act of 1980. Arizona Revised Statutes, Title 45, Ch. 2, secs. 401, 403, 411, 461, 491, 452, 454, 511, 576, 591.

2

Shaped by Water

An Arizona Historical Perspective

Jack L. August, Jr. and Grady Gammage, Jr.

Four basic commodities make human existence possible: land, air, sunshine, and water. Where these are present, humans are able to exist and make everything else they need. Of those four commodities, only one is easily captured and transportable: water. The history of Arizona is largely written in the ability to hold, store, and move water.

Land in American society is the quintessential private good—it can be owned. Even as to public land, we think of government as the owner. Air, on the other hand, is the classic common-use good: available to everyone and free for the taking. The "tragedy of the commons" is the conundrum presented by the rational exploitation of a common-use good by any individual, which leads to the unfortunate overexploitation of that commodity by society as a whole (Hardin 1968).

Water has been regarded sometimes as a private-use good (for example, when it is beneath our land and we have the right to pump it up and use it) and sometimes as closer to a common-use good (for example, when it is in a free-flowing river available for capture and use at no cost, but not readily subject to alienation). When water exists in abundance, this distinction does not matter much or may not even be noticed. But when it is scarce, institutions, laws, and societies are structured around its management. The unique qualities of water as a commodity have been played out in Arizona's history of shaping a harsh and arid environment to make it habitable for large numbers of people. The early part of that history is about agriculture. Since the middle of the twentieth century, the hydropolitics of Arizona have turned toward accommodating the increasingly urban nature of the state.

Water, Culture, and Tradition

Soon after the outbreak of war between the United States and Mexico in 1846, Colonel Stephen Watts Kearny and his Army of the West encountered the Pima Indians farming along the Gila River. The invading Americans, en route to their military destination in California, marveled at the agricultural abundance and the extensive irrigation works and realized immediately, as the Spaniards and Mexicans had before them, that irrigation along the river predated the Pimas (Kupel 2003). By the time Spanish explorers of the seventeenth century discovered prehistoric ruins in central Arizona, their builders, the Hohokam, had been gone for more than 200 years. Archeologists continue to debate the nature and extent of the more than 350 miles of canals along the Salt River in the Phoenix area and the additional canals in southern Arizona (Haury 1965). It was the most extensive prehistoric irrigation system in North America, and the Hohokam, according to recent scholarship, irrigated approximately 100,000 acres of land in the Salt River Valley alone. One scholar has noted that while the Hohokam are recognized as the premier desert irrigation specialists of the pre-historic era, they actually used many methods to control and use water. Besides an extensive canal system, they developed terracing, check dams, rock piles, and linear and grid borders. Additionally, like other prehistoric cultures in Arizona, Hohokam water resource development fell into two categories: irrigation methods (canals and ditches) and indirect methods reflected in soil moisture conservation. These methods provided palpable technological precedents for the region's European successors (Logan 1999; Kupel 2003).

The irrigation works built by the Hohokam evidence the earliest impact of water management on Arizona's traditions. We think of the West as a place born of rugged individualism, but the reality is that in an arid region it is impossible to survive unless you get along well enough with your neighbors to share a plumbing system. In fact, the earliest forms of government in the world may have arisen in the Middle East over the need to construct and share water-distribution facilities (Worster 1985). In the Southwest, the irrigation works of the Hohokam present similar early evidence of the necessary cooperative endeavor that leads to an institutionalized civilization.

As Spaniards colonized the Southwest in the sixteenth and seventeenth centuries, they consciously adopted Native American settlement patterns, often displacing existing towns and villages where water could easily be conveyed for irrigation. Beyond these effects, Spaniards introduced and reconfigured agriculture in the region. They brought a myriad of new crops and at the same time introduced livestock and domesticated animals. The Spanish also created a new language of water use, much of which dates from the Moorish occupation of Spain from 711 to 1492. The Spanish word *acequia*, or canal, is still used today, and water users in Arizona continue to refer to the *zanjero*, or ditch tender. The acequia districts of northern New Mexico are the oldest extant governmental units of European settlement in North America.

The most significant Spanish influence in Arizona and the Southwest was in the law. The Spanish maintained a near obsessive interest in water regulation, reflected in volumes of land grant documents and government officials' diaries about interminable water rights disputes. The single most important Spanish water legacy is reflected in the Latin phrase "qui prior est in tempore, potior est in jure"—first in time, first in right. This legal doctrine of "prior appropriation" became the cornerstone of water law, not only in Arizona, but also throughout the trans-Mississippi West (Meyer 1984). Though Spanish law recognized "first in time, first in right" in theory, Spanish settlers in many cases used a more pragmatic, communal approach to water that acknowledged the inherent value of the scarce resource in an arid region (Reich 1995). Notably, the doctrine of prior appropriation remained in place during the Mexican period (1821–1848) and formed the legal framework regarding the use and distribution of water when Colonel Kearny promulgated his legendary code of 1846. That code resulted in continuing the Hispanic traditions of water and land use until the creation of the Arizona territory in 1863.

One of the first actions of the territorial legislature was to enact a comprehensive legal code. Known as the Howell Code for its author, Judge William T. Howell, the document contained several provisions that addressed water resources in the nascent Arizona territory. Howell was from the mining state of Michigan and, in an inspired notion, he attempted to reconcile local conditions with the emerging nation. The legal code retained the Spanish and Mexican customs of prior appropriation. Concerning the regulation of *acequias,* Howell asserted that water rights should be held appurtenant to the land; that is, as a right attached to the principal property that passes in possession with it. Mining law under the Howell Code also followed the theory of prior appropriation, giving the rights to the first person to discover minerals. As the pace of American settlement in Arizona territory quickened, the Howell Code and its implications loomed large for those who competed for land and water.

The Irrigation Era

As settlement in the arid region of Arizona grew, the suitability of portions of the region for growing crops became clearer. Flat land and sunshine were available in abundance in a mild year-round climate. However, to significantly expand the irrigation works that supported widespread agriculture, something more important than just getting along with your immediate neighbors was needed. Outside capital and expertise would have to be brought to bear. The distant government of the United States of America would be the source of that money and expertise.

The post-Civil War population influx into Phoenix and the Salt River Valley depended on the importation of American cultural, legal, and political institutions. Realizing that time and money could be saved by using the still-evident Hohokam canal system, entrepreneurs and schemers like Jack Swilling commenced the essential activity of water resource development. By 1870, Phoenix maintained a community of 240 residents with roughly 1,500 acres under cultivation, relying on the Salt River and a web of irrigation ditches or wells to address growing community demands (Sheridan 1996).

In the 1880s, an inexorable move toward government domination of development took off. Although imaginative individuals continued to pursue private initiatives, the advent of the National Irrigation Association (NIA), headed by reclamation pioneers William Ellsworth Smythe and George Maxwell, marked this shift. Maxwell in particular epitomized the noisy booster for a federal solution to the aridity of the West. With the passage of the Newlands Reclamation Act of 1902, Maxwell and his followers claimed victory, and the federal government became the dominant force involved in all aspects of irrigation and reclamation.

In many ways, however, the 1890s were a disaster for the Arizona territory. During mid-February 1891, "the biggest flood of the Salt River that had ever been known" erased years of human effort and toil. The flood reached the valley on February 20, and for several months thereafter, residents remained isolated from the outside world. After the floodwaters receded and settlers reclaimed what remained, they clamored louder than ever for river storage, regulation, and federal aid. Not surprisingly, they also wholeheartedly supported the efforts of Smythe and Maxwell. And, in what became a cruel irony, a decade-long drought followed the flood of 1891 (August 1985).

Intermittent floods and drought led, inevitably, to legal fights. In 1892, on the heels of the flood and an ensuing monsoon that dumped only about half of the average expected amount of rain, Judge Joseph H. Kibbey, the chief justice of the territorial supreme court, tried to resolve a number of water rights and canal company disputes that punctuated the increasingly chaotic community of water users. Kibbey's landmark decision in *Wormser v. Salt River Valley Land Company* (1892) reaffirmed the doctrine of prior appropriation. A significant aspect of the ruling held that water belonged to the land and not to any particular canal company and that it could not be sold as a separate commodity. The Kibbey decision, which linked water to land, would serve as a model for water law and subsequent legislation throughout the West.

Eighteen years later, on March 1, 1910, Judge Edward Kent essentially affirmed the Kibbey decision in *Hurley v. Abbott* (1910). The Kent decree determined the prior rights of all acreage in the Salt River Valley to Salt River water and even adjudicated when each parcel had first been cultivated. The Kent decree, in its determined complexity, took into consideration elements of the federal Newlands Reclamation Act and enabled Arizona to undergo a seamless transition into statehood in 1912, especially as it concerned water law administration. The decree stands as one of the great early monuments to Arizona's maturing legal system.

Meanwhile, Salt River Valley residents organized and successfully lobbied the Theodore Roosevelt administration to obtain the first great federal reclamation project for the new state. When a dam was constructed at the confluence of Tonto Creek and the Salt River, it was the largest dam built in the world up to that time. Roosevelt himself came to dedicate the dam bearing his name and noted that with a new water supply and flood protection, he could foresee a day when the Phoenix Valley might hold 150,000 people (SRP 2006). As the Kent decree unfolded, Roosevelt Dam was almost complete, and a new relationship developed between local water users and the federal government. Although the bulk of these users were farmers, on October 1, 1910, city of Phoenix officials executed a water contract with the federal Department of the Interior's Reclamation Service for the delivery of water. Judge Kent, to his enduring credit, had recognized the urban dimension of portions of the Salt River Valley in the Kent decree, and this was reflected in the map designating urban areas that accompanied his legal rendering in the *Hurley v. Abbott* (1910) case. Ultimately, the annual renewal of water-delivery contracts with the Department of the Interior's Reclamation Service became routine until 1917, when the Salt River Valley Water Users' Association (SRVWUA) took control of the project. On March 20, 1919, the city of Phoenix executed its first water contract with the SRVWUA. Public ownership and government stewardship characterized this Progressive Era evolution in water policy.

The SRVWUA evolved over decades into one of the most important institutions in Arizona—the Salt River Project (SRP). A series of five additional dams were added on the Salt and Verde Rivers, and in 1949 a special municipal power district (Salt River Project Agricultural Improvement and Power District) was formed to sell hydropower and other types of energy to the citizens of metropolitan Phoenix. This unique institution has been profiled as one of the most effective special-purpose governments in the United States (Smith 1986; Garreau 1991; Gammage 1999).

The early cooperation between urban and agricultural interests is also a continuing hallmark of Arizona water policy. In states like California and Colorado, urbanization takes place in a geographically different area than the land on which agriculture was historically practiced. As a result, in those states, urban water uses are often viewed as being in opposition to continuing agricultural uses. In Arizona, by contrast, houses tend to replace farmland as the areas around the city of Phoenix have grown. Farmers, therefore, have often not been at odds with the conversion of their water to urban purposes because their land is simultaneously being converted to the highest value crop: a housing subdivision. SRP itself has made a remarkable transition from a group of water users organized to lien their property to repay federal reclamation costs into a huge public utility serving largely urban needs. This trend of converting agricultural uses into urban uses has created a remarkably stable culture of water use for most of Arizona's population.

Fighting over the Colorado River

As the framework for Arizona water law and administration developed into a coherent and predictable enterprise, a broader regional struggle loomed on the horizon that would dominate Arizona's politics and law for most of the twentieth century.

The history of Arizona's struggles over the Colorado River illuminates another key aspect of the social and political traditions of the state: the tribal nature of water as a commodity. The people with whom we share our water are regarded as the members of our tribe. Those who would seek to take our water away are the enemy. In most of the history of Arizona's fight for Colorado River water, that enemy has been the huge nation-state to our west—California. Opposition to California's single-minded exploitation of the Colorado River has bound Arizonans together as a people and has built significant institutions.

From its source in the Rocky Mountains, the Colorado River drains some of the most stunning, hostile, and arid topography on the planet. Despite its large tributary system, the Colorado was never a truly major river or heavy flowing stream, as it ranks only sixth in volume among the country's rivers. As a result of the demands placed on that flow by seven states and Mexico, the Colorado, according to its most distinguished historian, Norris Hundley, Jr., has been the most litigated, regulated, politicized, and argued-about river in the world (1975).

California, from the advent of federal reclamation law in 1902, has been an assertive and active participant in water resource development along the lower Colorado River. California's aggressiveness at diverting Colorado River water for beneficial use prompted a basin-wide response that was noble in its conception but inadequate in its results: the Colorado River Compact of 1922. Its chief innovation, the brainchild of Colorado water law attorney Delph Carpenter, divided the Colorado River watershed into two basins, with the division point at Lee's Ferry in the canyon lands of northern Arizona. The compact allotted the upper basin—Wyoming, Colorado, Utah, and New Mexico—7.5 million acre-feet of water annually. The lower basin, composed of Nevada, Arizona, and California, received 7.5 million acre-feet of mainstream water per year, plus an additional 1 million acre-feet under the vaguely worded and controversial Article III (b) (*Congressional Record* 1928). Despite its limitations, omissions, and ambiguities, the compact was soon heralded as the "Law of the River," a label implying that the agreement would somehow keep the river out of the courts.

When Arizonans began debating the pros and cons of the compact in their state legislature in 1923, few foresaw that it would take Arizona 22 years to ratify the compact, an unusual and frustrating chapter in Arizona's water history. But as Arizona debated, California marshaled her forces and in 1922 introduced in the U.S. House of Representatives the first Swing–Johnson bill. The bill had provisions for storage, power production, and an All-American Canal to divert large portions of the river into California. Arizona's lone congressman, Carl Hayden, opposed the bill and used his senior position on the House Committee on the Irrigation of Arid Lands to bottle up the objectionable legislation for as long as possible (Moeller 1971; Hundley 1975; August 1989).

At the same time as Arizona's congressional delegation fought off California's attempts to pass the bill, Arizona moved into an even more intransigent position regarding ratification of the compact. Delph Carpenter suggested to Herbert Hoover and other federal officials that the agreement become effective after six states had agreed to its provisions, and so by mid-1925 the compact passed into law. Simultaneously, California worked to secure the approval of a "storage dam" at or below Boulder Canyon (*Congressional Record* 1926; Mayo 1964).

From 1926 to the end of 1928, Arizona's leaders fought bitterly to stop California from getting its canal and the accompanying great dam. But ultimately, after a filibuster, threats of fistfights, and an executive session that "deprived the Senate gallery of one of the wildest scenes since war days," the Seventieth Congress on December 16, 1928, passed the Boulder Canyon Project Act by a vote of 64–11. The House approved the Senate version two days later by a vote of 167–122. President Calvin Coolidge signed the legislation into law three days later on December 21, 1928, ending one phase of the controversy and signaling the beginning of another (Moeller 1971; Hundley 1975).

Few measures have had a greater impact in the region than the congressional action that authorized Hoover Dam and the All-American Canal. The legislation repealed the law of prior appropriation as it applied between the upper and lower basins and, much to the chagrin of Arizonans, codified the terms of the Colorado River Compact of 1922. The act also contained the Pittman Amendment, named for Nevada Senator Key Pittman, under which Nevada received 300,000 acre-feet of water annually, California 4.4 million, and Arizona 2.8 million, plus "exclusive rights to the Gila River." Finally, under the terms of the Pittman proposal, Arizona and California divided equally any surplus mainstream water (August 1999). Most pundits thought that the legislation gave California everything and Arizona nothing.

Between 1930 and 1936, Arizona was a party to four U.S. Supreme Court cases—all with negative results as they pertained to the Colorado River. Arizona seemed to stand alone in the West as a pouting, intransigent little state unable to play in the sandbox. Even Arizona's congressional delegation found itself at odds with state leaders. They questioned a dogmatic adherence to a "state's rights" water policy and disavowed Governor B.B. Moeur's histrionics concerning the calling out of the National Guard to halt construction of Parker Dam. Whereas the celebrated miniature war with California made exciting press, sold newspapers, and focused attention on their perceived aggressors, the days of "saving" the Colorado River for Arizona were over, and alternative approaches needed to be explored (August 1999).

With the election of Sidney P. Osborn as governor in 1940, Arizona underwent a water policy revolution at the state level. Once a state's rights advocate and ardent opponent of the regionalism inherent in the Colorado River Compact, Osborn now told Arizona lawmakers that with the passage of the Boulder Canyon Project Act of 1928, the era of philosophizing and theorizing about the river had ended: "Whatever our previous opinions about the best place or plan, we can only recognize that decisions have been made and the dam constructed" (Hundley 1986).

In a special session called specifically to deal with the Colorado River, the legislature, on February 9, 1944, passed a bill authorizing a water-delivery contract with the Secretary of the Interior providing the annual delivery of 2.8 million acre-feet of mainstream water, plus half of "any excess or surplus ... to the extent for use in Arizona ... under the compact." On February 24, 1944, Osborn signed the bill that ratified the compact, thereby ending more than two decades of controversy within Arizona. Importantly, these actions enabled Arizona to fight its reclamation battles within, rather than outside of, federally approved guidelines.

Arizona's reentry into the sandbox of water players allowed Senator Carl Hayden, in typically discreet fashion, to secure congressional appropriations in 1943 for the U.S. Bureau of Reclamation to conduct an inventory of irrigation and multiple-use projects in the lower Colorado River basin that could be made ready for construction when servicemen returned home at the end of World War II. This apparently innocuous proposal marked the first meaningful step in Arizona's already decades-long quest to divert its share of Colorado River water to the burgeoning heart of the state.

On July 31, 1944, a subcommittee convened five days of hearings in Arizona to discuss the bureau's recently completed preliminary reports on importing Colorado River water and to survey the state's various irrigation needs. Shortly after the conclusion of the Arizona hearings, Hayden directed funds to the Bureau of Reclamation for the purpose of commencing full-scale feasibility studies for what the bureau's engineers were now calling the "Central Arizona Project" (CAP) (Johnson 1974).

By February 1947, federal and state officials picked one alternative—the "Parker Pump Plan"—for diverting Colorado River water to central Arizona. Secretary of the Interior J.A. Krug signed the final feasibility report on February 8, 1948, and justified construction of CAP because it was essentially a rescue project designed to avert serious disruptions in Arizona's predominantly agricultural economy. CAP would transform the Colorado River into a truly multipurpose natural resource that would replace depleted groundwater, create hydroelectric power for a developing region, provide supplemental water to lands currently in production but not adequately irrigated, and increase Tucson's domestic water supply.

Three issues needed resolution before any further action took place. First, the lingering water allocation question between Arizona and California required a

final answer. California contended that the annual flow of the Gila River, estimated at 1 million acre-feet, should be included in Arizona's allotment of
Colorado River water. Arizona, of course, countered that the Gila was exempt
from allocation formulas.

Second, Arizona also needed to adopt a groundwater control law to limit the
average annual withdrawal from groundwater basins within the areas served by
CAP. Finally, the state had to organize an improvement district to help repay
construction costs and oversee local management of the project (USBR 1948;
Rusinek 1985).

Because of these issues, Arizona's delegation had no success in pushing CAP
legislation in the late 1940s. Unable to exact a compromise acceptable to both
parties, in 1952 Congress turned over the mosaic of contested issues to the U.S.
Supreme Court. As several students of *Arizona v. California* (1963) have noted,
the case was one of the most complex and fiercely contested in the history of
the high court. In the course of 11 years and at a cost of almost $5 million, 340
witnesses and 50 lawyers produced 25,000 pages of testimony. When a sharply
divided court announced its opinion on June 3, 1963, and its decree on March
9, 1964, it greatly modified the legal framework governing the apportionment
and use of Colorado River water previously claimed by California and thereby
cleared the way for final legislative action on CAP (Akin 1982; Hundley 1986).

The next five years of legislative wrangling brought forth the Colorado River
Basin Project Act of 1968, which sanctioned construction of CAP and served as
the capstone to 89-year-old Carl Hayden's towering career (August 1999). The
legacy of hundreds of miles of canals, pumping stations, and water-delivery systems that today wind their way through the desert stand as a testament to the
careers of leaders whose names are now beginning to flicker out on the horizon of history. The authorization of the CAP marked the end of Arizona's
sometimes quixotic relationship with the United States over the Colorado River.
Instead of fighting for more of the resource based on perceptions of fairness
and past ill treatment, the state moved aggressively to develop the resource it
was given: 2.8 million acre-feet. However, cooperation came at a price: in accordance with the act, Arizona's rights to the river were made junior to California's
and Nevada's, meaning shortages in times of drought would hit Arizona first.

The Arrival of CAP, the Groundwater
Management Act, and Beyond

Passage of the Colorado River Basin Project Act in 1968 brought Arizona
municipal leaders to the forefront as staunch supporters of CAP because they
viewed it as the best source of augmentation to address dwindling water supplies. In this way, what began as an agricultural rescue project emerged, by the
mid-twentieth century, as a lifeline to Arizona's growing cities and a substantial gain to the state's tribal residents. Ultimately, Arizona's tribes, cities, and

farmers would play a major role in the use and distribution of the benefits of CAP, and how these Arizona stakeholders managed their hard-won good fortune depended on an efficient administration of CAP construction and finance, a constructive and open relationship with the federal government, and a unified approach to these and future challenges (Kupel 2003).

There was also a simultaneous need for the U.S. Congress to appropriate monies for the Bureau of Reclamation to complete plans for construction of CAP. Additionally, the Department of the Interior needed assurances that the federal government would be repaid for construction. In 1970, Congress appropriated $1.2 million to begin CAP construction, but the U.S. Office of Management and Budget (OMB) refused to release the money "until such time as a project cost repayment contract between the Secretary of the Interior and Arizona water users had been negotiated." Only then did Arizona water leaders react. Arizona considered several alternatives before enacting legislation that created the multicounty (Maricopa, Pinal, Pima) Central Arizona Water Conservation District (CAWCD) on June 16, 1971, as the political and administrative agency designated to oversee repayment to the federal government (Zarbin n.d.).

In 1977, President Jimmy Carter, in a political miscalculation of enormous proportions, commenced a campaign against 19 western water projects, including CAP. Carter's mishandling of western water policy was one of a host of problems that beset the new president and further cemented a growing Republican domination of the inland West.

Ultimately, Carter was forced to back down, but even after the project was reinstated, Secretary of the Interior Cecil Andrus, on October 5, 1979, informed Arizona that it must demonstrate a greater commitment to controlling groundwater use in the state before he issued final recommendations for CAP allocations. There is widespread belief that Arizona Governor Bruce Babbitt suggested using the federal government as a threat to unify Arizona water interests as a tactic to get groundwater use under control. The Carter administration reasoned that because CAP had been promoted as a rescue project to alleviate overdrafting of groundwater supplies, Arizona had to demonstrate that it maintained the political will to curtail the use of groundwater in exchange for surface-water deliveries from CAP (Kupel 2003; CAWCD 1992).

As a result of these political and fiscal realities, Arizona, under the prodding of Democratic Governor Bruce Babbitt and a cooperative Republican-led legislature, responded with the adoption of the Groundwater Management Act of 1980. The act established a timeline for reduction and elimination of groundwater pumping in certain areas of the state by creating active management areas (AMAs) and irrigation nonexpansion areas. Within AMAs, it limited development to areas with an "assured water supply," which means an area with an amount of water adequate for the needs of development for 100 years. Any city with a CAP contract automatically had a 100-year assured water supply designation. Additionally, it recast Arizona water law in substantive ways and resulted in the creation of a new agency of government, the Arizona Department of Water Resources, which replaced the governor-appointed Arizona Water Commission. In fact, the prompt, decisive action reflected in the Groundwater Management Act of 1980 prompted the federal government to put CAP in the forefront of reclamation activities.

The Groundwater Management Act stands 26 years after its passage as one of the towering innovations of Arizona's water management history. The AMA-based regulations further strengthened the role of water as a "binding agent" in Arizona's urban growth by discouraging groundwater-dependent development within AMAs.

As the CAP neared completion in the early 1990s, a series of problems appeared on the horizon. First, the ultimate cost of the canal vastly exceeded the original estimates. The repayment contract between the Central Arizona Project and the federal government was exceedingly complicated and was interpreted differently by Arizona and the United States. As a result, in 1994 when the notice of completion triggered Arizona's obligation to repay its share of the cost of the canal, the state and federal repayment calculations differed by nearly $1 billion.

Second, the original concept for charging CAP customers was that any water not used by cities would be paid for and used by Arizona farmers. The farmers had therefore entered into a series of contracts referred to as "take or pay" obligations, which required them to pay for certain portions of the water supply. Whereas agricultural water under the CAP contract did not bear any interest on the federal debt, simply the cost of repaying the principal amount to the federal government meant that the water was far more expensive than had originally been anticipated. Also, additional debt accumulated within those irrigation districts that had built CAP delivery systems to distribute the CAP water to farms within their districts. At the same time, the value of cotton, the CAP area's principal irrigated crop, had dramatically fallen in international markets. As a result, CAP deliveries to agriculture between 1993 and 1994 dropped from 500,000 to 50,000 acre-feet, and agricultural customers were threatening to file for bankruptcy.

Third, when CAP deliveries commenced to the city of Tucson, the largest municipal customer, the pipes spewed forth water containing what many consumers described as "brown gunk." Some in Tucson thought that this was a plot by Phoenix residents to poison them, but the problem was actually that Tucson had switched overnight from an entirely groundwater-based system to an entirely surface-water-based system, and there were serious engineering and water quality effects. Tucsonans responded with anger and used the voter initiative process to shut off all direct delivery of CAP water to Tucson consumers. This prohibition remains in place today.

The little-known political institution of the CAWCD suddenly had to react to all three of these crises simultaneously. As to the first, the CAWCD attempted to negotiate a compromise with the federal government over the repayment cost. In doing so, CAWCD quickly discovered that the federal government was less interested in the amount of the repayment than in the question of how much CAP water might be reallocated to Arizona's Native American tribes. The claims of Arizona's Native American tribes to waters in central Arizona stemmed from the U.S. Supreme Court case *Winters v. United States* (1908). The water rights claims of *Winters* are based on a doctrine under which the federal government was held to have implied that they had reserved enough water to irrigate all practically irrigable acres on Native American reservations when those reservations were created. The claims in central Arizona were predominantly claims against the Gila River and its tributaries, the Salt and the Verde. But no water from the Gila could be made available to satisfy those claims because the Gila's waters were essentially fully appropriated by the Salt River Project. The federal government's plan, therefore, was to acquire some of Arizona's CAP appropriation and use it to satisfy the Native American claims. During 1995 and 1996, an attempt to negotiate a compromise with the federal government over the Native American water claims and the repayment amount collapsed. In those negotiations, the federal government was ironically represented by the Secretary of the Interior, former Arizona Governor Bruce Babbitt, and his Assistant Secretary for Water and Power, Betsy Rieke, the former director of the Arizona Department of Water Resources.

The dispute with the federal government over the cost of CAP repayment and Native American water rights settlements resulted in a suit being filed by the CAWCD against the United States in 1995. Four years later, after hundreds of pages of depositions, interrogatories, motions, court hearings, and a marathon of settlement negotiations taking place all over the United States, a tentative agreement was announced. Under that agreement, CAP's overall repayment obligation would be fixed at $1.65 billion, and a total of 653,000 acre feet of water would be reallocated to satisfy the claims of Native American tribes, principally the Gila River Indian Community in central Arizona. The Native Americans would control 48% of the CAP water supply.

This intricate settlement was decried by some in central Arizona as a "give away" of huge quantities of water to a handful of Native American communities, which would simply remarket the water to Arizona cities at a profit. However, the reality was far more complex. For almost a century, courts have upheld claims of Native American communities to federally reserved water rights. Because of the senior status of Native American tribal claims to waters from rivers like the Gila, this reserved water rights doctrine could result in water being taken away from the Salt River Project and the cities of central Arizona and giving that water to the Gila River Indian Community (August 2003; Pearce 2003). Realizing this, Arizona Senator Jon Kyl, himself a former water rights attorney, took the lead in helping structure a settlement for the claims of the Gila River Indian Community and other Arizona Native American tribes. These settlements resulted in the Arizona Water Settlements Act, which President George W. Bush signed into law on December 10, 2004 (King 2005). The agreement is one of the most complex and far-reaching water settlements in U.S. history. (For a description of the settlement provisions, see Chapter 14.)

According to a statement issued by Secretary of the Interior Gale Norton after the president signed the bill, the settlement provided "a comprehensive resolution to some of the most critical water use issues facing Indian tribes and Arizona." Arizona tribes will now control almost half of the water of the Colorado River coming through the CAP canal. The cities would be able to add a small amount of new water to their existing shares of the river and could bargain with tribes to get more. Central Arizona's farmers, long a part of Arizona's history and culture, face the prospect of losing water to tribal claims. Though rooftops will replace cotton fields throughout central Arizona, agriculture will survive primarily on Native American lands, in part because of this water settlement.

As to the second problem—agricultural water deliveries—then-Governor Fife Symington appointed a 16-member Governor's Task Force that met during the first six months of 1992. Its purpose was to propose strategies for use of the state's CAP entitlement. Unfortunately, this first task force was unable to develop any recommendations, and several members claimed that they needed more information. In response to this initial disappointing outcome, the governor's office and the Arizona Department of Water Resources requested another CAP study that resulted in "An Economic Assessment of Central Arizona Project Agriculture," written by Paul N. Wilson of the University of Arizona's Department of Agricultural and Resource Economics. Among other thoroughgoing recommendations, Wilson suggested restructuring economic formulas to recognize a "target price" (Gelt 1993). Essentially, this meant that CAP would sell water to agriculture below even the marginal cost of delivery, with the difference being made up by Arizona cities. This program was implemented by CAP in 1995 and 1996. In exchange for cheap water and relief from "take or pay" contracts, agriculture was asked to give up its long-term CAP allocations. This proved to be a resounding success, and CAP agricultural deliveries bounced back to more than 500,000 acre-feet annually in 2001 (Hanemann 2002).

As for the third issue, the city of Tucson slowly worked through its problems and, with the pronouncement "Start Your Pumps" on May 3, 2001, Mayor Bob Walkup announced delivery of clean and safe CAP water to the citizens of Tucson. However, in part because of these three issues, Arizona was not using its full CAP allocation in the mid-1990s. California, meanwhile, continued to vastly overuse its 4.4 million acre-feet because it had the right to take any water Arizona left in the river. This led Arizona to adopt additional innovative water management institutions designed to encourage using as much Colorado River water as possible.

One innovation, "water banking," involves taking CAP water and putting it back underground in central Arizona, so that the state can protect itself against its junior status in times of drought on the river. Groundwater banking was also a deliberate mechanism to protect Arizona's allocation from California's hands. Water banking began when the SRP, CAWCD, and Arizona municipalities agreed to purchase excess Colorado River water from CAP and put it underground in central Arizona. This could be done either through direct recharge—letting the water physically seep into the aquifers—or through a process called "indirect" recharge—which meant that the water would be sold to farmers at a heavily subsidized price and the groundwater that the farmers would otherwise have pumped would be counted as "recharged" surface water, which could be used in the future by cities or whoever had paid the subsidy.

In 1996, Governor Symington signed legislation establishing the Arizona Water Bank Authority as a separate state agency designed for the purpose of acquiring excess CAP water and banking it in central Arizona. A brilliant stroke of western water diplomacy, the Arizona Water Bank, was authorized to make deals with neighboring states to allow them to bank in Arizona for their future needs. This mechanism proved particularly effective with Nevada, buying Arizona a critical ally in the always complex relationships over the Colorado River.

Three years earlier, in 1993, an additional innovative water banking mechanism was created, the Central Arizona Groundwater Replenishment District (CAGRD). The CAGRD, another monument to Arizona's water ingenuity, was designed to make it possible for developers to build housing subdivisions where they did not have direct access to CAP water or to a municipality with a CAP contract. The CAGRD, with legislative approval, expanded its powers and spheres of public policy influence in 1999. The CAGRD is a separate legal entity administered by the CAWCD. It has the authority to acquire excess Colorado River water from CAWCD and store it underground on behalf of developers seeking to build subdivisions without direct access to CAP water. The subdivision "joins" the CAGRD, and each house is subject to an assessment to pay for the water put underground. By virtue of joining the CAGRD, a subdivision is deemed to have the key criterion in establishing a 100-year assured water supply. (For a discussion of CAGRD and Arizona's Assured Water Supply Rules, see Chapter 13.)

The CAGRD has been heavily criticized as opening a loophole in the Groundwater Management Act's link between renewable water supplies and urban development. It has proved far more popular than originally anticipated, with more than 165,000 lots enrolled in the CAGRD mechanism as of 2005 and many thousands more likely to come.

Conclusion

Frank Herbert's science fiction classic *Dune* (1965) posits a world so dry that its culture is built around individual hoarding of water by Bedouin-like nomads who wear special suits to conserve their fluids and who recapture water from the dead. Their existence is an extreme exercise in aggressive self-reliance. Arizona, a place not quite so devoid of water, offers a contrasting experience. Here, water is the consummate shared enterprise. We have created institutions to obtain, protect, and manage our supplies. We have used the power of government to build vast public plumbing systems. We have crafted laws, contracts, decrees, and decisions to give order to the sharing of our most precious resource. And we celebrate as our greatest statespersons those who have focused on this collective endeavor.

For at least the past century, water has provided Arizona's clearest consensus: we need more, we will use all we can get, we will stretch it as far as we can, and we will fight anyone who tries to take it away.

References

Akin, Wayne. 1982. Oral History Interview with Jack L. August, Jr., Sept. 18. Oral History Collection. Department of Archives and Manuscripts, Hayden Library. Tempe, AZ: Arizona State University.

Arizona v. California, 373 U.S. 546 (1963).

August, Jack L., Jr. 1985. Carl Hayden: Born a Politician. *Journal of Arizona History* 26 (Summer): 127–130.

———. 1989. Carl Hayden, Arizona, and the Politics of Water Development in the Southwest. *Pacific Historical Review* 58 (May): 207.

———. 1999. *Vision in the Desert: Carl Hayden and Hydropolitics in the American Southwest.* Fort Worth, TX: Texas Christian University Press.

———. 2003. Hopis Seek Their Water Rights. Special to the *Arizona Republic,* September 21.

Central Arizona Water Conservation District (CAWCD). 1992. *Chronological History of the Central Arizona Water Conservation District.* Unpublished manuscript. Phoenix, AZ: Central Arizona Water Conservation District, 6–8.

Congressional Record. 1926. 69th Cong., 2d sess., 5822.

———. 1928. 70th Cong., 2d sess., 459, 466-472.

Gammage, Grady, Jr. 1999. *Phoenix in Perspective: Reflections on Developing the Desert.* Tempe, AZ: Arizona State University.

Garreau, Joel. 1991. *Edge City: Life on the New Frontier.* New York: Doubleday.

Gelt, Joe. 1993. Long Awaited CAP Water Delivers Trouble for State. *Arroyo* 6 (3) (Fall–Winter).

Groundwater Management Act of 1980. Arizona Revised Statutes, Title 45, Ch. 2, secs. 401, 403, 411, 461, 491, 452, 454, 511, 576, 591.

Hanemann, Michael. 2002. *The Central Arizona Project.* Working Paper No. 937. Berkeley, CA: Department of Agriculture and Resource Economics, University of California, October.

Hardin, Garret. 1968. The Tragedy of the Commons. *Science* 162: 1243–1248.

Haury, Emil. 1965. *The Hohokam: Desert Farmers and Craftsmen: Excavation of Snaketown, 1964–1965.* Tucson, AZ: University of Arizona Press.

Herbert, Frank. 1965. *Dune.* Philadelphia, PA: Chilton Books.

Hundley, Norris. 1975. *Water and the West: The Colorado River Compact and the Politics of Water in the American West.* Berkeley, CA: University of California Press.

————. 1986. The West against Itself. In *New Courses for the Colorado River: Major Issues for the Next Century*, edited by G.D. Weatherford and F.L. Brown. Albuquerque, NM: University of New Mexico Press, 30.

Hurley v. Abbott, Maricopa County Territorial Court Case No. 4564 (1910).

Johnson, T. Richmond. 1974. *The Central Arizona Project, 1918–1968*. Tucson, AZ: University of Arizona Press.

King, Patti Jo. 2005. Bush Signs Water Settlement Act. *Indian County Today*, January 17.

Kupel, Douglas E. 2003. *Fuel for Growth: Water and Arizona's Urban Environment*. Tucson, AZ: University of Arizona Press.

Logan, Michael. 1999. Head-Cuts and Check-Dams: Changing Patterns of Environmental Manipulation by the Hohokam and Spanish in the Santa Cruz Valley, 200–1820. *Environmental History* 4 (July): 405–430.

Mayo, Dwight. 1964. "Arizona and the Colorado River Compact." M.A. thesis, Arizona State University, Tempe, AZ, 30–34.

Meyer, Michael C. 1984. *Water in the Hispanic Southwest: A Social and Legal History 1550–1850*. Tucson, AZ: University of Arizona Press.

Moeller, Beverly Bowen. 1971. *Phil Swing and Boulder Dam*. Berkeley, CA: University of California Press.

Pearce, Michael. 2003. Indian Water Rights Settlement: The Arizona Landscape. *Western Water Law and Policy Reporter* (May).

Reich, Peter L. 1995. The "Hispanic" Roots of Prior Appropriation in Arizona. *Arizona State Law Journal* 27: 649–662.

Rusinek, Walter. 1985. *Bristor v. Cheatham*: Conflict over Groundwater Law in Arizona. *Arizona and the West* 27 (Summer): 143–162.

Salt River Project (SRP). 2006. SRP History. http://www.srpnet.com/about/history/default.aspx (accessed January 12, 2006).

Sheridan, Thomas. 1996. *Arizona: A History*. Tucson, AZ: University of Arizona Press, 77–99.

Smith, Karen L. 1986. *The Magnificent Experiment: Building the Salt River Reclamation Project 1890–1917*. Tucson, AZ: University of Arizona Press.

United States Bureau of Reclamation (USBR). 1948. *Report on the Central Arizona Project, United States Department of Interior Planning Report No. 3-Sb.4-2*. Washington, DC: Government Printing Office.

Winters v. United States, 207 U.S. 564 (1908).

Wormser v. Salt River Valley Land Company (1892).

Worster, Donald. 1985. *Rivers of Empire: Water, Aridity and the Growth of the American West*. New York: Pantheon, 3–21.

Zarbin, Earl. n.d. Central Arizona Water Conservation District: A Miracle of Unity. http://www.cap-az.com/about/index.cfm?action=founding&subSection=5 (accessed January 12, 2006).

3

Balancing Competing Interests

The History of State and Federal Water Laws

Michael J. Pearce

Arizona water law is a blend of federal and state law. It varies across the state and according to the type of water. It is complex and substantial, yet surprisingly incomplete at times. Some laws were intended simply to memorialize historic practices, and others were clearly intended to change the course of future events. At times, large compromises were struck and a system of laws was developed by methodical planning. At other times, a single case between disputing parties set the course of the law for all future generations. The water law of Arizona is more a fabric than a code. It can best be explained by examining its evolution because in that way we can understand what these laws were trying to accomplish. A timeline of the development of Arizona water law appears at the end of this chapter.

Origins of Water Law in Arizona

In the eastern United States, the English doctrine of riparian water rights prevailed. This doctrine attached the stream to the adjacent land and protected the streamside owner from those who would diminish the flow (and therefore the power) of the river. The concept of owning the water separate from the land was unheard of. The arid environment in the western United States, however, created the absolute need to divert water out of the stream to make beneficial use of the water. This led to the widespread rejection of riparian law and adoption of the western doctrine of prior appropriation, where the first person to make beneficial use of the water had the property right to continue that use unimpeded by those who come later. In the 1888 case of *Clough v. Wing*, Arizona adopted this rule while still a territory.

In territorial times, percolating groundwater (water oozing in the pores of the earth and not flowing in any defined channel) was accessible only through hand-dug wells. Such groundwater was believed to belong to the overlying landowner, to be extracted and used in the same manner as the soil and its nutrients. As decided in the 1906 case *Howard v. Perrin*, Arizona generally declined to apply the doctrine of prior appropriation to water found beneath the surface of the earth.

By the 1920s, Arizonans began to discover that there were substantial basins of freshwater under the surface of the state—hundreds of millions of acre-feet of water stored in large aquifers spanning thousands of square miles—free for the mere cost of drilling and operating a well. Exploitation of percolating groundwater drove the mid-century economic development of Arizona until, in a classic example of the tragedy of the commons, significant overdraft of Arizona's groundwater basins in the latter half of the twentieth century threatened that economic base and caused a sharp revision of Arizona's water management policy.

Meanwhile, two new types of water emerged on the Arizona legal landscape—federally controlled Colorado River water, and "effluent," a name given to wastewater collected in sanitary sewers and treated to a level allowing discharge. Thus, we have four types of water recognized by Arizona water law: surface water flowing from springs or in natural channels, groundwater, Colorado River water, and effluent. Each will be examined in this chapter.

Surface Water and the Law of Prior Appropriation

When Arizona's constitution was drafted, it expressly rejected the riparian doctrine and assured that appropriative rights would be preserved (Arizona Constitution, art. 17). This was important because, by the time of statehood, most of the surface water in Arizona had already been appropriated. The Salt River Water Users' Association had been formed, Roosevelt Dam on the Salt River had been constructed, and the water rights of the farmers in the Salt River Valley had already been decreed in *Hurley v. Abbott* (1910). The individual members of the water users' association had staked their land and their livelihood on the orderly administration of these water rights.

Orderly administration, however, proved to be a bit of a challenge. In territorial times, one could appropriate water merely by making beneficial use of it. Multiple claims on the same stream led to the need to quantify the competing rights and prioritize them in the "first in time, first in right" hierarchy of the prior appropriation system. It was apparent that the Arizona streams were overappropriated, with more claims than water to fill them. To rein in overappropriation, Arizona adopted a comprehensive codified version of the prior appropriation doctrine in 1919. Still referred to as the 1919 code, the Public Water Code represents a line of demarcation between pre-1919 and post-1919 water rights (the latter requiring a certificate issued by the state to be valid).

However, Arizona had never settled the rights of the Native American tribes. Though the tribes did not have perfected water rights under the laws of the Arizona territory, life on the reservation would be impossible without water. This reality led the U.S. Supreme Court in *Winters v. United States* (1908) to conclude that the federal government must have intended to "reserve" water rights when the Native American reservations were created. These water rights were potentially large, but the tribes and the federal government, as their trustee, were immune from suits to determine their relative rights. In 1952, Senator Patrick McCarran of Nevada amended a bill in Congress to provide for a waiver of federal sovereign immunity for stream adjudications. The McCarran Amendment opened a new horizon for water litigation. In Title 45, Section 251 of the Arizona Revised Statutes, the state adopted laws authorizing comprehensive general stream adjudications to take advantage of the McCarran Amendment and bring all potential water claimants, including the federal government, into one forum.

Two general stream adjudications were commenced in Arizona in the 1970s—one covering the Gila River watershed (the southern half of the state), and one covering the Little Colorado watershed (the northeastern quarter of the state). They have been pending in our state courts for three decades now, winding back and forth between the trial courts and the state and federal appellate courts, arguing matters of jurisdiction, due process, the limits of federal reserved water rights, and other issues, but not adjudicating any rights. In the 1992 *Gila River I* case, the Arizona Supreme Court determined that service of process by certified mail on the more than 70,000 potential claimants was constitutionally permissible. In the 1999 *Gila River III* case, the court found that federal reserved water rights may extend to groundwater and that federal reserved rights in streams may be entitled to more protection from adjacent groundwater pumping than state-based rights. Finally, in *Gila River V* (2001), it was decided that in Arizona, federal reserved rights would be measured against their purpose, e.g., the creation of a permanent homeland for Native Americans on reservations. To say that they have been contentious is an understatement, but they have encouraged Native American water rights settlements and have resolved some issues of federal law.

Aside from Native American water rights, the general stream adjudications have raised another old and contentious issue in Arizona—the relative rights of the surface-water appropriator vis-à-vis the groundwater user with wells near the stream. This issue has vexed Arizona water policy for more than 70 years and, as discussed in the following sections, is far from resolved.

Arizona Groundwater Law

In the late 1920s, Southwest Cotton Company was extracting irrigation water from large wells located in the alluvial fan of the Agua Fria River below a proposed dam site. Concerned that the new dam would dry up the wells, the company sued to prevent the construction and claimed that it had "appropriated" the water flowing beneath the ground. In a long and scholarly opinion for *Maricopa County Municipal Water Conservation District No. 1 v. Southwest Cotton Company* (1931), the Arizona Supreme Court declared that, under Arizona law, one can only appropriate water flowing in a defined channel, with ascertainable bed and banks. The court explained that, although streams could have an underground "subflow," it denied relief to the company on the grounds that it failed to prove such a channel existed at this particular location.

Ironically, the ruling in the Southwest Cotton Company case caused groundwater pumping to expand. Without proof of a natural underground channel, landowners were free to pump groundwater without worrying about prior appropriation. Pumping accelerated at such a rate that civic leaders recognized something had to be done, or the entire state's groundwater supply would be consumed. The legislature passed a groundwater act in 1948, which did little except designate "critical" groundwater basins. Dissatisfied, established groundwater pumpers again urged the courts to rule that groundwater was subject to prior appropriation. At first, they succeeded. In *Bristor v. Cheatham* I (1952), the Arizona Supreme Court held in a 3 to 2 decision that prior appropriation did control groundwater. The losing side requested a rehearing and, in the interim, one judge retired and a new judge was elected. On rehearing in *Bristor v. Cheatham II* (1953), the court reversed its prior determination and adopted the "American rule" of groundwater use. This rule allowed the owner of land to access the groundwater beneath that land for "reasonable use" so long as the water was not transported "off the land." Thus, for the second time in the twentieth century, the court issued a major order promoting groundwater use.

The American rule did little to ease the situation in the most rapidly declining groundwater basins, but it was the rule's prohibition against transporting water off the land that eventually precipitated the largest reform in Arizona groundwater law. When the courts eventually enforced the rule in *Jarvis v. State Land Department I, II, III* (1969, 1970, 1976) and *Farmers Investment Company v. Bettwy* (1976), it became apparent that such a restriction just would not work in rapidly developing Arizona. These cases led to the adoption of the Arizona Groundwater Management Act of 1980 (GMA), a law heralded at its inception, and since, as the most comprehensive groundwater law ever adopted in the United States.

The GMA is found in Arizona Revised Statutes title 45, section 401. It contains several articles, but the basic elements can be described briefly. First, it created the Arizona Department of Water Resources (ADWR) to assume control of state groundwater management. It required ADWR to delineate the groundwater basins of the state in one comprehensive map. Certain of these basins were singled out for active management and became the four initial active management areas (AMAs) (the Tucson AMA was later split into the Tucson and Santa Cruz AMAs, thus making five). In these AMAs, groundwater use is quantified and limited by state law. The intention is to stop widespread expansion of groundwater use, while at the same time enforcing water conservation measures that will cause existing uses to decline. Although the specific goals of the AMAs vary, most AMAs focus on obtaining safe yield within the groundwater basin by encouraging use of alternative supplies, conserving groundwater, and eventually, by the year 2025, achieving equilibrium between groundwater withdrawals and natural (and artificial) recharge of the basin.

The GMA created a series of grandfathered groundwater rights in the AMAs, intended to allow existing users to continue their enterprise at the same level as before the new law came into effect. The grandfathered rights fall into three categories:

- irrigation grandfathered rights (allowing application of groundwater to two or more acres for production of plants),
- Type 1 rights (covering formerly irrigated land that has been retired for the purpose of nonagricultural development), and
- Type 2 rights (covering industrial uses such as mining and electricity generation).

The GMA also provides for a few types of groundwater withdrawal permits and for service area rights for municipal water providers (cities, towns, private water companies, and some irrigation districts) that serve water for typical urban or suburban use. Significantly, the GMA also allows "exempt" wells—wells with a pumping capacity of less than 35 gallons per minute—for domestic and household use. The exemption of these small wells has led to a large loophole in the GMA's ability to manage groundwater, but the ability to construct a small well for domestic purposes is still considered an inalienable right by most Arizonans. Attempts to curtail the use of exempt wells have generally met with resounding defeat in the state legislature.

Three tenets of the GMA deserve special attention. First, the GMA prohibits new irrigation within the AMAs with *any* type of water. This means that once agricultural land goes out of production (usually for housing developments), it cannot be replaced. Thus, the agricultural land base in all of the AMAs is shrinking, and use of groundwater for irrigated agriculture is declining. Second, the GMA regulates the construction of all water wells within the state. By allowing only state licensed drillers to construct wells, ADWR can regulate construction standards and accumulate valuable data on hydrogeology and water use patterns across the state. Third, the GMA implemented the "assured water supply" requirement for all new residential subdivisions in the AMAs. To develop a housing subdivision, either the developer or the municipal water provider must prove a 100-year supply of water that is physically, legally, and continuously available to that subdivision and is consistent with achieving the overall management goal of the AMA. With the rapid residential growth rate in Arizona, the Assured Water Supply Rules in the Arizona Administrative Code have made a marked difference on the use of groundwater.

Because the GMA purported to restrict the use of groundwater, particularly in the AMAs, it was immediately challenged in the courts as an unlawful taking of property without just compensation. In *Town of Chino Valley v. City of Prescott* (1982) and *Cherry v. Steiner* (1982), the GMA survived these challenges in both state and federal court. With these constitutional challenges resolved, the GMA has become the major law of Arizona water management.

Meanwhile, the old issue of wells near streams threatens to affect groundwater use significantly, not through the GMA, but through the courts. The effect of pumping wells on appropriative surface-water rights and the meaning of *Maricopa County v. Southwest Cotton Company* has been litigated in the general stream adjudications for almost two decades. In *Gila River II* (1993), the Arizona Supreme Court determined that the adjudication court's jurisdiction over the "river system and source" extended to wells that may be pumping subflow, whereas in *Gila River IV* (2000), the court defined subflow as water within the "saturated floodplain Holocene alluvium." Recently, the Gila River adjudication court has issued yet another order attempting to define the elusive subflow zone so that the relative rights of groundwater and surface-water users can be determined.

The importance of subflow cannot be overestimated. In Arizona, wells are often drilled in areas near a stream, in part because these wells provide a much more reliable and cleaner source of water than the stream itself. For decades, Arizona developed on the ability to drill a well almost anywhere. That era is rapidly coming to an end. As populations in rural areas increase, wells near streams have also increased, potentially diminishing the flow available to senior surface-water appropriators. To the extent that these wells are in the subflow zone, they can be enjoined from pumping by the general stream adjudication courts. Such injunctions would be devastating to some small communities, and clearly a compromise must be found to protect the investment of both the pumpers and the appropriators. To date, however, that compromise has yet to materialize, and the adjudication courts do not appear to be solving the problem.

Colorado River Water Law

The Colorado River originates in Colorado, flows generally southwest to the Sea of Cortez, draining land in Wyoming, Colorado, Utah, New Mexico, Nevada, Arizona, and California. It is known for extreme and unpredictable floods. For years, would-be irrigators attempted to harness the river for agricultural production, only to have their diversion works destroyed by flooding. At the beginning of the twentieth century, economic leaders in California were demanding a federal reclamation project that would dam the Colorado and provide a new "all-American" canal to transport the water to the Imperial and Coachella Valleys in southern California.

Arizona had deep concerns about this plan. Under the law of prior appropriation, which was applied to cases between states by the U.S. Supreme Court in *Wyoming v. Colorado* (1922), California could rapidly appropriate the entire river and leave nothing for the other states. The tensions resulted in a series of meetings to discuss apportioning the river by interstate compact, culminating in the meetings at Bishop's Lodge in Santa Fe, New Mexico, in 1922. Arizona went into these meetings with two objectives: that Arizona would be free to develop and use all tributaries within Arizona, regardless of their contribution to the Colorado; and that any such compact specifically allocate the water to each state.

Arizona achieved neither objective. Instead, the proposed 1922 compact divided the river at Lee's Ferry, Arizona, into an artificial upper and lower basin. The estimated annual yield of 18 million acre-feet was apportioned as 7.5 million acre-feet to the upper basin (Wyoming, Colorado, Utah, New Mexico, and a small portion of Arizona) and 7.5 million acre-feet to the lower basin (Arizona, California, and Nevada). The proposed compact recognized that the United States may have to give some water to Mexico and split that burden between the upper and lower basins. Finally, the proposed compact gave the lower basin the right to increase its beneficial consumptive use by 1 million acre-feet per annum but was otherwise silent on the tributaries.

Arizona refused to ratify the proposed compact. However, in 1928, Congress passed the Boulder Canyon Project Act authorizing the construction of Hoover Dam by the U.S. Department of the Interior's Bureau of Reclamation and approving the 1922 compact if six of the seven states, including California, ratified it. Six states ratified the compact, Hoover Dam was constructed, and entities in California were quick to accept the opportunity, provided under the Boulder Canyon Project Act, to enter into "permanent service" contracts with the Secretary of the Interior for the newly regulated water supply. By 1931, California interests had contracted for 5.36 million acre-feet of the lower basin's 7.5 million acre-feet supply. Arizona continued to object, at one point even calling out the state's National Guard troops to the site of the Parker Dam construction.

By World War II, Arizona was beginning to see the light. The United States was about to enter into a treaty with the Republic of Mexico that would guarantee 1.5 million acre-feet of water deliveries across the border. California had rapidly developed and was using the 5.36 million acre-feet limit of its contracts, notwithstanding the fact that the Boulder Canyon Project Act had only authorized 4.4 million acre-feet for California and 2.8 million acre-feet for Arizona. In 1944, Arizona finally ratified the 1922 compact, entered into a contract with the Secretary of the Interior for 2.8 million acre-feet, and began to petition Congress for Arizona's own large-scale reclamation project: the Central Arizona Project (CAP).

California tried to block the CAP. It contended that it had appropriated 5.36 million acre-feet of water from the Colorado River by virtue of its contracts and its already constructed diversion works, leaving nothing for Arizona beyond the existing agricultural uses in Yuma. Arizona eventually filed suit against California in the U.S. Supreme Court, seeking an apportionment of the river that would support the CAP. That litigation was successful, and in *Arizona v. California* (1964) the U.S. Supreme Court decreed that Arizona was absolutely entitled to 2.8 million acre-feet of mainstream Colorado River water by virtue of the congressional apportionment of the river in the 1928 Boulder Canyon Project Act.

The result was important in many ways. It confirmed the basic allocation of the lower basin in accordance with the provisions of the Boulder Canyon Project Act; namely, 2.8 million acre-feet of consumptive use for Arizona, 4.4 million acre-feet for California, and 0.3 million acre-feet for Nevada. It enjoins the Secretary of the Interior from allowing any state to exceed its apportionment, except in surplus years or years when one state is not using its entitlement. It also authorized the Secretary of the Interior to manage the river system and control the use of water among the various users. This authority has placed significant responsibility on the Secretary of the Interior and "federalized" the river's management, including the authority to declare shortage conditions and curtail water use.

Immediately after the decree was entered, Arizona again introduced legislation to construct the Central Arizona Project. That bill eventually passed in the form of the Colorado River Basin Project Act of 1968. This act authorized the construction of the CAP canal, required the creation of a state-based entity (now the Central Arizona Water Conservation District, or CAWCD) to repay Arizona's share of the cost of construction and, in a final nod to California's political strength, subordinated the CAP diversion to all existing diversions in California, up to California's 4.4 million acre-feet entitlement. Thus, if there is ever a shortage on the river, deliveries to Arizona's CAP will be reduced to zero before California's apportionment is reduced at all.

Nonetheless, the CAP was constructed and is currently delivering 1.5 million acre-feet of water to central Arizona through a 336-mile-long uphill canal. It is an engineering marvel, delivering water on a steady, predictable basis at moderate costs. It has displaced large amounts of agricultural groundwater pumping in the Pinal and Phoenix AMAs and has become a major new source of municipal supply in the Phoenix and Tucson metropolitan areas. The CAP has also greatly facilitated Native American water rights settlements. CAP water, or the proceeds from the sale or lease of CAP water, has factored heavily into almost every congressionally authorized Native American water rights settlement in Arizona to date (see Chapter 14).

The CAP is administered at the state level by the Central Arizona Water Conservation District. Water is delivered under the terms of a contract in four major categories representing their descending order of priority in times of shortage: (1) Native American, (2) municipal and industrial, (3) non-Indian agriculture, and (4) excess water. All such contracts must be approved by the Secretary of the Interior, although CAWCD is allowed to enter unilaterally into excess water contracts on a year-to-year basis under an approved allocation formula. Although low in priority, excess water contracts are extremely important to Arizona's water management scheme because they allow CAP water that is under long-term contract, but not being currently used, to be put to beneficial use today. Notably, Arizona learned from one of California's challenges and clearly subordinated agricultural CAP use to municipal demands. Thus, in times of moderate shortage, municipal supplies are protected.

The Law of Effluent

Human activity does not consume 100% of the water diverted from the system. Gravity-fed irrigation works along the Colorado River typically return 50% or more to the stream after the consumptive use of the crops. In the agricultural context, this "return flow" has consistently been accounted for and used in the administration of western water rights. In the municipal context, "effluent" has traditionally been considered a nuisance, to be disposed of in the most cost-efficient manner possible. Even today, some cities are recapturing only 20% or less of the municipal effluent. Recent years have seen a sharp reversal of this trend. Because it can be readily sold and transferred, effluent is becoming a valuable commodity, and these same cities, including Surprise, Arizona, are predicting more than a 50% recapture and reuse of effluent in the future (Surprise, Arizona, Water Services Department 2004).

Such was not always the case. In the 1970s, six cities in the Phoenix area negotiated an agreement to sell effluent to two public utilities for cooling the proposed Palo Verde nuclear generating station approximately 50 miles west of Phoenix. The proposal caused much controversy, and two ranches downstream from the wastewater treatment plant challenged the basic right of the cities to enter into the agreement because the sale would mean that the effluent would no longer be discharged into the river, where it had traditionally been captured by the ranches and used for agricultural production. The challenge led the Arizona Supreme Court in *Arizona Public Service Company v. Long* (1989) to make an in-depth analysis of the nature of effluent and the ownership rights to this heretofore nuisance commodity.

In the *Arizona Public Service Company v. Long* case, the Arizona Supreme Court was confronted with the difficulty that the water used by the cities was composed of both surface water and groundwater. Thus, some parties contended that the surface-water component retained the character of surface water and therefore could not be severed from the appurtenant land base from which it was originally appropriated. Other parties contended that, as groundwater, the effluent would be subject to all of the restrictions of the GMA, including the restrictions on transportation. The court rejected these theories and held that effluent is not regulated by either the prior appropriation doctrine or the GMA, and in fact was not regulated at all. In the absence of such regulation, the cities were at liberty to contract for the sale of the effluent in any manner they saw fit. The court nevertheless concluded that, whereas effluent is neither surface water nor groundwater, it is *water* within the meaning of Arizona law, and thus a public commodity subject to regulation by the state legislature, if and when the legislature decides to act.

Since the *Arizona Public Service Company v. Long* decision, the state legislature has not acted to regulate the use or sale of effluent in any significant way. Municipal and county governments and private sewer utilities are still at liberty to sell effluent, and the demand has steadily increased, particularly for use as a nonpotable supply for golf course, park, and common-area irrigation in new planned developments. Some local governments, such as Pima County, even require the use of effluent for golf course and turf irrigation in many circumstances (Pima County Code n.d.).

The *Arizona Public Service Company v. Long* decision has yet to reach its full effect. With the boom in housing in Arizona, and the concomitant generation of large volumes of effluent, the state legislature's ability to regulate effluent comprehensively represents an entirely new field of water management. Meanwhile, characterizing effluent as a separate and distinct type of water opens opportunities to use this water in ways that would otherwise be prohibited. This unique aspect of effluent is particularly relevant in the field of underground storage and recovery.

Underground Storage, Savings, and Replenishment in Arizona

Of all the water laws created by Arizona, the laws relating to underground water storage and recovery are perhaps the most innovative and provide the most flexibility for large-scale water management. These laws, found in Arizona Revised Statutes title 45, section 801.01 and the sections that follow, allow anyone the opportunity to store water underground for future use. Significantly, they also provide a means of underground "transportation" of water, by allowing the entity storing the water to interject it at one location within the groundwater basin and remove it from another location in the same basin. In the large AMA basins, this rule can allow transportation of water underground for many miles. Furthermore, once stored, the water retains its legal character when recovered. Thus, if a municipality stores effluent at a recharge facility near its wastewater treatment plant, it can recover that effluent, as effluent, miles away at its water production facilities.

Underground storage facilities come in two basic types: direct storage facilities and groundwater savings facilities. Direct storage facilities are either constructed (human-made spreading basins or injection wells) or managed (natural water course channels managed for recharge purposes). In direct storage facilities, a supply of "renewable" water (usually effluent or CAP water) is imported to the site and deposited into the aquifer.

Groundwater savings facilities are groundwater-dependent uses, such as groundwater-based irrigation districts, that agree to accept a substitute water supply (usually CAP water) in exchange for their groundwater. The groundwater saved is deemed to be transformed into the exchanged water. Thus, if the storing entity provides CAP water to the groundwater savings facility, the facility still reports having used "groundwater," and the aquifer is deemed to have received CAP water, held in the name of the storing entity.

Underground storage facilities must receive permits before water can be stored. To store water in a permitted facility, the storer must also have a storage permit, indicating that the storer has the legal right to use the water for storage purposes, and that the water is of a type approved for storage by ADWR. Once properly stored, the storer earns long-term storage credits for the amount of water determined by ADWR to have reached the aquifer. These credits are somewhat like a warehouse receipt, entitling the bearer to recover the water at some future time. In some cases, the storer may only receive credits that can be used in that same year—annual storage and recovery credits—as, for example, when the storer wants to store surface water, but "recover" the water by pumping from groundwater wells. In any case, the storer must have a recovery well permit to be able to extract the stored water legally.

Arizona's underground storage laws enhance many management objectives. They facilitate the state's goal to maximize the use of renewable water resources such as effluent and CAP water. Also, because Arizona's CAP water supply is a junior priority use on the Colorado River, storage builds up prudent reserves as a hedge against some future shortage. Storage of water also helps fill depleted aquifers and prevent subsidence, fissuring, and other ill effects of groundwater pumping. Perhaps most importantly, Arizona's underground storage laws facilitate economic development by making water easier to use. For example, effluent still carries a certain social stigma for direct use. The ability to store it underground and extract it from the ambient groundwater provides both a great natural filter and a separation from the direct use stigma of effluent. Similarly, CAP water, coming directly from the river through an open canal, must be treated before it can be served to municipal domestic customers. The ability to store and recover the water makes it much easier to use and has accounted for a significant increase in Arizona's usage of the CAP for municipal purposes.

These laws have also fostered two other major water management programs. The Arizona Water Banking Authority (AWBA) was created in 1996 amid speculation by California and Nevada that Arizona would never be able to use the CAP fully. Arizona recognized that the CAP water was valuable, but the cost to use it was often prohibitive. To bridge the time until the state can fully absorb the CAP supply, Arizona Revised Statutes title 45, section 2401 and the sections following authorize the AWBA to purchase CAP water and store it in the central aquifers for future use. Since its inception, AWBA has stored much more than 2 million acre-feet of CAP water. This water has been used to create an innovative interstate water bank, making additional Colorado River supplies available to the state of Nevada, and has provided a source of banked water to use for Native American water rights settlements. It has also provided a substantial cushion of CAP water for municipal use in the event that shortage conditions are declared on the Colorado River and CAP diversions are curtailed.

The Central Arizona Groundwater Replenishment District (CAGRD) was formed in 1994 to allow new development in the Phoenix, Pinal, and Tucson AMAs to be based on readily available groundwater, but with the promise that the government would "replenish" the groundwater by acquiring and storing alternative supplies, such as effluent and excess CAP water. Both the AWBA and the CAGRD are examples of using existing laws in new ways to create entirely new water management options.

Federal Water Laws

Although state law has traditionally governed the use and allocation of water in the United States, Congress has adopted a series of laws that bear directly on water. Although they have caused disruption in the administration of water rights, the federal laws relating to safe drinking water standards, point source pollution control, and environmental protection have undoubtedly enhanced the quality of life in the United States. They are briefly summarized here, to put them in context with state water management policy.

The Federal Water Pollution Control Act, or Clean Water Act of 1972, is designed to stop discharge of pollutants into the nation's rivers. It requires a permit (known at the federal level as a National Discharge Elimination System [NPDES] permit) for the discharge of pollutants from a point source, and it also provides for adoption of programs, in cooperation with the states, for the total maximum daily load of pollutants that a stream may lawfully carry. A curious aspect of the NPDES permit program is the case of *South Florida Water Management District v. Miccosukee Tribe of Indians* (2004), in which the U.S. Supreme Court held that a transfer of water from one distinct body of water to another, even if nothing was added to the water so transferred, would require an NPDES permit if the transfer introduced a different, lower quality water. This ruling could significantly affect the western states, where different sources of water are often commingled, sometimes with the deliberate intent of diluting poorer quality water. For example, the importation of CAP water into other non-Colorado River water bodies, even though practiced for years with the express consent of Congress, could now suddenly require an NPDES permit.

The Safe Drinking Water Act of 1974 provided the maximum contaminant level for toxins in our drinking water and set the requirements for an entity to act as a public water provider. This program has largely been delegated to the states, which are entitled to set their own standards, as long as the minimum requirements are met. As an example, and amid much controversy, the U.S. Environmental Protection Agency has recently decreased the allowable quantity of arsenic in drinking water. In Arizona, arsenic is a naturally occurring component of groundwater and is found in varying quantities throughout the state. The new standard, allowing only 10 parts per billion of arsenic, will mean that many water providers will have to treat the otherwise acceptable Arizona groundwater to remove arsenic.

The National Environmental Policy Act (NEPA) of 1969 is designed to require that any major action undertaken by the federal government first be analyzed for its impact on the environment before it is approved. NEPA is strictly a procedural statute that requires due consideration of the impact of actions before those actions are undertaken. Nevertheless, NEPA has had a significant impact in Arizona. Often, the extent of compliance is uncertain and large federal projects have been suspended indefinitely while litigation ensued over NEPA compliance. In recent years, NEPA's environmental assessments or more comprehensive environmental impact statements have become a built-in planning component of any project involving a connection with the federal government.

The Endangered Species Act (ESA) of 1973 is designed to protect threatened and endangered species from "take" (killing, harming, or destruction of habitat) and "jeopardy" (federal actions that diminish the likelihood that species can survive). All federal agencies are required to consult with the U.S. Fish and Wildlife Service about any activity that may adversely affect a threatened or endangered species, including the issuance of federal contracts for deliveries of water. All persons are prohibited from taking species, except as authorized by permit, and many private enterprises have taken extraordinary mitigation measures to obtain such a permit and avoid the possibility of harming an endangered species. The ESA has had a dramatic effect on water issues across the West, including in particular, the Klamath River and the Rio Grande. The ESA has had impacts within Arizona through the multispecies conservation plan for endangered species along the Colorado River, mitigation requirements related to willow flycatcher habitat that was inundated when Roosevelt Dam was raised, and issues associated with managing the San Pedro River.

The System at Work: Managing Arizona's Water Future

Arizona water law is designed to encourage the use of water for economic development. At the same time, these laws must protect the property rights of those who have lawfully appropriated water and attempt to preserve common supplies, such as groundwater, for future generations. All these goals cannot be accomplished simultaneously, and the fabric of Arizona water law, such as it is, is an attempt to find a balance among the competing interests.

There are, however, a few significant problems. The litigation over wells near streams in the adjudication courts has the potential for causing widespread disruption, to either the groundwater or surface-water users, depending on the ultimate outcome. Litigation, with its all-or-nothing tendencies, is a poor forum for resolving this most perplexing problem in Arizona water management. New attempts should be made to resolve this problem through legislation, including new laws that restrict the ability to drill wells that will have a demonstrable effect on the stream, but allowing wells where the effect is slight and economic conditions favor groundwater development.

Despite the efforts of the GMA, Arizona is still experiencing overdraft throughout the state. With the rapidly expanding population and limited opportunities to expand the water portfolio, new development will have to become more efficient. Great advances have been made in effluent reuse through recharge and nonpotable direct use, but effluent is still discharged to waste. New laws and enhancement of existing laws and programs, such as the AWBA and the CAGRD, can help optimize this efficiency. Likewise, we will have to address the ability to transfer water rights with more efficiency and create an atmosphere where entrepreneurial ability can bring water supplies to new development.

References

Arizona Administrative Code. Rule 12–15–701 et seq. (Assured Water Supply Rules).

Arizona Constitution, art. 17.

Arizona Public Service Company v. John F. Long, 773 P.2d 988 (Ariz. 1989).

Arizona Revised Statutes, Title 45, sec. 401.

Arizona Revised Statutes, secs. 45–251 et seq.

Arizona Revised Statutes secs. 45–801.01, 45–811.01, 45–831.01, 45–834.01, 45–841.01, 45–851.01.

Arizona Revised Statutes secs. 45–2401 et seq.

Arizona v. California, 373 U.S. 546 (1963) (opinion); 376 U.S. 340 (1964) (decree).

Boulder Canyon Project Act of 1928. U.S. Code. Vol. 43, sec. 617 et seq.

Bristor v. Cheatham I, 240 P.2d 185 (Ariz. 1952).

Bristor v. Cheatham II, 255 P.2d 173 (Ariz. 1953).

Cherry v. Steiner, 543 F. Supp. 1270 (D. Ariz. 1982); aff'd. 716 F.2d 687 (9th Cir. 1983); cert den. 466 U.S. 931 (1984).

Clean Water Act of 1972. U.S. Code. Vol. 33, sec. 1251 et seq.

Clough v. Wing, 17 P. 453 (Ariz. 1888).

Colorado River Basin Project Act of 1968. U.S. Code. Vol. 43, secs. 1501, 1521(b).

Endangered Species Act of 1973. U.S. Code. Vol. 16, sec. 1531 et seq.

Farmers Investment Company v. Bettwy, 558 P.2d 14 (Ariz. 1976).

Gila I. 1992. 830 P.2d 442 (Arizona).

Gila II. 1993. 857 P.2d 1236 (Arizona).

Gila III. 1999. 989 P.2d 739 (Arizona); cert den. 530 U.S. 1250 (2000).

Gila IV. 2000. 9 P.3d 1069 (Arizona); cert den. 533 U.S. 941 (2001).

Gila V. 2001. 35 P.3d 68 (Arizona).

Groundwater Management Act of 1980. Arizona Revised Statutes, Title 45, Ch. 2, secs. 401, 403, 411, 461, 491, 452, 454, 511, 576, 591.

Howard v. Perrin, 17 P. 460 (Ariz. 1904); aff'd. 200 U.S. 71 (1906).

Hurley v. Abbott, Maricopa County Territorial Court Case No. 4564 (1910).

Jarvis v. State Land Department, City of Tucson I, II, III, 456 P.2d 385 (Ariz. 1969); mod. 479 P.2d 169 (Ariz. 1970); injunction mod. 550 P.2d 227 (Ariz. 1976).

Maricopa County Municipal Water Conservation District No. 1 v. Southwest Cotton Company, 4 P.2d 369 (Ariz. 1931); mod. and reh. den., 7 P.2d 254 (Ariz. 1932).

McCarran Amendment of 1952. U.S. Code. Vol. 43, sec. 666.

National Environmental Policy Act of 1969. U.S. Code. Vol. 42, sec. 4321 et seq.

Pima County Code, Chapter 18.59.

Public Water Code. 1919. Arizona Revised Statutes, Title 45, Ch. 1, secs. 45–101 et seq.

Safe Drinking Water Act of 1974. U.S. Code. Vol. 42, sec. 300f et seq.

South Florida Water Management District v. Miccosukee Tribe of Indians, 541 U.S. 95 (2004).

Surprise, Arizona, Water Services Department. 2004. Water Resources Master Plan. http://www.surpriseaz.com/documents/Water%20Services/Water%20Resources% 20Master%20Plan%20-%20Executive%20Summary.pdf (accessed March 9, 2006).

Town of Chino Valley v. City of Prescott, 638 P.2d 1324 (Ariz. 1982).

Winters v. United States, 207 U.S. 564 (1908).

Wyoming v. Colorado, 259 U.S. 419 (1922).

Timeline of the Development of Arizona Water Law

1863 Arizona Territory Established
President Lincoln declared Arizona a U.S. territory on February 24, separating it from New Mexico territory.

1864 Howell Code
The first Arizona territorial legislature passed the Howell Code, which adopted the prior appropriation system for surface-water rights in Arizona.

1904 *Howard v. Perrin*
The Arizona Territorial Supreme Court ruling in this case (upheld in 1906 by the U.S. Supreme Court) established that percolating groundwater was not subject to appropriation as surface water.

1908 *Winters v. United States*
The U.S. Supreme Court recognized that Native American water rights may be implied when a land reservation is created, regardless of whether a tribe had previously put the water to beneficial use.

1912 Arizona Statehood
Arizona was accepted for statehood by President Taft on February 14.

1919 Public Water Code
Legislation was enacted on June 12 to establish procedures for perfecting a prior appropriation right to use surface water.

1922 Colorado River Compact
The compact divided the Colorado River basin into an upper and lower basin and apportioned 7.5 million acre-feet of Colorado River water per year to each basin. Arizona refused to ratify the compact until 1944.

1928 Boulder Canyon Project Act
This act authorized the construction of Hoover Dam and provided a mechanism for approval of the Colorado River Compact despite Arizona's refusal to ratify it.

1931 *Maricopa County Municipal Water Conservation District No. 1 v. Southwest Cotton Company*
The Arizona Supreme Court indicated that an underground "subflow" component of a flowing stream may be appropriable as surface water.

1944 Arizona Approval of the Colorado River Compact
Arizona ratified the compact in hopes of getting approval for a large reclamation project to deliver Colorado River water to central and southern Arizona.

1948 Critical Groundwater Code
In response to declining groundwater levels, the Arizona legislature limited new wells for irrigated agriculture in 10 designated critical groundwater areas in the state.

1952 McCarran Amendment
After passage of this law by the U.S. Congress waiving federal sovereign immunity for comprehensive general stream adjudications, federal reserved water rights could be quantified in state court proceedings.

1952 *Bristor v. Cheatham I*
This controversial ruling by the Arizona Supreme Court reversed almost 50 years of common law rulings and held that percolating groundwater is subject to prior appropriation. A request for reconsideration was immediately filed.

1953 *Bristor v. Cheatham II*
Reversing *Bristor I*, this decision by the Arizona Supreme Court adopted the rule of reasonable use for groundwater pumping and confirmed that groundwater would not be subject to the prior appropriation system for surface water.

1963 *Arizona v. California*
The U.S. Supreme Court confirmed the apportionment of water between the lower Colorado River basin states under the Boulder Canyon Project Act. Arizona was awarded 2.8 million acre-feet per year from the Colorado River, plus exclusive use of the river's tributaries within the state.

1968 Colorado River Basin Project Act
This act authorized the construction of the Central Arizona Project and provided that in the event of shortage on the Colorado River, deliveries of water to the Central Arizona Project would be curtailed as necessary to allow full delivery of California's 4.4 million acre-feet basic apportionment.

1972 Clean Water Act
This law required a federal permit for pollutant discharge into waters of the United States.

1973 Endangered Species Act
This act required all federal agencies to consult with the U.S. Fish and Wildlife Service about any activity that might adversely affect a threatened or endangered species, including the issuance of federal contracts for deliveries of water.

1976 *Farmers Investment Company v. Bettwy*
This Arizona Supreme Court decision enforced the reasonable use doctrine's prohibition on transporting groundwater away from the land from which it is pumped. This decision was unfavorable to Arizona mining companies and cities, which had been relying on transported groundwater. This case was a catalyst in the adoption of Arizona's 1980 Groundwater Management Act.

1978 Ak Chin Native American Community Water Rights Settlement Approved by U.S. Congress

1980 Groundwater Management Act
Under pressure from the U.S. Secretary of the Interior, Arizona passed the most comprehensive groundwater law ever adopted in the United States to secure final funding for the Central Arizona Project. The Groundwater Management Act enabled the Arizona Department of Water Resources to establish active management areas to stop widespread expansion of groundwater use, while at the same time enforcing water conservation measures that would cause existing uses to decline.

1982 Southern Arizona Water Rights Settlement Act (Tohono O'odham Nation) Approved by U.S. Congress

1988 Salt River Pima–Maricopa Water Rights Settlement Act Approved by U.S. Congress

1989 *Arizona Public Service Company v. Long*

The Arizona Supreme Court ruled that treated effluent is not subject to existing regulations for surface water or groundwater and that the city that produces the treated effluent owns it and may sell it to others.

1990 Ft. McDowell Native American Community Water Rights Settlement Act Approved by U.S. Congress

1991 Groundwater Transportation Act

The act restricts the ability of municipal water providers to transport groundwater from rural subbasins to active management areas. The groundwater transportation restrictions were implemented in response to rural interests asking the legislature to protect their water from being used by the growing urban areas. Under the act, groundwater may be transported within the subbasin without penalty.

1992 San Carlos Apache Water Rights Settlement Act Approved by U.S. Congress (Salt River drainage only)

1993 Groundwater Replenishment District Act

This act allowed for creation of the Central Arizona Groundwater Replenishment District (CAGRD) in 1994. With the creation of CAGRD, new housing developments in active management areas that are members of the replenishment district may rely on groundwater for their physical supply. The CAGRD then buys and recharges renewable sources of water to replace its members' groundwater pumping.

1994 Creation of Central Arizona Groundwater Replenishment District

1994 Underground Water Storage, Savings and Replenishment Act

This act allowed anyone to store water underground for future use. The storing entity earned credits for the water stored, and the credits entitled the bearer to recover the water at some time in the future. The act also gave farmers an incentive to irrigate with renewable surface-water supplies so that underground storage credits could be earned for later use.

1994 Yavapai Prescott Native American Tribe Water Rights Settlement Act Approved by U.S. Congress

1995 Assured Water Supply Rules Adopted

These rules were adopted by the Arizona Department of Water Resources to ensure that all new housing subdivisions use renewable water supplies and do not contribute to depletion of the state's groundwater resources. Before land within an active management area is sold, the developer must demonstrate an assured (renewable) water supply.

1996 Arizona Water Banking Authority

The Arizona Water Bank was created as a mechanism for Arizona to use its Central Arizona Project water allotment fully and to protect its citizens from future shortages by storing currently available excess water underground. The Arizona Water Bank also stores water on behalf of Nevada.

1999 Gila River III

In this case, the Arizona Supreme Court found that to the extent groundwater is necessary to accomplish the purpose of the reservation, federal reserved water rights may include groundwater. This case recognized potential Native American reserved water rights to groundwater.

2003 Zuni Native American Tribe Water Rights Settlement Act Approved by U.S. Congress

2004 Arizona Water Settlements Act Approved by U.S. Congress (Gila River Native American Community and Tohono O'odham Nation)

In addition to settling the Gila River Native American Community's water rights claims and finalizing the Tohono O'odham water rights settlement, this act set the state of Arizona's Central Arizona Project repayment obligation to the federal government at $1.65 billion.

4

The Water Supply of Arizona

The Geographic Distribution of Availability and Patterns of Use

Mark T. Anderson, Donald R. Pool, and Stanley A. Leake

Water is the most widely used natural resource in Arizona, consumed daily by all residents. A stable water supply is essential to the state's economic stability. Water supplies in Arizona originate with precipitation and some surface and groundwater inflow from adjacent states and Mexico. More water is consumptively used in the state than is available from the renewable sources. Fortunately, there are geologic formations (aquifers) in the state that are capable of storing vast quantities of water from past climatic eras, recent precipitation events, or artificial recharge. The aquifers of the state constitute the largest reservoir of freshwater available for use. Groundwater is still under active development and is sustaining much of the state's population and economic expansion.

The state can be divided into three water resource provinces—the Basin and Range Lowlands Province, the Plateau Uplands Province, and the Central Highlands Province (Figure 4-1). Groundwater occurs in all three provinces, but there are separate types of aquifers: stream alluvium along the major streams, alluvial basin fill within the Basin and Range Lowlands Province, and sedimentary rock and fractured rock systems. Rates of storage and depletion need to be quantified so that the sustainability of the current and projected overdraft can be evaluated.

The Renewable Supply—Surface Water

Surface water is defined by hydrologists as water that is present on the surface of the earth in streams, lakes, and reservoirs (for lawyers' definition of surface water, see Chapter 3). The surface-water portion of the supply is generally con-

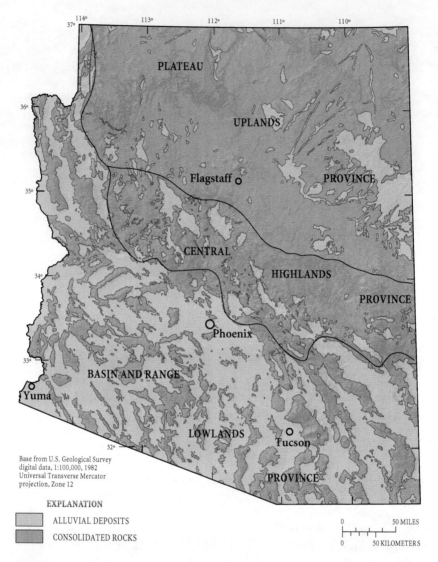

FIGURE 4-1. Water Resource Provinces in Arizona and the Extent of Alluvial Deposits and Consolidated Rocks
Source: Modified from Reynolds 1988.

sidered to be renewable, although rates of precipitation and runoff vary greatly from year to year. Reservoirs provide an effective buffer to the annual variation in surface runoff by allowing storage of water in seasons and years of surplus and release of water in seasons and years of shortage. The geographic distribution of surface water in Arizona is strongly influenced by elevation, with the greatest amounts of precipitation and runoff coming from the mountainous areas of the east-central portions of the state (Figures 4-2 and 4-3). The renew-

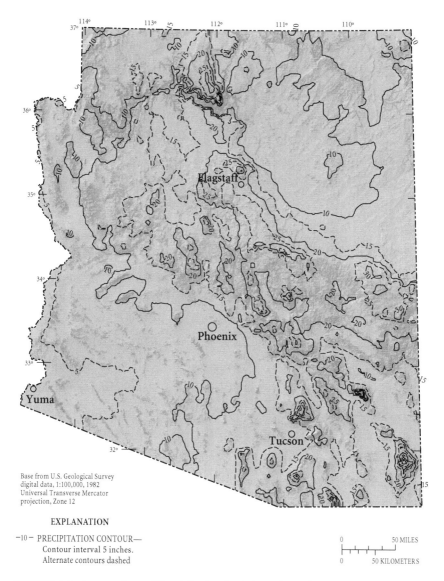

FIGURE 4-2. Average Annual Precipitation for Arizona in Inches, 1971–2000
Source: Oregon State University 2005.

able surface-water supply is largely developed, and few opportunities remain for further enhancement of the supply. The water supply in central Arizona (Phoenix and Tucson) is augmented by Colorado River water delivered by the Central Arizona Project canal system, but this aspect of Arizona's water supply will not be addressed in this chapter; see Chapter 11.

The surface-water resources of the state are well quantified by a network of 270 streamflow gages operated by the U.S. Geological Survey (Figure 4-4). About

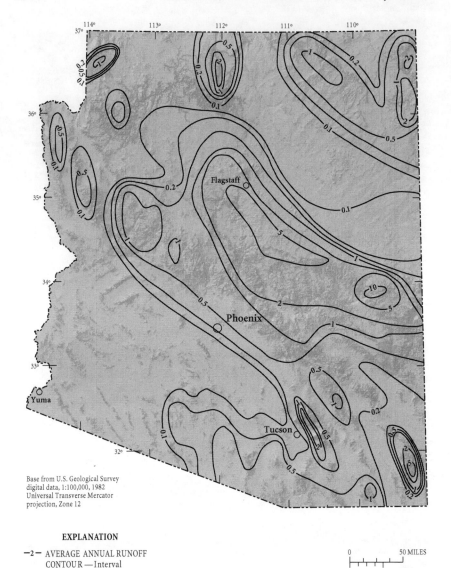

Base from U.S. Geological Survey
digital data, 1:100,000, 1982
Universal Transverse Mercator
projection, Zone 12

EXPLANATION

−2− AVERAGE ANNUAL RUNOFF
         CONTOUR — Interval
         variable, in inches

0   50 MILES

0   50 KILOMETERS

FIGURE 4-3. Average Annual Runoff for Arizona in Inches
Source: Gebert et al. 1987.

61 million acre-feet is delivered annually to the state by precipitation (Figure 4-2), but only about 4.5 million acre-feet results in runoff (Figure 4-3), and an even smaller fraction results in recharge to the state's groundwater aquifers. The total amount of surface water available varies along with the climate, but no trend is evident that the availability of water is changing outside of historical precedent. There is evidence, however, that the distribution of flow is changing throughout the year. Analysis of historical streamflow data for the western

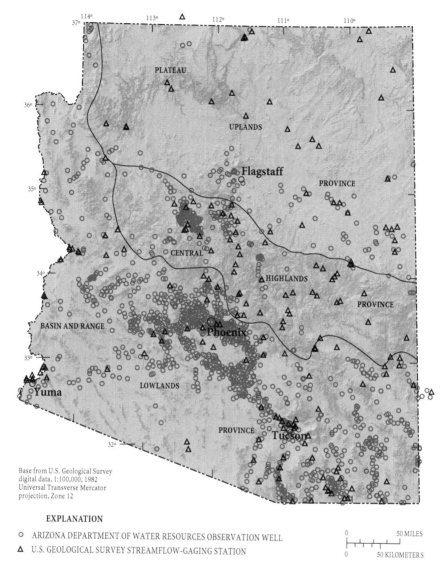

FIGURE 4-4. Surface and Groundwater Monitoring Networks in Arizona

United States indicates that there is a widespread trend toward earlier occurrence of the major seasonal flows (Stewart et al. 2003), especially in snowmelt-dominated basins in the West (Roos 1991; Knowles and Cayan 2002; Mote 2003; Stewart et al. 2004). The earlier timing of snowmelt-derived streamflow is probably connected to warmer winter and spring temperatures (Dettinger 2005). In Arizona, summer season flows are declining at some gaging stations (Figure 4-5) and may be related to an apparent trend of a progressively later onset of the North American monsoon (Anderson et al. 2005).

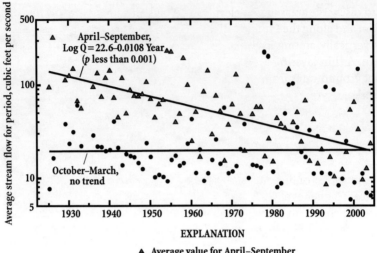

FIGURE 4-5. Change in Seasonal Distribution of Streamflow at the San Pedro River at Charleston Gage in Southern Arizona

The Supply in Storage—Groundwater

Water is present under the land surface in all areas but can only be withdrawn in amounts sufficient for use by humans where hydrogeologic conditions are favorable. Most groundwater in the state is stored in two types of regionally extensive aquifers—thick alluvial deposits of basin fill within the Basin and Range Lowlands Province and extensive sedimentary rock units throughout the Colorado Plateau. The Central Highlands Province includes both of these types of aquifers. These regional aquifers are also the main source of groundwater for agricultural and public uses. Minor amounts of water can also be available locally for domestic and stock supply in fractured crystalline and sedimentary rock aquifers. Water stored in thin layers of stream alluvium is accessed by domestic and agricultural wells near many major streams. Aquifer size is limited by non-aquifer sedimentary and crystalline rocks that form most of the mountains in the Basin and Range Lowlands Province and underlie aquifers on the Colorado Plateau.

Groundwater readily flows between the aquifers in many areas where they lie adjacent to one another. The basin-fill aquifers form a system of hydraulically connected aquifers that decant water to adjacent basins that lie down gradient. This decanting system of aquifers mimics the surface-water drainage system, with water generally flowing toward the Gila and Colorado Rivers. Groundwater flow in the sedimentary rock aquifers of the Colorado Plateau is generally from high-elevation areas near the Mogollon Rim and Coconino Plateau toward discharge areas in low-elevation springs and streams below the Mogollon Rim and along the Little Colorado and Colorado Rivers. Groundwater also flows vertically among layers of sedimentary rock aquifers on the Colorado Plateau. A thin layer of stream alluvium is often an excellent conduit for the flow of groundwater from the underlying regional aquifers to discharge at the streams and springs.

Water Resource Provinces

For the purposes of this discussion, Arizona is divided into three water resource provinces (Ligner et al. 1969; Cooley 1977): 1) the Basin and Range Lowlands Province in the south, 2) the Plateau Uplands Province in the north, and 3) the Central Highlands Province or transition zone between the two other provinces (see Figure 4-1). The influence of this geology creates distinctly different water resource conditions in these areas. A brief description of the hydrogeologic setting within each province is helpful to understand the implications for water availability.

Basin and Range Lowlands Province

The Basin and Range Lowlands Province is characterized by broad alluvial basins surrounded by mountain ranges that are as much as 6000 feet above the valley floor. The mountains in the Basin and Range Lowlands Province are primarily composed of igneous and metamorphic rocks. A few mountains are capped by volcanic rocks. These rocks are largely impervious to water and as a result, precipitation at higher elevations runs off to the valley floor and contributes to basin recharge. In the subsurface, these rocks also form an impermeable barrier to flow, which bounds and underlies the permeable sediments, creating structural troughs that hold large amounts of water in storage (Ligner et al. 1969). This component of water in storage is valuable for sustaining groundwater withdrawals.

The basins are filled with hundreds to several thousand feet of alluvial sediments—the erosional remnants of the surrounding mountains. The basin-fill sediments in Arizona were deposited at different times under varying conditions, which has a substantial influence on their water-bearing characteristics (Anderson et al. 1992). The alluvial deposits are characterized into three units based on grain size, color, degree of consolidation, and sedimentary position: lower basin fill, upper basin fill, and stream alluvium (Figure 4-6) (Anderson et al. 1992). Hydraulic conductivity of the lower basin fill ranges from 1 to 50 feet per day (Anderson et al. 1992). Substantial differences in hydraulic characteristics between the upper and lower basin fill are the result of different depositional environments. Generally, the lower basin-fill unit was

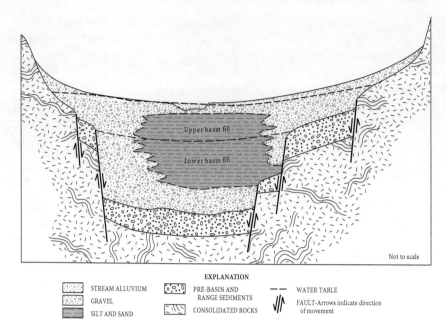

EXPLANATION

STREAM ALLUVIUM		PRE-BASIN AND	– –	WATER TABLE
GRAVEL		RANGE SEDIMENTS		FAULT-Arrows indicate direction
SILT AND SAND		CONSOLIDATED ROCKS		of movement

FIGURE 4-6. Generalized Cross-Section of the Principal Hydrogeologic Units in the Basin and Range Lowlands Province
Source: Anderson et al. 1992.

deposited under internal drainage conditions and is more highly consolidated, deformed, and finer grained than the upper basin-fill unit. Mudstone and evaporite deposits are common in the lower basin fill of deeper basins, which portends poorer water quality and lower yields to wells. The upper basin fill was deposited during the last stages of basin infilling and transition to an integrated drainage system among basins. As a result, upper basin fill is generally more coarse-grained than lower basin fill. The upper basin fill ranges in thickness from less than 100 to about 1000 feet but typically is 300–500 feet thick in the deeper basins. Sediments range from coarse-grained on the basin margins to fine-grained toward the center of most basins. Hydraulic conductivity of the upper basin fill ranges from 1 to 100 feet per day (Anderson et al. 1992).

Thin stringers of stream alluvium were deposited along the major drainage channels after the establishment of the present surface-water drainage system. Stream alluvium consists of highly permeable flood-plain material, channel deposits, sand, and gravel. This unit is generally less than 100 feet thick, and hydraulic conductivities range from 30 to 1000 feet per day (Anderson et al. 1992).

Plateau Uplands Province

The Plateau Uplands Province is composed of consolidated sedimentary rocks, which underlie the entire province. Surface water is rare on the Colorado

Plateau, despite abundant precipitation in certain areas. Several regionally extensive aquifers are present and developed for groundwater use—the C-aquifer (composed of the Coconino Sandstone, Kaibab Formation, Schnebly Hill Formation, and Supai Group), the D-aquifer (composed of the Dakota Sandstone, Morrison Formation, and Entrada Sandstone), the N-aquifer (composed of the Navajo Sandstone, Kayenta Formation, and Wingate Sandstone), and the much deeper Redwall-Muav limestone aquifer. The Redwall-Muav is used for water supply in the Coconino Plateau west and south of the Little Colorado River basin, but it is largely unexplored within the basin (Hart et al. 2002). The amount of groundwater available in these plateau aquifers has not been well defined or quantified.

Central Highlands Province

The Central Highlands Province, also known as the transition zone, divides the state and separates the other provinces. The province is characterized by numerous mountain ranges made of igneous, metamorphic, and sedimentary rocks. Aquifers of regional extent are uncommon in this province but are significant in a few basins, mainly along the Verde River. Alluvial basin-fill deposits are generally restricted in extent except in a few basins. In most basins of the province, groundwater is present in fractures, cracks, and solution features in crystalline and sedimentary rocks. Yields to wells are highly variable, depending on the local fracture systems and the degree to which they are interconnected.

Groundwater Availability

Groundwater recharge and the amounts of water in storage under predevelopment conditions were estimated for most of the groundwater basins in Arizona by the U.S. Geological Survey as part of the Regional Aquifer Systems and Analysis Program (Freethey and Anderson 1986). Large amounts of groundwater are in storage within the state's aquifers. About 900 million acre-feet of recoverable water was estimated to be within 1200 feet of the land surface in the Basin and Range Lowlands Province aquifers (Freethey and Anderson 1986). This amount of water represents about five times the total volume of water that was pumped from these aquifers between 1915 and 1980 and is almost 400 times the estimated rate of annual groundwater depletion in 1980 (Freethey and Anderson 1986). The groundwater basins contain varying amounts of water in storage (Figure 4-7). Estimates of groundwater in storage alone, however, can be misleading. Groundwater storage depletion can result in undesirable consequences, such as land subsidence or capture of stream and spring flow long before the estimated volume in storage is depleted. Moreover, storage depletion can be a mining of water, which is a nonrenewable, unsustainable use.

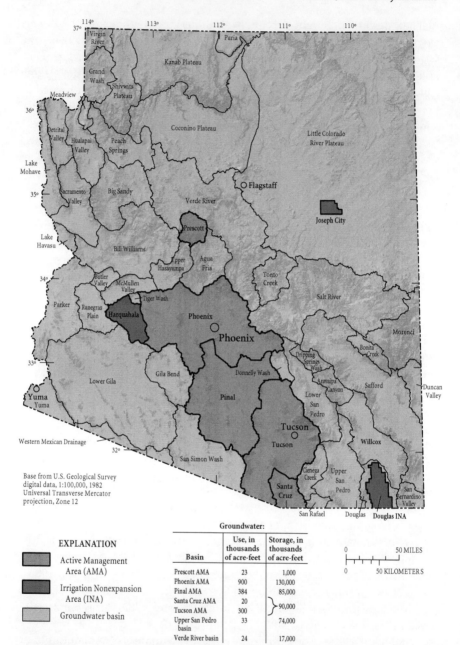

Basin	Groundwater: Use, in thousands of acre-feet	Groundwater: Storage, in thousands of acre-feet
Prescott AMA	23	1,000
Phoenix AMA	900	130,000
Pinal AMA	384	85,000
Santa Cruz AMA	20	90,000
Tucson AMA	300	
Upper San Pedro basin	33	74,000
Verde River basin	24	17,000

EXPLANATION

Active Management Area (AMA)

Irrigation Nonexpansion Area (INA)

Groundwater basin

Base from U.S. Geological Survey digital data, 1:100,000, 1982 Universal Transverse Mercator projection, Zone 12

FIGURE 4-7. Groundwater Basins, Active Management Areas, and Irrigation Nonexpansion Areas in Arizona

Note: Groundwater use and storage are shown in the table for selected basins.

Sources: Storage estimates are from Freethey and Anderson 1986; water use estimates for the AMAs are from Arizona Department of Water Resources; water use for the Upper San Pedro and Verde River basins are from Tadayon 2005.

The value of consistent long-term monitoring of aquifer conditions is critical to sustainable management of aquifers. In contrast to surface water, the systematic monitoring of groundwater availability is far more challenging. A useful monitoring strategy is to structure data collection in support of the terms in a simple hydrologic budget (equation 4-1).

$$\text{Inflow} - \text{Outflow} = \Delta\text{Storage} \qquad (4\text{-}1)$$

Changes in storage occur because of differences in the rates of inflow and outflow. Estimates of inflow and outflow can be highly uncertain. Therefore, derivative estimates of storage change include the cumulative uncertainty of both recharge and discharge estimates. Recharge occurs diffusely across the aquifer and cannot normally be measured. Natural discharge to the land surface at springs, streams, and wetlands normally occurs in specific areas and can often be measured accurately or estimated within reasonable bounds of certainty. Natural groundwater flow to adjacent basins also can be estimated, but with less certainty. Human withdrawals at wells and drains can be measured accurately, but for some time periods and locations such measurements have not been done.

Water Use in Arizona

The amounts and the geographic distribution of water use in Arizona are presented in this section. Water is accounted for by type (surface water or groundwater), by the various uses (agriculture, public supplies, mining, etc.), and by groundwater basin. There are also distinctions made regarding the amount of water consumptively used (without discharge to a stream or aquifer) and the total amount withdrawn or diverted. In the most recent U.S. Geological Survey accounting of water use (total amount withdrawn or diverted in 2000), irrigation used 80% of all water in Arizona (Hutson et al. 2004). Public supplies account for about 16% of use, followed by several other uses in minor proportions (Figure 4-8). The portion of groundwater use in total water use for Arizona has declined from more than 60% in the 1950s to less than 50% for most of the 1990s (Figure 4-9). Total water withdrawals in Arizona have increased from about 5.37 million acre-feet in 1950 to about 7.53 million acre-feet in 2000 (Konieczki and Heilman 2004). All water-use categories have shown increases, but the largest rate of increase is for domestic use, which changed from about 100,000 acre-feet in 1950 to about 1,240,000 acre-feet in 2000. During the same time period, agricultural use increased from 5.22 million acre-feet in 1950 to 6.05 million acre-feet in 2000 (Konieczki and Heilman 2004). However, it should be noted that there are overall decreases in agricultural *groundwater* use since 1990, in part due to increased use of surface water, and in part due to urbanization of agricultural lands. Groundwater use outside of the active management areas (AMAs) in Arizona was compiled for the

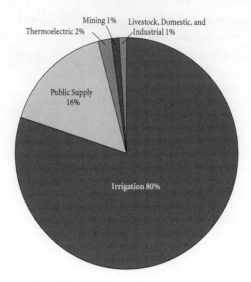

FIGURE 4-8. Water Use in Arizona by Category
Source: Hutson et al. 2004.

period 1991 to 2000 by Tadayon (2005). The groundwater basins and water-use statistics for the AMAs and selected rural basins where development is particularly active are shown in Figure 4-7.

The statewide increase in domestic use is primarily related to increases in population. Per capita water use rates have actually decreased due to conservation efforts in some metropolitan areas within AMAs. Growth rates in the rural parts of the state are extremely high, greater than 5% annually in some communities along the Colorado River, and between 2% and 5% in multiple communities in the southeastern part of the state and the Central Highlands Province (ADWR 2004a). Water supply issues are critical in some areas in the Central Highlands Province, where aquifers are not as productive as in other parts of the state and drought effects are more significant. The towns of Pine, Payson, and Strawberry have not been able to meet delivery requirements during summer months in several recent years, and trucking of water supplies was common in northern Arizona from 2002 to 2004, during the peak of recent drought conditions (ADWR 2004b). On the Navajo and Hopi reservations, access to potable water supplies through delivery systems is limited, and more than 50% of the rural population hauls water for domestic and stock use on a regular basis.

Monitoring Aquifer Conditions

Although it is useful to improve estimates of all water-budget terms for any aquifer, substantial improvement can be achieved by improving estimates of

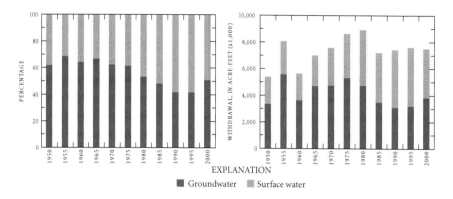

FIGURE 4-9. Groundwater and Surface-Water Withdrawals and Percentage of Groundwater and Surface Water in Total Withdrawal, 1950–2000 for Arizona
Source: Konieczki and Heilman 2004.

withdrawals (one of the outflow terms) and storage change. Withdrawals at wells can be monitored, but it is difficult to monitor adequately the thousands of wells that may tap an aquifer. Rates of storage change are also difficult to quantify. Methods of evaluating storage change include water-budget methods and monitoring water levels in index wells, base flow discharge to streams and springs, and gravity. Each method includes uncertainties that may render it unsuitable for some aquifers. Water-budget methods rely on estimated recharge rates and measured and estimated rates of groundwater discharge. Most of the water-budget method error occurs because rates of recharge are often highly variable on seasonal, annual, and decadal time scales. Typically, water-budget methods assume that recharge rates are equivalent to an estimated long-term average recharge rate.

Water-level change in index wells is an indicator of the extent of storage change. The Arizona Department of Water Resources collects annual water levels from a network of about 1600 index wells (Figure 4-4). Rising water levels indicate increases in storage and an excess of recharge over discharge. Falling water levels indicate an excess of discharge over recharge. Estimates of the volume of storage change require a well-defined spatial distribution of water-level change and well-defined estimates of the aquifer storage coefficient. Aquifer storage coefficient is a measure of the volume of water that the aquifer yields with water-level change. Storage coefficients of aquifer materials can vary greatly. As a result, estimates of groundwater storage change are highly uncertain when based on water-level change.

Changes in groundwater discharge to streams and springs can be a useful method of monitoring changes in groundwater storage where they are the primary modes of groundwater discharge. Winter base flow in many streams is composed entirely of groundwater discharge, and analysis of long-term streamflow gaging records can often reveal trends and cycles in groundwater discharge. Discharge through groundwater use by riparian vegetation also occurs in these areas, but variations are not easily monitored. A drawback of this method is that it measures the capture of groundwater discharge, which is the end effect of groundwater storage change. In many cases, the capture of groundwater discharge occurs decades or more after the storage change occurs.

Gravity methods apply Newton's law of gravitational attraction and use sensitive instruments to measure changes in gravity (Zohdy et al. 1974; Pool and Eychaner 1995). Greater amounts of water in an aquifer will produce a stronger downward gravitational force when instrument measurements are made above the aquifer. Instruments include land- and space-based methods. Land measurements are capable of measuring the gravitational field to an accuracy of 6 inches of water or better. Space-based methods measure the gravitational field at a distance of 500 km or more to an accuracy of about 1 cm of water, which is a high level of accuracy. However, the space-based measurement is influenced by mass across a large area of the earth and is not currently capable of accurately measuring storage change in basins that are much smaller than the Colorado River basin.

Conclusions

The residents and visitors of Arizona depend on surface water and groundwater as the sources of the water supply. The renewable portion of the supply is largely surface water, which is fully appropriated and developed. Groundwater, however, is under active development and sustaining much of the state's economic expansion. Groundwater is present in various types of aquifers, and because of geologic conditions, the volumes of water in storage are large in some groundwater basins. Depletion of groundwater in storage is occurring in many basins, and undesirable consequences, such as land subsidence and streamflow capture, can occur long before the estimated volume of water in storage is depleted. The systematic monitoring of aquifer conditions is useful to develop sustainable management strategies of groundwater use.

References

Anderson, M.T., D.R. Pool, and J.M. Leenhouts. 2005. Changes in Seasonality of Streamflow in the Southwestern United States [abs.]. *Eos Transactions* 86(52), Fall Meeting Supplement, Abstract H21A–1328.

Anderson, T.W., G.W. Freethey, and Patrick Tucci. 1992. Geohydrology and Water Resources of Alluvial Basins in South-Central Arizona and Parts of Adjacent States. U.S. Geological Survey Professional Paper 1406-B, 67 pp.

Arizona Department of Water Resources (ADWR). 2004a. Rural Water Resources Study: Rural Water Resources 2003 Questionnaire Report. October 2004, 29 pp.

————. 2004b. Arizona Drought Preparedness Plan. October 2004.

————. n.d. Data for Active Management Areas http://www.azwater.gov/WaterManagement_2005/Content/AMAs/default.htm (accessed December 2005).

Cooley, M.E. 1977. Map of Arizona Showing Selected Alluvial, Structural, and Geomorphic Features. U.S. Geological Survey Open-File Report 77-343, p. 20, 1 sheet.

Dettinger, M.D. 2005. Changes in Streamflow Timing in the Western United States in Recent Decades. U.S. Geological Survey Fact Sheet 2005-3018. http://pubs.usgs.gov/fs/2005/3018/ (accessed February 9, 2006).

Freethey, G.W., and T.W. Anderson. 1986. Predevelopment Hydrologic Conditions in the Alluvial Basins of Arizona and Adjacent Parts of California and New Mexico. U.S. Geological Survey Hydrologic Investigations Atlas HA–664, 3 sheets.

Gebert, W.A., D.J. Graczyk, and W.R. Krug. 1987. Average Annual Runoff in the United States, 1951–1980. U.S. Geological Survey Hydrologic Investigations Atlas HA–710, scale 1:7,500,000.

Hart, R.J., J.J. Ward, D.J. Bills, and M.E. Flynn. 2002. Generalized Hydrogeology and Groundwater Budget for the C Aquifer, Little Colorado River Basin and Parts of the Verde and Salt River Basins, Arizona and New Mexico. U.S. Geological Survey Water-Resources Investigations Report 02-4026, 55 pp. http://az.water.usgs.gov/pubs/pdfs/WRIR%2002-4026%20WEB.pdf (accessed February 23, 2006).

Hutson, S.S., N.L. Barber, J.F. Kenny, K.S. Linsey, D.S. Lumia, and M.A. Maupin. 2004. Estimated Use of Water in the United States in 2000. Reston, VA: U.S. Geological Survey Circular 1268, 46 pp. http://pubs.usgs.gov/circ/2004/circ1268/ (accessed February 9, 2006).

Knowles, N., and D. Cayan. 2002. Potential Impacts of Climate Change on the Sacramento/San Joaquin Watershed and the San Francisco Estuary. *Geophysical Research Letters* 29(18), 1891; DOI: 10.1029/2001GL014339.

Konieczki, A.D., and J.A. Heilman. 2004. Water-Use Trends in the Desert Southwest: 1950–2000. U.S. Geological Survey Scientific Investigations Report 2004–5148, 32 pp. http://pubs.usgs.gov/sir/2004/5148/pdf/sir20045148.pdf (accessed February 23, 2006).

Ligner, J.J., N.D. White, L.R. Kister, and M.E. Moss. 1969. Mineral and Water Resources of Arizona, Part II, Water Resources, prepared by U.S. Geological Survey. In *The Arizona Bureau of Mines Bulletin* 180, 469–638.

Mote, P.W. 2003. Trends in Snow Water Equivalent in the Pacific Northwest and Their Climatic Causes. *Geophysical Research Letters* 30; DOI: 10.1029/2003GL0172588.

Oregon State University. 2005. Spatial Climate Analysis Service. http://www.ocs.orst.edu/prism/ (accessed October 2005).

Pool, D.R., and James Eychaner. 1995. Measurements of Aquifer-Storage Change and Specific Yield Using Gravity Surveys. *Ground Water* 33(3): 425–432.

Reynolds, S.J. 1988. Geologic Map of Arizona. Arizona Geological Survey, Map 26.

Roos, M. 1991. A Trend of Decreasing Snowmelt Runoff in Northern California. Proceedings of the 59th Western Snow Conference. Juneau, AK, 29–36.

Stewart, I., D.R. Cayan, and M.D. Dettinger. 2003. A Widespread Trend Towards Earlier Streamflow Timing across North America over the Past 5 Decades. Paper presented at American Geophysical Union 2003 Fall Meeting. December 8–13, San Francisco, CA. *Eos Transactions* 84(46).

Stewart, I., D.R. Cayan, and M.D. Dettinger. 2004. Changes in Snowmelt Runoff Timing in Western North America under a "Business as Usual" Climate Change

Scenario. *Climatic Change* 62: 217–232.

Tadayon, Saeid. 2005. Water Withdrawals for Irrigation, Municipal, Mining, Thermoelectric-Power, and Drainage Uses in Arizona outside of Active Management Areas, 1991–2000. U.S. Geological Survey Scientific Investigations Report 2004–5293, 28 pp. http://pubs.usgs.gov/sir/2004/5293/ (accessed February 23, 2006).

Zohdy, A.A.R., G.P. Eaton, and D.R. Mabey. 1974. Application of Surface Geophysical Methods to Groundwater Investigations. U.S. Geological Survey Techniques of Water Resources Investigations, Book 2, Chap. D1, 116 pp. http://pubs.usgs.gov/twri/twri2-d1/html/pdf.html (accessed February 23, 2006).

5

Drought, Climate Variability, and Implications for Water Supply and Management

Gregg Garfin, Michael A. Crimmins, and Katharine L. Jacobs

A rid regions are subject to periodic drought, a phenomenon likely to be exacerbated by climate change. This chapter summarizes the most important features of climate variability and climate change research from a water management perspective and describes management tools useful for responding to increased water supply variability and the conflicts that accompany increased variability.

Climatic Controls on Drought

Arizona is built for drought. During most of the year, the state is in the lee of the eastern Pacific subtropical high, a semipermanent feature of atmospheric circulation that imparts clear, dry conditions to the southwestern United States. The state sits at a climatic crossroads: the northern edge of the subtropics (approximately 15° to 35° N) and the southern edge of the middle latitudes (30° to 60° N). Due to this coincidence of geography, Arizona has two climatically unrelated precipitation seasons (Figure 5-1): summer monsoon (July through mid-September), with intense convective thunderstorms brought in from the south and east; and winter (November through mid-April) with infrequent, multiple-day frontal storms guided by the middle latitude and subtropical jet streams that bring Pacific Ocean moisture to North America.

Arizona's multipeaked (*bimodal*) seasonality is more dramatic in the east-central and southeastern parts of the state, where summer precipitation can

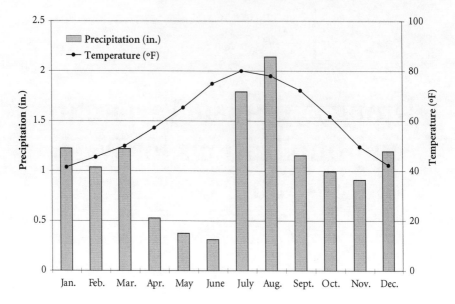

FIGURE 5-1. Average Statewide Arizona Monthly Precipitation (bars and left-hand scale) and Temperature (line and right-hand scale), 1971–2000

account for up to 60% of the annual total (Figure 5-2). A reliably arid foresummer occurs between mid-April and June, as the westerlies shift to the north and the monsoon circulation begins its slow heat-driven buildup. Post-monsoon autumn (mid-September through early November) is usually dry but is prone to high year-to-year (interannual) variability related to eastern Pacific Ocean tropical storm activity.

The fact that Arizona is at the periphery of the atmospheric dynamics and ocean moisture sources necessary to produce precipitation in any given season can help explain why it is arid and why it can experience high interannual precipitation variability. Relatively subtle shifts in the position and strength of the jet streams during the winter, or the Atlantic Ocean's Bermuda subtropical high-pressure system during the summer, can bring the moisture necessary for precipitation right over Arizona or move it far away. Variability in hemisphere-scale atmospheric circulation and sea surface temperature patterns, such as the El Niño–Southern Oscillation (ENSO), can cause these subtle shifts to occur, especially during the winter. Such shifts can persist for months to years, affecting precipitation totals over Arizona and western North America. In addition, because elevation influences precipitation and temperature, dramatic changes in topography can cause complex and subtle patterns of climatic variation over relatively short distances.

Seasonality, Variability, and Water Management

Bimodal precipitation seasonality presents a challenge to managers who must

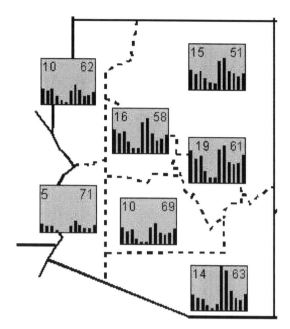

FIGURE 5-2. Arizona Climate Division Monthly Precipitation, 1971–2000

Notes: For each divisional graph, *y* axis scales range from 0 to 3 inches of precipitation; each bar is one month's precipitation, from January (left) through December (right). The number in the upper-left corner is the mean annual precipitation (in.), and the number in the upper-right corner is the mean annual temperature (°F).

Source: Adapted from Sheppard et al. 2002, Figure 3.

balance storage of winter precipitation for summer peak demand and seasonal-to-interannual drought with flood control protection for a variety of situations. Winter precipitation is more hydrologically effective because it is stored as snow and released gradually and because it coincides with cooler temperatures and lower evaporation rates. Whereas summer precipitation makes up the majority of annual precipitation totals in parts of Arizona and can contribute to reservoir and groundwater recharge, it falls in the form of spatially discontinuous (*heterogeneous*) downpours and is subject to extremely high evaporation rates.

High interannual variability presents an additional challenge to water managers because it underscores a lack of reliability. In contrast, decadal-scale persistence highlights phenomena, such as long-term drought, which can drastically reduce water supplies as was demonstrated in the exceedingly dry conditions between 1999 and 2004, as well as during the 1950s.

The Role of the Oceans

The most direct influences of the oceans on Arizona are the cool California current, which can reinforce Arizona's desert climate by inhibiting moisture transport and enhancing high pressure along the west coast of North America, and the equatorial countercurrent, which can impart energy and moisture to tropical storms moving north along the Mexican coast. Relative to the atmosphere, the oceans absorb and release heat slowly. Moreover, the oceans make up the majority of the earth's surface, so their influence on climate is pervasive. Slow fluctuations of ocean circulation at the surface and at different depths provide the so-called memory to the ocean–atmosphere system. In fact, long-term ocean memory can drive persistent multiseason to multidecade climate variations. Oceans clearly influence fluxes of moisture in the atmosphere, but their most important role in Arizona's climate might be their influence on storm tracks, through the episodic redistribution of heat and energy.

The Importance of the Upper Colorado River Basin

The Colorado River supplies 2.8 million acre-feet of water to Arizona annually. The river is the major renewable water supply for irrigated agriculture in central and southwestern Arizona and for municipal water use in Phoenix and Tucson, Arizona's major cities. The river derives more than 70% of its annual runoff from winter snowpack in the high elevations of the upper Colorado River basin (UCRB). (The UCRB includes portions of Wyoming, Utah, Colorado, and New Mexico.) Thus, the climate of this region is of paramount importance to distant water users in Arizona. Peak water use occurs in summer, accompanied by intense heat, especially in urban areas. Summer evaporation rates can exceed 350 mm per month in metropolitan Phoenix. A key factor with regard to drought in the Colorado River reservoir system is that system water uses are approximately equal to mean inflows, so reservoir deficits can accumulate rapidly during multiyear drought but are not rapidly compensated by years with average or slightly above average precipitation. This lag in hydrology can also result in a mismatch in perception when average or above-average precipitation occurs in the lower basin but reservoirs show only gradual and incremental increases. Redmond (2003) also points out that Arizona water supply status is affected by weather and climate occurring months earlier and at distant UCRB locations.

The seasonality of the UCRB differs from that of central and southern Arizona because the majority of UCRB precipitation falls in winter and spring. The climate of the UCRB is subject to shifts in the middle latitude and polar jet streams, and much of the region is semiarid desert. In addition, on interannual time scales, the ENSO signal in the northern UCRB is weaker than in Arizona, and extreme El Niño years tend to deliver less than average precipitation to the northern UCRB (Figure 5-3). Though notable Colorado River basin-wide droughts occurred in the late 1890s, 1950s, and during the early twenty-first century, droughts in the 1930s and mid-1970s were more pronounced in the UCRB than in Arizona. Nevertheless, in both instrumental and paleoclimate

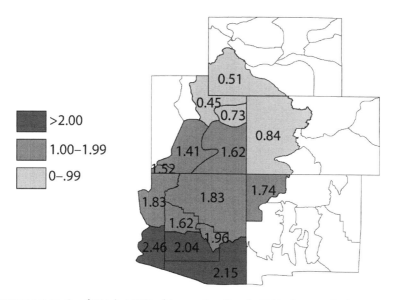

FIGURE 5-3. Ratio of Wet (>115% of Average) to Dry (<85% of Average) El Niño Event Winter (November–April) Total Precipitation
Source: Produced by Jenna McPhee.

records, Hirschboeck and Meko (2005) found a high coincidence of synchronous high and low streamflow years in the UCRB and in Arizona's rivers.

Temperature and Demand

Mean annual air temperatures increased throughout Arizona between 1931 and 2004, with the exception of climate division 7 in the southeastern part of the state (Table 5-1). Mean temperatures in the major urban areas, Tucson and Phoenix, increased by 1.1 °F per decade and 4.0 °F per decade, respectively, in winter, and 1.2 °F per decade and 6.0 °F per decade, respectively, in summer. Temperature increases were recorded in rural and urban areas, with the most pronounced trends generally occurring in winter and spring minimum temperatures. The magnitude of heat islands generated by increased paving and development in urban areas contrasts sharply with heating in surrounding desert and agricultural areas. Enhanced urban temperatures increase energy demand for cooling, as well as demand for landscape watering, which makes up the greatest portion of residential water use. The National Renewable Energy Laboratory (Torcellini et al. 2003) estimates that, nationally, thermoelectric freshwater use for power generation approximately equals freshwater use for irrigation. For Arizona, the laboratory estimates that 7.85 gallons of water are consumed for each kilowatt-hour of power consumed; thus, increases in urban temperature further tax water supplies.

TABLE 5-1. Arizona Climate Division Mean Annual Temperatures and Temperature Increases, 1931-2004

Climate division	1	2	3	4	5	6	7
Temperature increase °F	6.4	6.4	9.8	3.0	9.3	10.5	-2.0
Mean	62.9	51.2	58.5	61.2	71.6	69.4	62.8

Components of Climate Vulnerability in the Water Supply Context

Groundwater vs. Surface Water

Central Arizona, including the major metropolitan corridor from Phoenix to Tucson, has recently shifted from a dependence on overdrafted groundwater to a major new source of renewable water supplies: Colorado River water imported through the Central Arizona Project. In the short term, this water supply supports agricultural uses as well as municipal contractors. In the longer term, the supply will go primarily to municipalities and Native American nations. This new source is critical to achieving the state's management goals because it relieves the pressure on overdrafted groundwater supplies, but it is much more vulnerable to climate variability.

Although groundwater availability is affected by climate, the groundwater reservoirs in most of central Arizona are large enough that short-term climate variability does not have an immediately discernible effect, except in the vicinity of streams that support recharge to groundwater. In contrast, surface-water supplies are affected more rapidly by changes in temperature and precipitation.

The Role of Imported Water Supplies

Importing water supplies, particularly in the context of the vast Colorado River watershed, has a number of implications for water management. As described above, the climate impacts on the upper Colorado River basin are not always synchronous with conditions in the lower basin. To the extent that the water supplies are not affected by the same climate regime, there are advantages to drawing supplies from a broader geographical area. On the other hand, also described above, synchronous long-term drought is more common than the alternative. From a climate prediction standpoint, it is more likely that regional conditions can be more accurately projected than conditions for small watersheds. As prediction skill increases, this may prove useful for managers who have access to Colorado River supplies.

Lessons from the Past, Lessons for the Future: Interannual and Multidecadal Variability

Our most trusted sources for examining interannual-to-decadal climate variability in the western United States are instrumental climate records from the past century. These records show that ENSO is the strongest and most important influence on interannual climate and weather variations in Arizona, particularly in winter. ENSO, defined by significant changes in equatorial Pacific Ocean temperatures, is known for one- to two-year extreme episodes, called El Niño and La Niña. The episodes recur every 3 to 7 years on average, although instrumental and paleoclimate records indicate long-term variations in the recurrence interval. ENSO extremes can disrupt the location and track of jet streams that bring winter weather systems to the southwestern United States.

Researchers have linked El Niño with increased probability of high-intensity winter precipitation and enhanced streamflow (Cayan et al. 1999), Arizona floods (Cayan and Webb 1992), and groundwater recharge (Dettinger et al. 2001). La Niña, on the other hand, brings reliably dry winters to Arizona that seldom exceed long-term average precipitation. Investigators have linked La Niña with sustained drought in the southwestern United States through observational and modeling studies. ENSO also has been linked with summer monsoon precipitation through its effect on one of the many controls on the monsoon: North American winter snowpack and subsequent late spring land-surface heating (Hawkins et al. 2002). In addition, ENSO has an effect on North Pacific Ocean temperatures and downstream atmospheric circulation (Castro et al. 2001). The aforementioned research indicates a tendency for the summer monsoon to be characterized by a late onset and lower than average precipitation in Arizona when it follows an El Niño winter.

Considerable attention recently has been focused on variations at longer time scales, associated with multidecadal variations in the Pacific and Atlantic Oceans. The Pacific decadal oscillation (PDO) is characterized by persistent ENSO-like ocean temperature patterns that are pronounced in the North Pacific Ocean (Mantua and Hare 2002). Multidecade regimes of sustained warm and cool PDO behavior are associated with winter half-year precipitation variations in the western United States, including below-average winter precipitation and episodes of sustained drought in the Southwest, as seen during the 1950s, and above average precipitation, such as the post-1976 wet period. The physical mechanisms behind the PDO are not currently known, and explanations range from complex North Pacific Ocean–atmosphere dynamics to delays in the emergence of ENSO-related tropical ocean perturbations in the northern oceans. Even in the absence of a precise understanding of the mechanisms governing PDO, statistical associations between PDO and Arizona climate yield insights into past episodes of sustained drought and their influence on water resources.

Multidecadal fluctuations in Atlantic Ocean temperatures, called the Atlantic multidecadal oscillation (AMO), are also associated with persistent dry conditions in the southwestern United States (Enfield et al. 2001), such as the 1950s drought. Recent research shows that the AMO in conjunction with the PDO can produce atmospheric circulation patterns conducive to persistent La Niña-like conditions and a higher frequency of drought years in the southwestern United States (McCabe et al. 2004). However, some researchers question whether the AMO is independent of Pacific Ocean variations. Multidecadal climate phenomena have the following ramifications for water resources management: managers cannot count on conditions, dry or wet, to return to "normal" for any significant stretch of time, and expectations regarding future seasonal precipitation are linked with long-term states of the oceans.

The Paleoclimate Record of Drought

The semiarid southwestern United States is a treasure trove of dendroclimatic records derived from long-lived trees and well-preserved stumps and logs on the landscape. Dendroclimatic records of drought and winter precipitation show dry episodes longer and more severe than any that have occurred during the past 100 years. In Arizona, notable multiyear droughts occurred in virtually every century in the past 1,000 years. Particularly notable are winter droughts during the early 1400s, the late 1500s, the late 1600s, and the late 1700s (Table 5-2). The mid-to-late twentieth century is the warmest period in a southern Colorado Plateau reconstruction (Salzer and Kipfmueller 2005), as well as in reconstructions of summer precipitation for a region stretching from west Texas to eastern California.

Spatial Heterogeneity

The Palmer Drought Severity Index (PDSI) is well reconstructed by trees because the index models soil moisture variations by integrating precipitation and temperature measurements, much as a tree integrates precipitation, temperature, and soil moisture in its annual growth. PDSI reconstructions by Cook et al. (2004) for the western United States illustrate an important lesson about increasing temperatures and severe sustained drought. Vast areas of the western United States experienced greater aridity and droughts more sustained and severe than the early twenty-first century drought during centuries characterized by greater warmth, such as during the medieval warm period. Such spatially extensive droughts probably stretched simultaneously across major western river basins, a phenomenon witnessed during the 1999–2004 western U.S. drought. Multi-proxy climate reconstructions, using information from tree rings (PDSI) and corals (ENSO), show that spatial variation in drought in the contiguous United States is due partly to the influence of frequent and persistent La Niña episodes, which result in characteristic patterns of drought across the southwestern United States (Cole et al. 2002). It should be noted,

TABLE 5-2. Notable Consecutive Below-Average Arizona Statewide Winter (November–April) Precipitation Seasons of the Preinstrumental Record

Rank	Starting year	Ending year	Duration	Magnitude	Severity
1	1423	1440	18	260	4681
2	1662	1672	11	392	4311
3	1772	1783	12	348	4171
4	1582	1593	12	289	3471
5	1735	1742	8	310	2482
6	1146	1151	6	395	2369
7	1214	1218	5	414	2068
8	1442	1450	9	229	2060
9	1250	1254	5	387	1934
10	1728	1733	6	319	1916

Notes: Ranked by drought severity. Magnitude is defined as the average winter precipitation departure from the mean of the period 1000–1989 A.D. Severity is the duration times the magnitude. Values have been rounded to the nearest whole number.
Source: Data from Ni et al. 2002.

however, that not all droughts in the paleoclimate record were simultaneously and equally severe across Arizona.

Streamflow

The key lesson for water resource managers from paleohydrologic streamflow reconstructions is that Colorado River water resources were overallocated based on one of the highest streamflow regimes in the past 500 years (Meko et al. 1995). The other important perspective comes from a recognition that periods of extended low flows, such as those in the 1580s, early 1620s to 1630s, 1710s, 1770s, and 1870s were either more severe or longer than droughts we have experienced in more recent times. The late 1500s low-flow period is associated with widespread drought conditions across North America (Stahle et al. 2000). Such periods of widespread drought are characterized by low streamflows in both the upper Colorado River basin and interior Arizona River basins, such as the Salt–Verde–Tonto River system.

Climate Change Predictions

Evaporation, Variability, and the Potential for Extreme Events

The most up-to-date assessment of climate change suggests the following effects over most land areas, including Arizona and the southwestern United States: higher minimum and maximum temperatures, increased precipitation intensity, enhanced rates of evaporation, and increased precipitation variability (IPCC 2001). The assessment also suggests that global warming is likely to increase the risk of extreme droughts and floods that occur with ENSO episodes. Observations from instrumental records show increasing temperatures over the course of the past 75 years throughout most of rural and urban Arizona. The March 1 snow water equivalent at snow courses along the Mogollon Rim and Colorado Plateau has been approximately 2 to 4 inches less during the drought of the early twenty-first century than during the cooler, wetter 1950s drought. (Snow water equivalent is defined as the depth of water that would result by melting the snowpack at a given site. The depth depends mainly on the density of the snow. Given two snow samples of the same depth, heavy, wet snow will yield a greater snow water equivalent than light, powdery snow.) The Colorado River reservoirs that provide renewable water resources to central Arizona's large urban areas are currently subject to evaporation rates of 1.5 million acre-feet per year. Enhanced evaporation rates, combined with earlier snowmelt in the upper Colorado River basin, which provides around 85% of the inflow to Lake Powell, would likely increase water supply vulnerability. Moreover, Redmond (2003) cautions that past climate records may not indicate future climate patterns, due to warming-induced changes in ocean circulation and land surface heating. Such changes could plausibly alter the frequency and persistence of ENSO and PDO episodes.

Arizona and the Colorado River Basin

Between 1950 and 2003, most of the Colorado River basin (CRB)—particularly the lower basin—exhibited a trend toward increasing winter precipitation. This trend is attributable to changing ocean conditions and is believed to be related to an increased occurrence of El Niño episodes after 1976. Although scientists anticipate that global warming will contribute to an enhanced hydrologic cycle, there is no evidence for a cause–effect relationship between the known increases in greenhouse gases and the observed wet trend in the lower Colorado River basin. Global climate model precipitation predictions for the CRB and the western United States must be viewed with caution because they yield inconsistent and sometimes conflicting results. In contrast to inconsistent *precipitation* predictions, western United States and CRB *temperature* projections are relatively consistent. Models show increased CRB temperatures in both summer and winter, with seasonal increases of 2 °C by 2050 and annual increases of 4–5 °C by 2099. The increases are based on greenhouse gas emission scenarios with assumptions of continuously increasing population and regionally oriented economic development. Temperature increases, especially in urban areas, have implications for increased residential water use and energy consumption.

Studies by scientists at the Scripps Institution of Oceanography, using a climate model that projects modest temperature increases of about 2.5 °C in the

CRB by the end of the twenty-first century, found peak snowmelt runoff in the upper basin occurring one to three weeks earlier by mid-century and two to five weeks earlier by the end of the century (Stewart et al. 2004). Although these projections should not be taken as specific predictions, but rather as indications of hydrologic sensitivity to increased temperatures, they are consistent with observed trends toward temperature-driven earlier snowmelt during the twentieth century in western North America and with observed changes in atmospheric circulation that favor high pressure over western North America.

Several studies looking at the effect of increasing temperatures on CRB runoff and system reliability (Gleick and Chalecki 1999; Strzepek and Yates 2003; Christensen et al. 2004), have found that earlier streamflow runoff is likely with increasing temperatures, regardless of precipitation projections. Given the high sensitivity of the CRB due to overallocation of water resources and high demands on the system, increased temperatures are likely to degrade CRB system performance. Ramifications of degraded system performance include decreases in reservoir storage, hydroelectric power output, and deliveries to the Central Arizona Project. The results of these and other climate change studies beg the following water resource management considerations:

1. How will earlier peak streamflows affect the abilities of reservoir operators to balance management objectives with regard to winter and spring floods and summer drought peak demands?
2. Is additional legal flexibility necessary to govern water use in the face of decreasing runoff reliability and predictability?

Arizona Drought Monitoring Tools and Forecast Innovations

Background on the Arizona Drought Preparedness Plan

Recent severe drought conditions prompted the development of Arizona's first drought plan, the Arizona Drought Preparedness Plan (ADPP). Completed in October 2004, the ADPP seeks to limit drought impacts and delineates planned drought responses in four stages of drought severity (ranging from "abnormally dry" to "extreme drought," based on a specific set of indicators). Mitigation and response activities are triggered by monthly drought status reports submitted by a multiagency monitoring committee to the governor's office. These reports are submitted in coordination with the Arizona Department of Water Resources. Monitoring committee activities are linked to communities and subregions of the state through local area impact assessment groups (LAIAGs). The LAIAGs report local and regional drought status and impacts to the monitoring committee once "abnormally dry" conditions are experienced in one of seven drought-reporting regions. LAIAGs also coordinate local drought planning, mitigation, assessment, and adaptation activities at the county level.

Triggers and Indicators

The monitoring committee assesses drought severity through the use of a science-based system of drought indicators and drought status triggers for management actions. An indicator is defined as a quantity that reflects drought conditions, such as streamflow. A trigger is defined as a threshold of a drought indicator that is associated with mitigation or response actions, such as stream-flow at least 15% below average for three consecutive months. Short-term (up to 12 months) and long-term (12 months to 4 years) drought status is calculated separately for each of the seven Arizona climate divisions, using a combination of drought indicators with data dating to 1948. These data include the Standardized Precipitation Index (SPI), streamflow, and reservoir levels. The trigger requirements are designed to ensure that the monitoring committee will not trigger a false alarm going into drought or prematurely remove preparedness measures going out of drought.

Citizens Monitor Precipitation Data

Precipitation data collected by existing meteorological networks are often used as a primary means for tracking changes in drought status, but they are difficult to access in near real time and are unevenly distributed across the state. The current distribution of near-real-time precipitation observations is heavily weighted toward populated areas in the state, with relatively little coverage in rural or wilderness areas. Moreover, the existing network is not dense enough to monitor the spatial heterogeneity in precipitation that is generated by complex topography and summer thunderstorms. This presents a challenge when trying to monitor high-resolution changes in drought status on a monthly-to-seasonal time scale.

A supplementary volunteer observer network to monitor precipitation and other drought-related variables provides an alternative to more expensive and elaborate traditional monitoring approaches. Precipitation is an easy and inexpensive variable to monitor using simple measuring devices (e.g., backyard plastic rain gauges). In conjunction with the LAIAGs, efforts are currently under way to develop a volunteer rainfall monitoring network in Arizona, using recruits from existing programs that have some stake in monitoring rainfall, such as the Cooperative Extension Master Gardener program.

Volunteer monitoring follows standard reporting procedures developed by the National Weather Service. An online reporting and mapping system allows users to enter and store their personal rain gauge data and visualize all volunteer data in near real time. Citizen monitoring cannot replace high-quality automated instrumentation, but it can be used to increase the density of observations and to complement existing networks.

In addition to the aforementioned volunteer precipitation monitoring data, the Arizona drought monitoring committee receives quarterly drought status reports for rural Arizona from the U.S. Department of Agriculture's Natural Resources Conservation Service. These reports give information on the status of drought-sensitive water features, such as seeps, springs, and stock ponds, as well as drought impact information, including range conditions and needs for supplemental feed or water hauling.

Challenges and Lessons Learned

The greatest challenges for Arizona drought monitoring are improving the density and variety of indicator measurements (including the dire need for soil moisture, real-time current groundwater levels, and high-elevation precipitation), integrating subjective indicators and data with short-term records, and effectively communicating long-term drought status that might appear inconsistent with observed conditions, such as seasonally heavy precipitation.

Seasonal Forecasts at the Beginning of the 21st Century

During the past decade, increased understanding of the ocean–atmosphere system and improved observational capabilities through satellite data have given us the capability to make skillful climate forecasts. Each month, the National Oceanic and Atmospheric Administration's Climate Prediction Center (NOAA-CPC) produces probabilistic temperature and precipitation forecasts for three-month overlapping seasons (e.g., September–November, October–December, and so on), with lead times ranging from about two weeks to slightly more than a year. The NOAA-CPC also produces single-month forecasts about two weeks in advance.

The forecasts are derived from a combination of several empirical models that are based on past relationships between ocean–atmosphere parameters and observed U.S. temperature and precipitation and on the output of runs of many different dynamic models that predict temperature and precipitation. Whereas daily forecasts aim to predict individual storms, and thus are sensitive to the initial state of the atmosphere, climate forecasts depend on slower variations in ocean and land conditions, such as shifts in sea surface temperatures associated with ENSO, and long-term trends, such as the sustained increase in western U.S. temperatures since the 1960s. These forecasts attempt to identify regional changes in average conditions across the United States; even modest shifts in the average can result in large changes in the probability of extremes (Dole 2003). Because most of the high-precipitation winters in Arizona have occurred during El Niño episodes, knowledge of impending El Niño conditions enhances the ability to respond to probabilities of above-average winter precipitation totals.

When and Why the Forecasts Are Skillful

The NOAA-CPC temperature forecasts derive most of their accuracy (commonly referred to as *skill*) from long-term trends, especially in the western United States. For precipitation in Arizona, predictions of winter (December–February) and early spring (March) precipitation are most skillful, and forecast accuracy is generally greatest when made with lead times of one to six months. Summer precipitation forecasts are seldom made because of the spatial heterogeneity of summer precipitation, imperfect understanding of the interactions between the factors influencing summer monsoon circulation, and the lack of reliable statistical relationships between Arizona summer precipitation and dominant modes of ocean–atmosphere circulation.

Caveats and Limitations

Uncertainty in probabilistic forecasts is inherent because of the chaotic nature of the climate system; thus, forecasters always leave a small probability for conditions of the opposite extreme to occur. However, knowledge of the decreased probability of unfavorable conditions can be as useful to a decisionmaker as knowledge of increased probability of desired conditions. Key limitations of the NOAA-CPC probabilistic forecasts are the following:

- They have limited skill when not influenced strongly by temperature trend or extreme ENSO phases.
- They make no attempt to resolve regional topography.
- They cannot resolve precipitation forecasts into snow and non-snow components.
- The forecasts cannot resolve the timing or frequency of precipitation within a three-month season.

PDO information has the potential to improve climate forecasts for Arizona because of its strong tendency for multiseason and multiyear persistence (Mantua and Hare 2002).

Decisionmaking in the Context of Uncertainty

Using seasonal forecasts to inform water management decisionmaking requires knowledge of management tolerances for forecast failures. For example, frequent forecasts with a small shift in probability may be correct most of the time (a high "hit rate"), but they may also generate a high rate of false alarms. Most forecasts may only indicate small shifts (5–10%) in the probability of above- or below-average precipitation, which may challenge managers' abilities to use seasonal forecasts. Hartmann et al. (2002) have developed an online forecast evaluation tool that provides decisionmakers with the capability to evaluate forecast skill and biases. The tool also allows users to compare NOAA-CPC forecasts with analogs showing how similar past conditions played out. The tool can be accessed from the following URL: http://hydis6.hwr.arizona.edu/ForecastEvaluationTool/.

Current official and experimental seasonal climate forecasts are conveyed in ways that may not be intuitive to nonexpert users. Some forecast users are unfamiliar with probabilistic information and may be daunted by the additional work necessary to translate a 5–10% shift in seasonal precipitation probability into the range of potential runoff or reservoir inflows. Building confidence in today's seasonal forecasts requires users who are well educated in the nuances of forecast interpretation and the variety of inputs to the forecasts. Forecast users are likely to make the best use of seasonal forecasts if they are well informed about temporal and spatial variations in forecast accuracy and if they are aware of their own tolerances for forecast failure and their ability to take advantage of small shifts in probability. Tools, such as Hartmann's online forecast evaluation tool, and outreach efforts of forecast science agencies and forecast users are among the best means available to develop well-informed forecast users.

The Prospects for Multiyear Forecasts

As mentioned earlier, current climate forecast skill is limited to situations governed by strong temperature trends and extreme ENSO phases. Our ability to forecast beyond ENSO time scales is limited in part by observational capabilities and by computing power. Improved computing capabilities are essential to producing reliable forecasts at the resolutions required for water management (Dole 2003). Other limitations include gaps in our understanding of the land–atmosphere feedbacks, global atmosphere–ocean interactions, and the mechanisms behind drought-producing multiyear persistence in the climate system. Improved forecasts will require better understanding of the interactions between the dominant modes of ocean–atmosphere circulations in the tropical oceans with those in the middle and polar latitudes.

Prospects for multiyear forecasts hinge on diagnostic studies of the mechanisms behind apparent multidecadal phenomena, such as PDO and AMO. Oceanographers are devoting considerable effort to identifying so-called "regime changes" in ocean circulation by using multiple indicators that range from physical ocean–atmosphere variables (ocean temperatures and atmospheric pressure) to biological variables, such as species abundance (Mantua 2004). Identification of these regime shifts can open the door for the diagnostic studies of PDO and AMO variations to be used in climate forecasts, as suggested by research on apparent PDO–ENSO interactions.

Options for Responding to Improved Climate Information

In some cases, water managers are so constrained by operating procedures, rules, and regulations that they do not have the flexibility to respond to new information. Critical to adaptive management is the institutional flexibility to respond to new sources of knowledge. Case studies in using improved climate information that have received the most attention to date focus on multiobjective reservoir management, where climate information can be used to maximize output from a water supply or economic perspective. However, much more can be gained from the use of climate information in the context of integrated water resource management, where surface water and groundwater are used conjunctively.

National Integrated Drought Information System

The National Drought Preparedness Act of 2005 (NDPA) was introduced in Congress in April 2005 to move the country toward a proactive, preparedness-oriented approach to drought. In coordination with the NDPA, the Western Governors' Association is spearheading an effort to encourage Congress to create and implement a National Integrated Drought Information System (NIDIS). The goal of NIDIS is to integrate a variety of hydroclimatic observations across multiple federal and state agencies in conjunction with coordinated drought analysis and forecasting efforts. It is hoped that NIDIS will enhance efforts to improve multiseason and multiyear drought prediction and to convey hydroclimatic observations and forecasts through easily accessible interactive Web-based tools that nonexperts can understand.

Perhaps most important, NIDIS is intended to support drought assessment and decisionmaking at all levels. Hydroclimatic observations, physical science and societal effects, drought research, Web tool development, and stakeholder engagement (including education, outreach, and feedback to researchers and tool development teams) will be enhanced if Congress provides adequate support for NIDIS. This ability to connect water management decisions to improved climate information represents a major step forward.

References

Castro, Christopher L., Thomas B. McKee, and Roger A. Pielke, Sr. 2001. The Relationship of the North American Monsoon to Tropical and North Pacific Sea Surface Temperatures as Revealed by Observational Analyses. *Journal of Climate* 14: 4449–73.

Cayan, Daniel R., and Robert H. Webb. 1992. El Niño/Southern Oscillation and Streamflow in the Western United States. In *Historical and Paleoclimate Aspects of the Southern Oscillation,* edited by Henry F. Diaz and Vera Markgraf. New York: Cambridge University Press, 29–68.

Cayan, Daniel R., Kelly T. Redmond, and Laurence G. Riddle. 1999. ENSO and Hydrologic Extremes in the Western United States. *Journal of Climate* 12: 2881–93.

Christensen, Niklas S., Andrew W. Wood, Nathalie Voisin, Dennis P. Lettenmaier, and Richard N. Palmer. 2004. The Effects of Climate Change on the Hydrology and Water Resources of the Colorado River Basin. *Climatic Change* 62: 337–63.

Climate Assessment for the Southwest. University of Arizona. http://www.ispe.arizona.edu/climas/, 2004.

Cole, J., J.T. Overpeck, and E.R. Cook. 2002. Multiyear La Niña Events and Persistent Drought in the Contiguous United States. *Geophysical Research Letters* 29(13): 1647; DOI: 10.1029/2001GLO13561.

Cook, Edward R., Connie A. Woodhouse, C. Mark Eakin, David M. Meko, and David W. Stahle. 2004. Long-Term Aridity Changes in the Western United States. *Science* 306: 1015–18.

Dettinger, M.D., D.S. Battisti, R.D. Garreaud, G.J. McCabe, and C.M. Bitz. 2001. Interhemispheric Effects of Interannual and Decadal ENSO-Like Climate Variations on the Americas. In *Interhemispheric Climate Linkages*, edited by Vera Markgraf. San Diego, CA: Academic Press.

Dole, Randall M. 2003. Predicting Climate Variations in the American West: What Are Our Prospects? In *Water and Climate in the Western United States*, edited by William M. Lewis, Jr. Boulder, CO: University Press of Colorado.

Enfield, D.B., A.M. Mestas-Nuñez, and P.J. Trimble. 2001. The Atlantic Multidecadal Oscillation and Its Relation to Rainfall and River Flows in the Continental U.S. *Geophysical Research Letters* 28(10): 2077–80.

Gleick, P.H., and E.L. Chalecki. 1999. The Impacts of Climatic Changes for Water Resources of the Colorado and Sacramento–San Joaquin River Basins. *Journal of the American Water Resources Association* 35(6): 1429–41.

Hartmann, Holly C., Thomas C. Pagano, Soroosh Sorooshian, and Roger Bales. 2002. Confidence Builders, Evaluating Seasonal Climate Forecasts from User Perspectives. *Bulletin of the American Meteorological Society* 83: 683–98.

Hawkins, Timothy W., Andrew W. Ellis, Jon A. Skindlov, and Dallas Reigle. 2002. Intra-Annual Analysis of the North American Snow Cover–Monsoon Teleconnection: Seasonal Forecasting Utility. *Journal of Climate* 15: 1743–53.

Hirschboeck, Katherine K., and David M. Meko. 2005. *A Tree-Ring Based Assessment of Synchronous Extreme Streamflow Episodes in the Upper Colorado & Salt–Verde–Tonto River Basins.* Tucson, AZ: University of Arizona Laboratory of Tree-Ring Research. http://fpcluster.ccit.arizona.edu/khirschboeck/srp.htm (accessed January 19, 2006).

Intergovernmental Panel on Climate Change (IPCC). 2001. *Climate Change 2001: The Scientific Basis. Contribution of Working Group I to the Third Assessment Report of the Intergovernmental Panel on Climate Change,* edited by J.T. Houghton, Y. Ding, D.J. Griggs, M. Noguer, P.J. van der Linden, X. Dai, K. Maskell, and C.A. Johnson. New York: Cambridge University Press.

Mantua, Nathan J. 2004. Methods for Detecting Regime Shifts in Large Marine Ecosystems: A Review with Approaches Applied to North Pacific Data. *Progress in Oceanography* 60(2–4): 165–82.

Mantua, Nathan J., and Stephen R. Hare. 2002. The Pacific Decadal Oscillation. *Journal of Oceanography* 58: 35–44.

McCabe, Gregory J., Michael A. Palecki, and Julio L. Betancourt. 2004. Pacific and Atlantic Ocean Influences on Multidecadal Drought Frequency in the United States. *Proceedings of the National Academy of Sciences* 101(12): 4136–41.

McPhee, Jenna, Andrew Comrie, and Gregg Garfin. 2004. Drought and Climate in Arizona: Top Ten Questions and Answers. Tucson, AZ: CLIMAS, University of Arizona, March.

Meko, David, Charles W. Stockton, and W. Randy Boggess. 1995. The Tree-Ring Record of Severe Sustained Drought. *Water Resources Bulletin* 31(5): 789–801.

Ni, Fenbiao, Tereza Cavazos, Malcolm K. Hughes, Andrew C. Comrie, and Gary Funkhouser. 2002. Cool Season Precipitation in the Southwestern United States Since A.D. 1000: Comparison of Linear and Nonlinear Techniques for Reconstruction. *International Journal of Climatology* 22: 1645–62.

Redmond, Kelly T. 2003. Climate Variability in the West: Complex Spatial Structure Associated with Topography, and Observational Issues. In *Water and Climate in the Western United States*, edited by William M. Lewis, Jr. Boulder, CO: University Press of Colorado.

Salzer, Matthew W., and Kurt F. Kipfmueller. 2005. Reconstructed Temperature and Precipitation on a Millennial Timescale from Tree-Rings in the Southern Colorado Plateau, U.S.A. *Climatic Change* 70: 465–87.

Sheppard, P.R., A.C. Comrie, G.D. Packin, K. Angersbach, and M.K. Hughes. 2002. The Climate of the U.S. Southwest. *Climate Research* 21: 219–38.

Stahle, D.W., E.R. Cook, M.K. Cleaveland, M.D. Therrell, D.M. Meko, H.D. Grissino-Mayer, E. Watson, and B.H. Luckman. 2000. Tree-Ring Data Document 16th Century Megadrought over North America. *Eos* 81(12): 212.

Stewart, Iris T., Daniel R. Cayan, and Michael D. Dettinger. 2004. Changes in Snowmelt Runoff Timing in Western North America under a "Business as Usual" Climate Change Scenario. *Climatic Change* 62: 217–32.

Strzepek, Kenneth M., and David N. Yates. 2003. Assessing the Effects of Climate Change on the Water Resources of the Western United States. In *Water and Climate in the Western United States*, edited by William M. Lewis, Jr. Boulder, CO: University Press of Colorado.

Torcellini, P., N. Long, and R. Judkoff. 2003. *Consumptive Water Use for U.S. Power Production*. Technical Report NREL/TP–550–33905. Golden, CO: National Renewable Energy Laboratory.

6

Water Transactions

Enhancing Supply
Reliability during Drought

Bonnie G. Colby, Dana R. Smith, and Katherine Pittenger

Voluntary water transfer between economic sectors and between locations of use is an important tool for achieving cost-effective response to drought. Water may be transferred from uses that generate low economic returns to uses that generate higher economic returns. Additionally, those sectors that generate low economic returns can be paid to refrain from their customary water uses to ensure that enough water is available in times of drought for municipal and industrial users. Although water transfers are valuable for maintaining reliable regional water supplies during drought, they can also create unintended social and environmental problems for parties not part of the transaction. Thus, water transfers may require complex negotiations among multiple interests. Transactions can be both a stimulus for conflict and a means of accommodating new demands and resolving conflict. This chapter examines the types of water transactions that have occurred in Arizona and how they may be used for drought preparedness.

Water Rights and Institutions

As discussed in Chapter 3, Arizona has a dual system of water rights. Surface water rights are developed under the prior appropriation system. Whereas groundwater withdrawals from land located outside of active management areas (AMAs) are essentially unregulated, groundwater rights within AMAs are managed under a permit system authorized by the Groundwater Management Act of 1980 (GMA). Before 1962, appropriative surface-water rights were not transferable, unless the original diversion site was destroyed or impaired. After the legal constraints on transferability of surface-water rights were removed, these water rights became transferable to new locations (Saliba and

Bush 1987). Now the only legal constraint on transferability of surface-water rights is that the transfer must not cause harm to or diminish the water available to other appropriators. Despite the relatively limited legal constraints on surface-water transfers, these types of transfers are still hindered by institutional, hydrologic, and infrastructure limitations. For example, "water wheeling" through convenient conveyance facilities with adequate capacity to make the transfer is essential to smooth transactions, but such conveyance facilities exist in only a few regions within Arizona.

The process of transferring groundwater rights in Arizona is a bit more complicated than that for surface-water rights because of the different types of permitted groundwater rights. First, groundwater rights are only regulated and permitted within AMAs. Outside of AMAs, groundwater rights are subject to little regulation or monitoring. However, there is a significant limitation on groundwater transfers in that pursuant to Arizona Revised Statutes, title 45, section 544, groundwater cannot be transferred between basins. Originally, this prohibition on interbasin groundwater transfers was designed to protect rural groundwater from being moved to thirsty urban areas within AMAs. However, now that rural communities are faced with drought conditions, interbasin groundwater transfers are an attractive option to increase rural supplies. There are some statutory exceptions to the prohibition on interbasin groundwater transfers. One of these legislatively approved exceptions involves transferring groundwater from the Big Chino Subbasin into the Prescott AMA.

The 1980 Groundwater Management Act governs groundwater rights within AMAs. Within the AMAs, groundwater rights are classified with reference to the year the Groundwater Management Act went into effect as either grandfathered (rights established pre-1980) or permitted (rights developed after 1980). Grandfathered rights are further subdivided into the following three categories:

- Type I nonirrigation, which is water formerly withdrawn for irrigation but has been converted to nonirrigation use since 1965;
- Type II nonirrigation, defined as water that was used for nonirrigation purposes at the time the AMAs were established; and
- irrigation rights, which are rights from lands that were irrigated between 1975 and 1980 (Brookshire et al. 2004).

An important distinction between Type I and II groundwater rights is that Type II rights can be separated from the land, but Type I rights must remain attached to the land. Because Type II water can be transferred anywhere within an AMA, this distinction makes Type II rights inherently more marketable than Type I rights.

In AMAs, in addition to grandfathered groundwater rights, there are also exempt withdrawals. Withdrawals of groundwater for nonirrigation use from wells with pump capacities of not more than 35 gallons per minute are exempt from most regulations on groundwater pumping within AMAs. Pumping from exempt wells is not monitored or permitted, though exempt wells do need to be drilled by licensed well drillers. Water from such wells is not marketable because these small-capacity wells are generally for household use only.

Municipal water companies, private water companies, and irrigation districts within AMAs also have service-area rights to withdraw and transport groundwater within their service areas. Service-area rights allow these water providers to transport and deliver groundwater to their customers. Expansion of service areas is regulated, and water providers are subject to mandatory conservation measures designed to reduce per capita water use within each service area as well as the assured water supply requirements discussed in other chapters. Service-area rights are not transferable to locations outside the service area for which they are designated.

History of Water Transactions in Arizona

Before Construction of the Central Arizona Project Canal

In the 1970s and 1980s, before construction of the Central Arizona Project (CAP) canal was complete, water transactions in Arizona were dominated by transfers of groundwater rights within active management areas (AMAs) and transfers from the agricultural sector to the municipal sector. Because Arizona law ties irrigation water rights to land ownership, water buyers historically were required to purchase irrigated land to obtain the appurtenant water rights.

Water transfers occurred as early as 1948, when the city of Prescott bought farmland in the nearby Chino Valley and developed a well field to pump water for domestic use. Controversy arose, with local farmers charging that the Prescott pumping exceeded the amount normally needed for agriculture and led to water declines in the basin (Woodard 1988). Another set of early water transactions involved the city of Tucson's purchase of irrigated farmland in Avra Valley, about 15 miles west of the city. During the eight years from 1971 to 1979, Tucson acquired more than 13,000 acres of irrigated land in Avra Valley. The city developed a well field on the land and a transmission system to deliver the water to city customers. After Arizona's Groundwater Management Act was implemented in 1980, the city's Avra Valley purchases were subject to regulation. Pursuant to a later amendment to the act, the city is able to use a maximum of three acre-feet of water rights per grandfathered, irrigated acre per year from the land it purchased in Avra Valley before 1980, and the total volume of groundwater credits that can be used for assured water supply was legislatively capped. Because of these agriculture-to-urban transfers, previously irrigated land bought by municipal interests became known as "water farms."

Once the GMA was enacted, rural communities considered themselves especially at risk from transfers from nonregulated areas to AMAs because they believed that the 1980 law encouraged transfers (Oggins and Ingram 1990).

When "water farming" first began in 1948, the water farms were near the place of intended use and the original understanding was that the cities would confine themselves to adjacent agricultural areas. Hence, no effort was made to address the consequences of water farming in remote rural areas located far from cities. In contrast, in the late 1980s, water farm purchases triggered intense controversy because of the large scale of the land purchases and the potential economic, social, and environmental costs. Water farming in western Arizona became possible because the CAP canal provided a means of transporting water to Phoenix during dry years if space in the canal was available. The Arizona legislature enacted policies such as the Groundwater Transportation Act to regulate transfers from outlying rural areas in 1991. At the same time, it became clear that excess CAP water would be available for many years and urban areas' interest in such transfers diminished (NRC 1992).

Surface-Water Transfers

Outside of the Colorado and Salt Rivers, surface-water use, and thus surface-water transfers, make up a minor portion of the state's total water consumption. Of the surface water in Arizona, which has been made more reliable through development of storage and delivery infrastructure, most is held within large water districts such as the Salt River Project and several irrigation districts located in western Arizona that use Colorado River water. The use of this water has shifted over time within each district, but surface water generally has not been transferred out of these districts, and changes in the location and purpose of use are handled as matters internal to the district. The Salt River Project has shifted from primarily serving water for crop irrigation to providing a significant portion of its overall water supplies for residential and commercial use as its service area has urbanized.

The city of Scottsdale, thinking ahead to possible shortages of local water supplies, acquired a large irrigated ranch (Planet Ranch) in northwestern Arizona in 1984. The ranch includes surface-water rights to approximately 14,000 acre-feet of Bill Williams River water (this river is a tributary of the Colorado River). Because the ranch is located 200 miles from the city of Scottsdale, the water needs to be transported a great distance to the point of use in Scottsdale, and several conveyance alternatives have been identified. These include constructing a 172-mile pipeline from the ranch to Scottsdale at a cost of several hundred million dollars or building a 16-mile overland pipeline to discharge Bill Williams River water into the CAP canal for delivery to Scottsdale, at a cost of less than $30 million.

If it were not for the complexities of Colorado River law, the most direct and least expensive plan would be to leave Planet Ranch water in the Bill Williams River to flow directly into the Colorado River and then be diverted a few miles down into the CAP canal for delivery to the city. However, this is not currently a realistic option because of problems involving the legal characteristics of the water once it enters the main stem of the Colorado River. To avoid abandoning its water rights during the interim period while it is arranging transport of the water by the CAP canal or another conduit, Scottsdale must continue to use the water. Irrigated acreage has expanded to increase the Planet Ranch water rights claim. As pumping has increased, the riparian forests adjacent to the ranch have died, and forests downstream in a U.S. Fish and Wildlife Service refuge are stressed, except where beavers have created ponds.

Colorado River water has been involved in a limited number of specialized transfers. One example involved the Ak-Chin Settlement ratified by Congress in 1978, in which a large portion of the Ak-Chin tribe's water entitlement was satisfied by transferring senior Colorado River water originally allocated to a large irrigation district located in western Arizona. The Ak-Chin tribe thereby received a senior water entitlement, and the irrigation district received substantial financial benefits from the transfer, which was a voluntarily negotiated arrangement. Given the large quantity and high priority of Colorado River water used in western Arizona agriculture, there are likely to be many more such transfers in the future. Some of these possibilities are discussed elsewhere in this chapter.

CAP Transfers

In addition to appropriated surface-water rights and permitted groundwater rights, once delivery of Central Arizona Project (CAP) water began in 1985, a new type of water right became available. CAP water is accessible to municipal water companies, private water companies, and irrigation districts through delivery contracts with the Central Arizona Water Conservation District (CAWCD). The users of CAP water are divided into three classes: municipal and industrial (M&I), Indian, and non-Indian agricultural. Each class has different delivery priorities and charges. In the event of insufficient CAP water to make deliveries to all users, delivery will be made first to M&I users and non-agricultural Indian users. Next are Indian agricultural users, and third are non-Indian agricultural users.

CAP water contracts can be marketed between users, as long as certain rules are followed. The Arizona Department of Water Resources (ADWR) and the CAWCD issued a policy statement in 1996 on transfers by non-Indian subcontractors of their CAP allocations. The ADWR is currently updating its policy on transfers by M&I users. The director of ADWR reviews the proposed transfer of CAP water and makes recommendations for approval to the Secretary of the Interior. The ADWR provides for a public review of the proposed transfer and reviews it for consistency with water management objectives. Before a transfer is authorized, the relinquishing contractor must submit water supply plans that show that water supplies will be adequate without their CAP allocation and without increasing overdrafts of groundwater. The CAWCD requires that the subcontractor relinquishing the subcontract not make a profit from the transfer; however, the entity is reimbursed for the accumulated carrying costs. ADWR rules provide that the party giving up a CAP allocation must use the proceeds of the sale to purchase alternative water supplies. The CAWCD serves as a clearing house for CAP transfers and relinquishments. Once a transfer has been approved, the contract is released to CAWCD and then may be reallocated to another entity by it.

Many CAP allocations have been made available by non-Indian agricultural districts. These agricultural users signed CAP contracts before the canal was complete. However, after delivery began, these agricultural districts found that CAP water was too expensive to use. The relinquishment of these agricultural contracts has made CAP water available for other users, including for use in settling Arizona Indian water rights claims. Another source of CAP transactions has been leasing of Indian CAP allocations. These CAP transactions are usually part of Indian water rights settlement agreements, which are approved by Congress. Additionally, the city of Scottsdale has acquired CAP allocations from the cities of Prescott and Nogales and other subcontractors for a total of 17,823 acre-feet of CAP water. Scottsdale has used these additional CAP entitlements to meet the city's projected growth needs.

Effluent Transfers

Another important source of water transactions in Arizona has been effluent transfers. As discussed in Chapter 3, the Arizona Supreme Court case *Arizona Public Service Company v. John F. Long* (1989) established that until the legislature declared otherwise, effluent would not be regulated as either surface water or groundwater. Instead, effluent is "owned" by the municipality that generates it and is available for transfer until it is discharged into a surface-water channel. Pima County, in the Tucson AMA, sells up to 3,500 acre-feet per year of secondary treated sewage effluent to farmers in the Cortaro–Marana Irrigation district. The city of Tucson requires all new golf courses to irrigate with effluent and encourages commercial water users to purchase and use effluent from the city's effluent delivery system. Treated effluent (about 140,000 acre-feet annually) from some Phoenix-area municipalities is sold to the Palo Verde nuclear power station for use in cooling the nuclear plant's reactors.

Effluent transfers have also been used as part of tribal water settlement packages. The 2004 settlement with the Gila River Indian community includes a provision that exchanges the city of Mesa's effluent for part of the tribe's potable water allocation. The Indian community will use the effluent for irrigated agriculture, and the city may use the water it receives for its potable water supply. The 2004 amendments to the Southern Arizona Water Rights Settlement Act (SAWRSA) also provide for the use of effluent in settling the Tohono O'odham nation's claims. Originally, SAWRSA required the city of Tucson to deliver about 22,000 acre-feet of effluent per year to the federal government to assist in filling the tribe's water claims. Because the tribe has declined to use effluent

TABLE 6-1. Arizona Water Transfers, 1987–2004

Type of water	Number of transactions	Total volume (acre-feet)
CAP	65	5,983,647.66
Groundwater (Type II)	47	19,762.70
Reclaimed	15	83,394.40
Groundwater (non-AMA)	11	20,347.20
Surface water	9	1,313,592.00
Groundwater (Type I)	1	1,724.00
Total	148	7,422,467.96

for its agricultural needs, the federal government will recharge the effluent in exchange for state groundwater or CAP credits. The nation may then use or save those credits according to the rules of the Arizona Groundwater Management Act.

Tribal Water Transfers

Arizona tribal governments have been involved in water transactions both as acquirers of water through water settlement processes and as lessors of water to others. For instance, the recent Zuni Settlement (discussed in Chapter 14) required acquisition of surface-water rights on behalf of Zuni Pueblo to provide flows for wetland and stream restoration. Most of the water settlements involving central Arizona tribes provide for leasing of tribal CAP water to municipalities, and many such leases are currently in effect. These are discussed in more detail in Chapter 14.

Water Transactions in Arizona, 1987–2004

Table 6-1 summarizes Arizona's water transactions from 1987 to 2004. Transactions are grouped by type of water right and total volume transferred. CAP refers to Colorado River water delivered via a network of canals by the Central Arizona Project. Surface water is any non-CAP water supplied by the state's lakes, rivers, and streams. Reclaimed water is defined as treated effluent. Groundwater is subdivided into Type I and Type II as described above, with the addition of groundwater outside of an AMA (non-AMA).

Figure 6-1 shows the average volume in acre-feet and average price per acre-foot for Arizona's Type II purchases from 1987 to 2003. Figure 6-2 shows the average price per acre-foot and average volume in acre-feet for Arizona's surface-water purchases from 1991 to 1999. Figure 6-3 shows the average volume in acre-feet and average price per acre-foot for Arizona's CAP leases in the years 1987 through 2002.

FIGURE 6-1. Arizona Type II Groundwater Purchases, 1987–2003

Arizona Water Banking Authority

The Arizona Water Banking Authority (AWBA) plays an important role in Arizona's plan for using water transfers to prepare for drought (Arizona Water Banking Authority 2004). The water bank was created in 1996 as a way to use Arizona's Colorado River allocation fully by storing water underground that had been allocated to the state but was not being used. The ability to store water underground to be used in case of future drought or shortage on the Colorado River was also an important consideration in creation of the water bank. (See Chapter 13 for more information on the AWBA.) The bank has since expanded its role in interstate water banking through agreements with Nevada and California to store water in Arizona for these states' future use (Gelt 2004).

Though the water bank does not facilitate water marketing in the traditional sense of buying and selling water, it does facilitate water transfers in the sense that it substitutes the use of one type of water for another in times of drought or shortage. In the interstate banking context, the water bank does not buy and sell water. Instead, it stores water underground in Arizona, which allows other states to take more water from the Colorado River in times of need. Arizona then recovers and uses the stored water in lieu of taking water from the Colorado River.

In 2001, an Interstate Water Banking Agreement was reached among the AWBA, the Southern Nevada Water Authority, and the Colorado River Commission of Nevada. The agreement provided that Arizona would use its "best efforts" to store 1.25 million acre-feet for Nevada's use after 2016. However, drought, increased demand, and threatened water shortages intervened, and Nevada approached Arizona to renegotiate the agreement to provide more security. The new agreement, signed on February 3, 2005, changes the "best

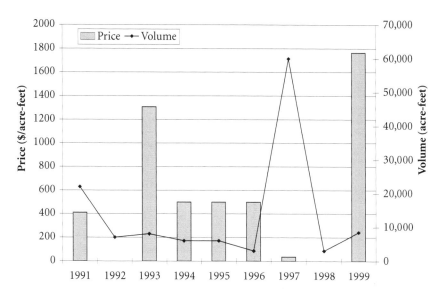

FIGURE 6-2. Arizona Surface-Water Purchases, 1991–1999

efforts" language to a *guarantee* that Arizona will store 1.25 million acre-feet on behalf of Nevada. In exchange for this guarantee, Nevada will pay Arizona $100 million above the actual cost of water delivery, storage, and recovery. The amended agreement allows Nevada to request at most 40,000 acre-feet of water (to be diverted at the intakes in Lake Mead) in any given year, except during shortage years (the 2001 agreement allowed Nevada to request up to 100,000 acre-feet per year). In theory, the agreement does not disadvantage Arizona water users because the AWBA only stores for Nevada water that is not being used by Arizona water users. By the end of 2004, Nevada had 125,260 acre-feet of stored credits in the Arizona Water Bank.

Potential Transfers Based on Land Fallowing

Drought, population growth, environmental protection programs, and other factors in the lower Colorado River region are driving an increase in demand for water and exposing the region to water supply variability. Balancing the shifting nature of supply and demand will likely be accomplished primarily with water transfers out of agriculture into other uses. Irrigated agriculture represents the largest portion of consumptive water use in Arizona. Because much of this water is used to irrigate crops that yield relatively low economic returns, even modest transfers out of agriculture for municipal or environmental use have the potential cost-effectively to fulfill changing demands and drought-induced shortage. Land fallowing and forbearance programs have been proposed and used

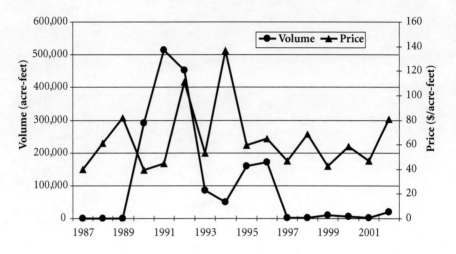

FIGURE 6-3. Arizona CAP Leases Yearly Averages, 1987–2002

throughout the western United States as a means of acquiring agricultural water, with varying degrees of success. Recent proposals by the Yuma Desalting Plant/Cienega de Santa Clara Workgroup and the lower Colorado River region of the Bureau of Reclamation all point to irrigation forbearance in Arizona and the lower Colorado River basin as a reallocation mechanism.

Conservation before Shortage

If a shortage were declared in the lower Colorado River basin, CAP water users would be among the first to experience reduced deliveries. At present, no criteria exist to guide the Secretary of the Interior in declaring a shortage, though a scoping process to develop shortage guidelines is under way, with an anticipated completion date of December 2007. Other concerned parties have also begun developing proposals for shortage sharing.

One such proposal is "Conservation Before Shortage" (2005), a document developed by several nongovernmental organizations (NGOs) released on July 18, 2005. The document proposes Colorado River drought management strategies aimed at avoiding extreme and uncompensated water shortages. The proposed conservation strategies hinge on the elevation of Lake Mead, such that when Lake Mead is drawn down to specific elevations, conservation through predictable, small-scale reductions in use by lower basin users is triggered. A fundamental element of the "Conservation Before Shortage" strategy is voluntary forbearance agreements in the form of part-year fallowing programs, dry-year options, and other similar arrangements.

The rationale for voluntary forbearance is that conservation of between 200,000 and 600,000 acre-feet of Colorado River water could be generated through forbearance of just 4–11% of Colorado River water used for crop irrigation in the lower basin. Based on current prices of short-term water leases between farmers and irrigation districts or municipal water districts, as well as economic analyses of the net return of irrigation water, the document suggests that water conserved through forbearance arrangements could be acquired for $20–$100 per acre-foot. An economic study undertaken by the NGO Environmental Defense suggests that more than 2.3 million acre-feet of irrigation water is currently being applied to crops in Arizona and California that yield profits under $100 per acre-foot. Of this, about 1 million acre-feet are being applied to crops that generate profits under $20 per acre-foot.

Yuma Desalting Plant

A consumptive-use reduction and forbearance program based on voluntary, temporary land fallowing has also been suggested as one of the solutions to the controversy surrounding the operation of the Yuma Desalting Plant (YDP) (see Chapter 7 for more discussion of the YDP). As laid out in the April 2005 document "Balancing Water Needs on the Lower Colorado River: Recommendations of the Yuma Desalting Plant/Cienega de Santa Clara Workgroup," the operation of the YDP (2005) would have both positive and negative effects in the lower basin and Mexico. Its operation would reduce the bypass of drainage water to Mexico from the Wellton–Mohawk Irrigation and Drainage District (WMIDD) in southwestern Arizona. This bypass would eliminate the need for additional releases from Lake Mead to make up for the bypass water, thus lessening the risk of shortage to lower basin water users. However, the operation of the plant would be costly, and depending on the volume of water treated, the reduced bypass flow could have severe environmental consequences in the Cienega de Santa Clara, a large wetland in Mexico sustained by drainage water from WMIDD.

One component of the workgroup's recommendations is a basinwide pilot consumptive-use reduction and forbearance program. The idea behind the program would be to pay farmers to voluntarily reduce their use of Colorado River water for irrigation and then credit the unused water to offset the obligation of the bypass flow. The irrigation forbearance could occur in the long term, on an annual basis, or temporarily through mechanisms such as dry-year options.

Participation in the forbearance program would be open to eligible irrigators in the United States and in Mexico. The workgroup suggests that a target volume of water conserved through forbearance could be tied to the elevation of Lake Mead, available funding, or another related limit. The pilot program would be undertaken for a defined period of time, at the end of which it would be determined, based on cost and effectiveness, if forbearance should be phased in as a component of the long-term YDP plan.

Bureau of Reclamation Pilot Forbearance Program

In 2004, the lower Colorado River region of the Bureau of Reclamation proposed a demonstration water-use forbearance program to be initiated in calendar year 2004 and run through December 31, 2006 (U.S. BOR 2004). The demonstration program was designed to evaluate the potential for voluntary forbearance to offset the effects of bypass water at WMIDD on the Colorado River storage system. Like the "Conservation Before Shortage" proposal, the water saved through land fallowing would make water available to replace the bypass water, and water not released for consumptive irrigation use would remain in the Colorado River storage system.

Under the bureau's proposal, participating irrigators would be eligible to forbear water use on up to 33% of their acreage. Forbearance proposals would be submitted by interested irrigators specifying how much consumptive-use water the irrigator planned to forbear, the expected financial compensation per acre-foot of forborne water, how verifiable reduced diversions and consumptive use would result from the proposed land fallowing, and any state-required approvals.

Although this pilot program was never implemented, the Bureau of Reclamation still espouses irrigation forbearance as a possible method to replace the bypass water to the Cienega de Santa Clara (U.S. BOR 2005).

Conclusions

Arizona's earliest experiences with water transactions involved purchases of large "water farms" by cities seeking to increase the quantity and reliability of their supplies. Although these water farm purchases caused concern in their areas of origin and led to numerous lawsuits, intense statewide controversy over rural-to-urban water transfers occurred later when it became clear that the Groundwater Management Act would limit pumping in the AMAs. After the passage of the GMA and the completion of the CAP canal, there was both incentive and conveyance infrastructure to move large quantities of water from rural areas of western Arizona to the central Arizona cities. Arizona moved into a new era of high rural–urban conflict over large-scale water transfers from western Arizona to the central municipalities. This round of "water farming" ended through state legislation that regulated such transfers and through recognition that the CAP canal would have excess supplies for many years to come.

In the past 20 years, there have been regular and relatively uncontroversial transfers of groundwater rights (within the AMAs), of CAP allocations, of effluent, and of Colorado River water through the Arizona Water Bank. Innovative transactions are being discussed to improve supply reliability through dry-year fallowing, as proposed in the "Conservation Before Shortage" strategy advanced in dialogue over the Yuma Desalting Plant. Such transactions will be temporary and will leave irrigated farming intact in normal water supply years. Whether they can be successfully implemented remains to be seen.

References

Arizona Public Service Company v. John F. Long, 773 P.2d 988 (1989).

Arizona Revised Statutes, sec. 45-544.

Arizona Water Banking Authority (AWBA). 2004. Annual Report 2004. http://www.awba.state.az.us/pubs/final2004report.doc (accessed November 30, 2005).

Brookshire, D., P. Ganderton, M. Ewers, B. Colby, and S. Stewart. 2004. Water Markets in the Southwest: Why and Where? *Southwest Hydrology* 3(March/April): 14–15.

Conservation Before Shortage: Proposed Shortage Criteria for Colorado River Operations. 2005. July. http://www.environmentaldefense.org/documents/4601_CBSshortage proposal2.pdf (accessed July 24, 2006).

Gelt, Joe. 2004. Arizona, Nevada Are Partners in Major Water Banking Deal. *Arizona Water Resource* 13(3). http://cals.arizona.edu/azwater/awr/novdec04/feature1.html (accessed November 30, 2005).

National Research Council (NRC). 1992. *Water Transfers in the West: Efficiency, Equity and the Environment.* Washington, DC: National Academy Press.

Oggins, C., and H. Ingram. 1990. Does Anybody Win? The Community Consequences of Rural-to-Urban Water Transfer: An Arizona Perspective. Issue Paper No. 2. Tucson, AZ: University of Arizona, Udall Center for Studies in Public Policy.

Saliba, Bonnie Colby, and David B. Bush. 1987. *Water Markets in Theory and Practice: Market Transfers, Water Values, and Public Policy.* Boulder, CO: Westview Press.

U.S. Bureau of Reclamation, Lower Colorado Region (U.S. BOR). 2004. *Policy Establishing a Two-Year Demonstration Program for the Forbearance of Colorado River Water.* USBR Draft. May.

U.S. Bureau of Reclamation, Lower Colorado Region (U.S. BOR). 2005. *Bypass Flow Replacement or Recovery Methods Alternatives.* http://www.usbr.gov/lc/region/programs/bypass/alternatives.html (accessed November 25, 2005).

Woodard, G.C. 1988. *The Water Transfer Process in Arizona: Analysis of Impacts and Legislative Options.* Tucson, AZ: University of Arizona, College of Business and Public Administration.

Yuma Desalting Plant/Cienega de Santa Clara Workgroup (YDP). 2005. Balancing Water Needs on the Lower Colorado River: Recommendations of the Yuma Desalting Plant/Cienega de Santa Clara Workgroup. http://ag.arizona.edu/AZWATER/publications/YDP%20report%20042205.pdf (accessed November 15, 2005).

7

Sustaining People, Habitats, and Ecosystems

The Challenge of Integrating Water Policy and the Environment

Patrick J. Graham

People are often surprised to learn that an arid western state ranks among the top five in the United States for natural diversity. Arizona is the most diverse state without a coastline and ranks second in the number of plant and animal species endemic specifically to itself. This diversity is a function of Arizona's geography, lying at the intersection of the Sonoran and Chihuahuan Deserts from the west and east and the Rocky and Sierra Madre Mountains from the north and south. Overlapping the range of both temperate and tropical species, Arizona is both a home and a migratory corridor for hundreds of species of birds, butterflies, and other creatures. With elevations ranging from the low desert to mountain peaks more than 12,000 feet high, diverse habitats often occur in close proximity in this state.

Water is as central to the existence of this rich diversity of life as it is to the human communities that are rapidly expanding across the land. Statewide, an estimated 35% of the perennial free-flowing stream miles have been lost or altered. Of the large lowland rivers in the Gila River basin, 70% of natural perennial flow miles have been lost (digital analysis of Brown et al. 1981). The intersection between water and the environment centers on the competition for water to meet the needs of people. Agriculture remains the largest consumer of both surface and groundwater, although population growth is converting both agricultural lands and water rights into domestic and commercial uses. All too frequently, the loser in this competition for water is the environment.

Life has adapted in form and function to the extremes of conditions in Arizona's climate. Subsurface water flows continue to support riparian vegetation during dry portions of the year in desert regions, and plants have adapted with smaller leaves and the ability to remain dormant during extended droughts only to reemerge in years when winter rains are abundant. Diverse arrays of animals seek water from desert plants and riparian corridors and modify their life cycles to accommodate harsh conditions. However, nature and wildlife are having a hard time keeping up with changing water-use patterns in Arizona.

The primary effect of water policy on the environment involves altered streamflow regimes. The most extensive diversions and flow regulation structures are on the main stem of the Colorado River, the Gila River, and the Salt River. Groundwater pumping of both regulated and unregulated wells has created cones of depression that have dried up entire river reaches. The conversion of natural habitat to agriculture or urban development, inappropriate grazing, and the suppression of fire have robbed the land of its ability to restore aquifers and streams and instead have contributed to flash floods and erosion. Alien species such as tamarisk (salt cedar) have invaded riparian areas along altered stream reaches and are competing for the valuable water and displacing native species. Under reduced flow regimes, native aquatic and riparian species such as fish, frogs, willows, and cottonwoods often are unable to compete with introduced species, such as bullfrogs and tamarisk. The result is loss or severe degradation of much of the aquatic and riparian habitat in the state.

Freshwater Biodiversity

Arizona is an arid to semiarid state with limited surface water. Nonetheless, freshwater systems, including rivers, streams, creeks, cienegas, and other wetland types, and their associated riparian habitats, support a disproportionately high number of species relative to their aerial extent. In addition, riparian areas provide migratory birds and pollinating insects and bats critical travel corridors.

Natural freshwater ecosystems provide a myriad of services, including clean water, mitigation of droughts and floods, recharge of groundwater supplies, regeneration of soil and soil fertility, nutrient cycling, and extensive recreational opportunities. Many of the top recreational attractions in Arizona are water-based, and hikers, birders, hunters, and fishers are a growing economic force.

The critical state of freshwater biological diversity in Arizona is best illustrated by examining native fish species in perennial streams. Arizona's native fish are found nowhere else on earth. They have survived droughts and flash floods for thousands of years. However, human-caused changes are taking a toll. One species, the Santa Cruz pupfish, is extinct, and 20 of the 35 remaining native species or subspecies are federally listed as endangered or threatened or are candidates for listing under the Endangered Species Act.

Arizona's rivers and streams also maintain Arizona's riparian systems, which support the highest densities of breeding birds found in North America. Riparian areas, particularly the cottonwood–willow forests, provide migratory corridors for birds, butterflies, bats, and many other pollinators that winter in Central and South America and summer throughout the western United States and Canada. Depth to groundwater is a critical factor for many native riparian species.

The most basic need of fish is permanent water. Diverse riparian forests are maintained by the natural hydrologic cycle—floods, periods of base flow, and shallow groundwater conditions. The majority of aquatic and riparian habitat in Arizona occurs in streams draining the Mogollon Rim and White Mountains. However, desert streams such as the Verde River, Aravaipa Creek, and Eagle Creek exhibit the highest native fish diversity. Important riparian and aquatic diversity also occurs at locations with permanent water in western and southeastern Arizona.

Perennial flow in streams is maintained by discharge of groundwater from adjoining aquifers. Even streams supported by extensive aquifers may eventually be affected by groundwater pumping at locations distant from the streams. Examples include the Verde and San Pedro Rivers, where rapid population growth is tapping groundwater aquifers whose discharge maintains high-diversity riparian or aquatic habitats.

There is growing awareness that riparian habitats are important for more than biological diversity. However, our understanding of how riparian areas work—the fluxes of water, carbon, and energy, the relationship between surface and groundwater and native plant communities, and how nutrients cycle through the systems—is incomplete, which makes preservation or restoration difficult. Riparian preservation and restoration efforts may include bank protection, fencing to exclude grazing, restoring the natural hydrologic regime, eradicating exotic species, and restoring native species.

There is inadequate recognition of the connection between human uses of water and effects on the environment and a lack of appreciation of the natural benefits provided by healthy landscapes. Sustaining water supplies, flood control, improved water quality, and recreation opportunities are some of the benefits of intact ecosystems that are not often appreciated, nor are they reflected in the public policy of Arizona. This chapter is a collection of case studies that reflect a range of environmental issues, challenges, tools, and potential solutions to sustain the needs of people and nature.

Regulated Rivers

The Lower Colorado River Multi-Species Conservation Plan

The Colorado River and its tributaries provide municipal and industrial water to about 27 million people and irrigation water to almost 4 million acres of land in the United States. The river also serves about 2.3 million people and 500,000 acres in Mexico. In addition, 12 billion kilowatt hours of electricity are generated from its flow. In the lower basin, only 3 of the 10 native species of fish that inhabited the main stem of the lower Colorado River remained by the 1940s, but by the 1960s, none remained. These uses, along with the introduction and establishment of nonnative fish species, have altered the river to the point where all native warm water fish are biologically imperiled. Because these fish are threatened, the federal Endangered Species Act protections are triggered, and water supply and power generation activities on the river must comply with the act's provisions. To create some certainty for the future, affected parties agreed to create the Lower Colorado River Multi-Species Conservation Plan (MSCP). The MSCP is a multiparty effort to mitigate the effects of reservoir operations on threatened and endangered species on the lower Colorado River, thus ensuring the certainty of existing water and power operations. The goal of the MSCP is to move threatened and endangered species toward recovery and to prevent the future listing of at-risk species, although the river is so altered that attaining this goal is unlikely.

The MSCP covers the historical flood plain of the Colorado River from Lake Mead to the United States–Mexico Southerly International Boundary, a distance of about 400 river miles, including the full-pool elevations of Lakes Mead, Mohave, and Havasu. The MSCP does not extend into Mexico and thus does not address environmental effects on the once vast Colorado River Delta, which has dried up because of water withdrawals.

The U.S. Bureau of Reclamation is the primary implementing agency for the MSCP, in consultation and partnership with a steering committee made up of representatives from the 56 participating entities, including federal, tribal, state, local, and private corporations and governments. Environmental groups initially involved in the process withdrew when Mexico was excluded from the geographic scope of the MSCP. Implementation of the program began in April 2005 with the signing of a record of decision by the U.S. Secretary of the Department of the Interior. The department will provide 50% of the program's estimated $626 million cost, and California, Nevada, and Arizona will jointly provide the other 50%.

The MSCP provides funding and a framework for the creation, maintenance, and monitoring of 8,100 acres of riparian, marsh, and backwater habitat for listed and sensitive species. Water rights will be acquired to irrigate the habitat in perpetuity. The plan also includes provisions for stocking more than 1.2 million juvenile razorback sucker and bonytail chub to augment the existing populations of these fish in the lower Colorado River. The plan does not address removal of nonnative fish or rising river temperature problems.

There are concerns that the implementing agencies will not continue to sufficiently support the plan over its 50-year time frame. Critics claim that the MSCP does not provide comprehensive and coordinated ecosystem management of the lower Colorado River, both because Mexico is excluded and because there are no provisions for restoring some portion of the natural flows. Some environmental groups have suggested that a more sustainable approach to preventing species extinction on the river would be to operate the river's infrastructure to mimic natural flow patterns. These groups argue that modest dam reoperation and commitments to in-stream flows for the environment could secure the future of the species that depend on the river for a much lower cost than MSCP implementation. However, the complexity of river management, combined with often-limited water availability, led the users to resolve that no power or water would be lost to environmental mitigation measures. The collaborative approach produced some modest gains for the environment, but debate continues about the long-term benefits.

Yuma Desalting Plant and the Cienega de Santa Clara

Increasing demand for water from the Colorado River and significant drought conditions since 1998 have led to pressure from water-using groups to operate the Yuma Desalting Plant (YDP) in Arizona to reduce the bypass of drainage water to Mexico from the Wellton–Mohawk Irrigation and Drainage District (WMIDD), thereby retaining more water for use in the United States. However, operation of the YDP would be expensive and could result in severe environmental effects to the Cienega de Santa Clara in Mexico, a 40,000-acre wetland, currently sustained by drainage water that the YDP was originally designed to treat. Although significant water supply benefits, up to 100,000 acre-feet, could result from operating the plant, there is major opposition from Mexican interests and environmental groups.

In an innovative attempt to find a win–win solution to this seemingly intractable problem, the YDP/Cienega Workgroup was created to develop solutions that would both offset the effect of the continued bypass of return flows from the Wellton–Mohawk Irrigation and Drainage District and preserve the Cienega de Santa Clara. This diverse group of environmentalists and water managers from the United States and Mexico negotiated behind closed doors for 11 months before issuing a white paper that summarized their recommendations (YDP Workgroup 2005).

The workgroup started by agreeing on fundamental objectives, such as reducing the risks of shortage to lower basin water users and protecting habitat and ecosystem values of the Cienega de Santa Clara. Among other recommendations, they agreed to allow YDP to be operational at a minimum of one-third capacity, using Yuma-area groundwater as an operational source, and that there should be a multipronged long-term plan that can be phased in over several years. The remainder of the water supply would come from conservation and supplies purchased through a shortage alleviation contingency fund described in the short-term plan. The recommended next steps involve initiation of a public process through the Bureau of Reclamation. It remains to be seen whether this intense effort will bear fruit in the context of ongoing concerns about shortages on the Colorado River. The proposed combination of Lower Colorado River basin initiatives may yield the ultimate integration of ecological needs and river management that is necessary to restore and maintain ecological processes on the entire length of the lower Colorado River, including the main stem in Mexico and the Colorado River Delta.

Managing Dam-Regulated Systems for Ecological and Direct Human Benefits: Alamo Dam and the Bill Williams River Watershed

Alamo Dam on the Bill Williams River in southwestern Arizona was completed in 1968. Built by the Army Corps of Engineers, its initial purposes were to provide flood control benefits to protect water control structures on the lower Colorado River, recreational opportunities on the newly created Alamo Lake upstream of the dam, and some water conservation. Water from the Bill Williams River watershed, however, does not become subject to the Colorado River Compact (see Chapter 2) provisions until it reaches Lake Havasu, 39 miles downstream from Alamo Dam. It was not until 1996 that Congress authorized Alamo Dam to be operated for fish and wildlife benefits upstream and downstream of the dam. Before that time, operations were inconsistent with the missions of natural resource agencies such as the U.S. Fish and Wildlife Service's Bill Williams River National Wildlife Refuge, downstream from the dam.

Mitigating effects and enhancing the ecological functioning of dam-regulated rivers are now becoming viewed as important public policy goals. The presence of dams alters surface flow volumes and timing, hydrologic function upstream and downstream of the dam, and sediment transfer and deposition processes. Changes to the ecological attributes of a riverine system affect not only in-stream aquatic resources but also the associated riparian, flood plain, and upland resources. The challenge of ecological flow management is to work with these altered conditions, within the constraints of the dam's physical limitations as well as with other user interests, to craft strategies that can restore lost ecological values or at least create more desirable ecological outcomes.

Riverine systems in the Southwest are unique in that they are extremely dynamic. Chronic low base flow conditions are punctuated by infrequent yet significant flood events—significant in terms of both their relative magnitude and ecological function. Flow regimes can have annual or decadal cycles in response to regional precipitation patterns; these flow variations are critical to a healthy dynamic system. Dampening the extremes of water flow and storing water through the use of dams reduces the risk of catastrophic flooding and provides other human benefits, but it significantly alters the inherent variability that makes the system function to support life that evolved in these extreme environments.

The extensive riparian forests of cottonwood, willow, and mesquite that border the Bill Williams River provide the largest remaining example of this habitat associated with the lower Colorado River system. On the refuge alone, more than 340 bird species have been observed. In recognition of the regional significance of the natural resources associated with the Bill Williams River watershed, state and federal resource agencies have been working together since the early 1990s to resolve user conflicts and improve the prospects for ecological benefit while continuing to meet other dam purposes.

This collaboration recently evolved into the Bill Williams River Corridor Steering Committee (BWRCSC), which in addition to agencies now includes such members as the Nature Conservancy. The Nature Conservancy and the U.S. Army Corps of Engineers signed a national memorandum of understanding that targets a number of Army Corps dams across the country, including Alamo Dam, for ecological restoration projects as part of these two organizations' Sustainable Rivers Project. As part of this effort for Alamo Dam, steering committee members recently defined ecological flow requirements for the Bill Williams River with the goal of ultimately restoring ecological values while meeting other dam purposes. Additional efforts include baseline data collection of abiotic and biotic characteristics to improve the ability of resource managers to monitor and adaptively manage upstream and downstream resources.

During the winter and spring of 2005, water was released from the dam to emulate modest flood flows and to enable scientists to gather information about ecological responses. Near record fall and winter rains forced the release of water over a long duration that could have altered desired ecological outcomes and also led to potential conflicts with other downstream interests. For example, inappropriate timing of flows favors nonnative plants such as tamarisk over cottonwoods and willows, and Central Arizona Project pumping operations at Lake Havasu can be adversely affected by increased turbidity. The solutions crafted by the BWRCSC to avoid these problems helped illustrate why stakeholder coordination rather than regulatory mandate may be the best approach to river operation. The establishment of the BWRCSC, use of collaborative approaches to dam and river management, and advances in the knowledge of how a dam-regulated river functions provide hope that amid the complexity of competing interests, ecological values can be maintained and even enhanced along the Bill Williams River.

Growth and Groundwater Management in the Upper San Pedro Basin

The geographic and sociopolitical context of the Upper San Pedro basin presents an extremely challenging situation for regional water management. The watershed spans an international boundary, and within the U.S. portion, two federal agencies: the Bureau of Land Management (BLM) and the Department of Defense (DOD). BLM manages the San Pedro Riparian National Conservation Area (SPRNCA), the first of its kind designated in the nation in 1988. SPRNCA serves as an avian migratory corridor of hemispheric importance. Fort Huachuca, managed by the DOD, is southern Arizona's largest employer and is critical to the U.S. Army's intelligence training operations. This facility provides essential services associated with today's growing national security concerns.

In recent years, the growing civilian communities in neighboring areas of Cochise County and Sierra Vista are also placing additional demands on regional groundwater supplies. Recent estimates of the amount of recoverable groundwater stored within the Sierra Vista subwatershed are approximately 15 million acre-feet (USPP 2005). However, even relatively small drawdowns of this aquifer will affect the lush riparian habitats that flank the San Pedro River, where cottonwood and willow trees can only access groundwater when it is no deeper than approximately 9 feet from the surface.

Federal laws exert considerable influence on the ways that both BLM and DOD interact with water management issues in the basin, through their respective federally reserved water rights claims established by the Endangered Species Act and section 321 of the 2004 National Defense Authorization Act (U.S. Statutes at Large 2003). Section 321 requires that the Secretary of the Interior, in consultation with the Secretary of Agriculture and the Secretary of Defense, and in cooperation with the Upper San Pedro Partnership, achieve the goal of sustainable yield of the regional aquifer by the year 2011.

However, water users within the private sector—whose numbers are increasing—are not subject to the influence of these federal laws. Current state law does not provide any effective mechanisms for regional water management authority or local ability to create funding mechanisms for water management outside of active management areas (AMAs). Within AMAs, groundwater resources are managed and regulated. The Arizona Department of Water Resources (ADWR) occasionally reviews areas not within established AMAs to determine if the criteria for AMA designation are met. Water availability for riparian ecosystem sustainability is not included in these criteria. Similarly, current state law does not address the needs of ecological systems when evaluating water adequacy for potential new developments.

There are no controls on the expansion of agriculture in the area because it is not designated as an AMA or an irrigation nonexpansion area (INA). The Nature Conservancy partnered with BLM and DOD to retire irrigated agriculture near the San Pedro River through the establishment of voluntary conservation easements, but unfortunately, with no limits on agricultural pumping, the irrigated agriculture was simply displaced to a nearby location. Although an INA designation for the Sierra Vista subwatershed may be appropriate and needed to accomplish local goals, this concept has met with resistance from local landowners.

The passage of House Bill 2364 by the Arizona state legislature in 2005 provides at least an initial mechanism for managing growth as it relates to water in rural areas of Arizona. This provision in Arizona Revised Statutes, title 11, section 821.03 (2005) establishes the authority for counties to adopt ordinances implementing the transfer of development rights. As part of such a program, counties can define "sending areas" where development densities are decreased, and "receiving areas" where development densities are increased. Property owners in sending areas would have development rights legally severed from their property and would be paid for those rights, whereas property owners in receiving areas who desire increased densities could purchase additional density credits. This tool could potentially benefit the San Pedro River in two ways. First, the closer that groundwater pumping occurs to a stream, the more direct and immediate is the impact, especially over shorter time frames. Second, based on existing water-use patterns in the area, transferring future development into urban areas and away from more dispersed rural settings is also likely to reduce total water consumption and the number of unmetered, unregulated, private exempt wells. Treated effluent from municipal wastewater treatment plants in urban areas can also be much more effectively managed for recharge purposes than sewage recharged via individual residential septic systems.

The Upper San Pedro Partnership (USPP) was established in 1998 as part of ADWR's Rural Watershed Initiative to facilitate and implement sound water management and conservation strategies in the Sierra Vista subwatershed "to ensure an adequate long-term water supply is available to meet the reasonable needs of both the area's residents and property owners (current and future) and the San Pedro Riparian National Conservation Area" (USPP 2002). After a decade of "dueling hydrologists," litigation involving Fort Huachuca's water use, and ongoing controversy, the USPP has proven to be the most successful collaborative effort to date in terms of building consensus regarding common water management goals, establishing sound hydrologic research and monitoring programs, and implementing on-the-ground projects. Dozens of water conservation projects have been initiated. Many of these projects would have never been possible without significant federal funding sources. The collaborative effort by the diverse interests represented within the USPP undoubtedly enhanced the ability of the group to lobby successfully for these funds. By 2004, approximately half of the groundwater deficit within the Sierra Vista subwatershed had been mitigated through projects to conserve, recharge, reuse, or augment water resources.

Yet, for all the progress that has been made, water demands continue to rise with increasing human population, and several years of decreased aquifer recharge in the face of drought has exacerbated the situation. Between 1990 and 2002, the population in the Sierra Vista subwatershed grew by 2.2% per year, and the population in the Benson subwatershed grew by 3.5% per year. The San Pedro River was dry at the Charleston gage in the summer of 2005 for the first time since the gage was established (see Chapter 8). As the water conservation projects most economically and politically feasible are implemented first, the remaining options, especially water transfers or import projects, present much greater challenges in terms of finding funding and political support. The successful implementation of these projects will require unprecedented levels of community engagement, cooperation, and funding from multiple levels of government. In the long run, these projects will also need to be paired with additional growth management tools to be truly sustainable.

The Verde River

The Verde River watershed is a 6,600-square-mile area in central Arizona. The watershed consists of large grassland valleys and high ponderosa pine-covered plateaus dissected by deep canyons and steep mountains. Central Arizona's most important aquatic and riparian corridor, the Verde River surfaces in the central part of the watershed and flows east and south for almost 180 miles through semidesert grasslands, conifer woodland, chaparral, and Sonoran desert scrub.

Two major ecological priorities in the upper Verde River watershed include the grasslands in the Big Chino Valley and the Verde River corridor and tributaries. The Big Chino grasslands are some of the largest, highest quality grasslands within the context of this 30-million-acre ecological region. Currently, no paved roads or large developments dissect this extensive grassland, and the dominant activity—ranching—is compatible with the large population of free-ranging pronghorn antelope, a key indicator of grassland ecosystem function. The Verde River is a significant resource in Arizona. It is one of the desert's last free-flowing rivers (above Horseshoe Reservoir) and sustains a large regional wildlife population and a lush riparian community. The Verde River contains Arizona's only congressionally designated wild and scenic river area and the state's only designated greenway. The river and its tributaries and riparian corridors support diverse communities of rare, endangered, and sensitive species. The Verde River contains eight fish species native to Arizona, including populations of three federally listed threatened or endangered species.

The Big Chino grasslands serve as an infiltration basin for water recharge for the underlying aquifer, which feeds the headwaters of the Verde River. The Big Chino aquifer supplies approximately 80% of the flow to the first 24 miles of the Verde River (Wirt and Hjalmarson 2000); this water contributes to the water supply for downstream cities, including Phoenix. Composed of a handful of large, private family ranches with alternating sections of state trust land, management of the Big Chino grasslands and the underlying aquifer is key to the future of the upper Verde River. Groundwater pumping from the Big Chino aquifer will, with time, reduce flow in the upper Verde River. Delineating the water needs of habitat and native species in the upper Verde River is critical to ensuring protection of this important ecosystem.

The Prescott active management area is within the Verde watershed and is made up of three rapidly growing communities (total population 81,000). It is in a water deficit condition, with groundwater overdrafted at a rate of 12,000 acre-feet (more than 4 billion gallons) per year in 2005. This deficit could double with the full building of those homes permitted before the assured water supply criteria went into effect in Prescott and Prescott Valley. Although they are located in a separate subbasin, communities within the Prescott AMA are counting on the statutorily permitted interbasin water transfer from the Big

Chino subbasin to balance their current and projected water budget. Retirement of irrigated agriculture and importation of a portion of that water to the Prescott AMA is recognized as the most feasible way to balance the water budget with minimal additional effect on the Verde River. No other reasonably accessible water source, such as Central Arizona Project water, supplies water to other AMAs in Arizona. However, the Prescott AMA communities have not yet begun pumping from the Big Chino aquifer, in part because of threatened lawsuits related to reducing the flow in the Verde River and potential resulting effects to threatened and endangered species and downstream water users.

Convening interest groups to resolve difficulties within watersheds is challenging because perspectives are diverse, and the institutional mechanisms to bring them to the table collectively to address water use, management, and conservation are generally lacking. Yavapai County has an active Water Advisory Committee, and the city of Prescott is meeting with interest groups about mitigating future water use. In addition, the U.S. Congress recently established a collaborative community-based partnership. To support a workable regional water management plan, a broader array of land and water protection tools is needed. In the Big Chino Valley, outside the Prescott AMA, there is no information available regarding how much groundwater is being pumped. Inside the Prescott AMA, although pumping records are maintained for the large wells, there are on the order of 10,000 exempt domestic wells that do not report when and how much they pump. This lack of data is a considerable challenge to water management and planning. The county has limited authority to regulate wildcat subdivisions, and this type of development is converting native grasslands over the aquifer and is contributing to increased groundwater pumping.

Protecting a large aquifer presents challenges: it is not possible to protect half an aquifer. Purchasing development and pumping rights through voluntary land protection agreements will contribute to maintaining the ability to recharge the aquifer naturally. The creation of an irrigation nonexpansion area would assist with aquifer protection, but INAs only limit agricultural uses, not municipal development. Options to fund the purchase of land protection agreements include local bonds or taxes and cooperative agreements with public agencies and nonprofit conservation organizations such as the Nature Conservancy.

Restoring Land Health

Arizona's deserts, grasslands, forests, and rivers have undergone substantial alteration over the past 150 years since European settlement began. As the human footprint has increased across the state, habitat for native biological diversity has been reduced and fragmented. Habitat loss is significant to resident fauna and flora, wherever it occurs. Given the number of bird species alone that use Arizona in migration between North America and tropical Central and South America, loss of habitat for these species is of hemispheric concern.

Another dimension to the change in Arizona's landscapes is the interruption or cessation of the processes and cycles that perpetuate our grasslands, forests, and riparian corridors. For example, before the twentieth century when substantial resources were committed to fire suppression, low-intensity fires occurred in central and southern Arizona's grasslands on average every 7–10 years. Frequent fire, it turns out, is essential for limiting the growth and expansion of shrubs and maintaining the open character of grasslands. A two-and-a-half-year study by the Nature Conservancy to document the ecological conditions of grasslands found that statewide, 22% of grasslands have been lost to encroachment by shrubs (Schussman and Gori 2004). Fire suppression, cyclical changes in climate, and inappropriate livestock grazing have been the primary drivers of this change.

Fire in Arizona's grasslands also plays an important role in the health of our streams and riparian habitats. In the Galiuro Mountains of southeastern Arizona, the Nature Conservancy jointly manages the 57,500-acre Muleshoe Ranch with the Bureau of Land Management. The ranch contains seven perennial streams with native fish, including Gila chub (*Gila intermedia*), which is listed as endangered under the Endangered Species Act. The ranch's streams are free of exotic species, a rare circumstance in Arizona. The Nature Conservancy and BLM jointly developed an ecosystem management plan in the 1990s that identified watershed restoration goals targeted at enhancing the area's grassland, riparian, and aquatic habitats. Frequent, intense floods had removed stream bank vegetation and in-stream cover for native fish. Soil erosion in the uplands had reduced the depth of aquatic habitat, thereby limiting the availability of deep pools for species such as Gila chub. The management plan called for deferment of grazing and a series of treatments with prescribed fire to reduce shrub cover and to increase the cover of native perennial grasses. The working hypothesis was that increasing perennial grass cover would attenuate floods and result in improved riparian and aquatic conditions.

Over a 12-year period, the Nature Conservancy and BLM burned approximately 26,000 acres, almost half of the watershed. Pre- and post-treatment monitoring of the uplands and riparian and aquatic areas yielded significant results. First, grass cover increased from 33% pretreatment to 48.7% post-treatment, and shrub cover was reduced from 27.4% to 6.4%. Total ground cover, a measure of the watershed's capacity to capture and retain runoff and prevent soil erosion, increased significantly from 56% pre-treatment to 71% post-treatment (Gori and Backer 2004).

Over the study period, three measures of aquatic habitat quality—in-stream plant cover, depth of habitat, and amount of undercut bank—all showed significant increases. Streamflows between 1991 and 1999 actually had decreased because of prolonged drought, so the improved aquatic habitat conditions were not due to increasing flows but rather to structural changes in the stream channel. Native fish responded positively to these changes. The number of Gila chub increased 10-fold over the study period, and the number of all native fish increased significantly. These numbers are particularly striking given the documented decrease in streamflows. The ability to manage grassland watersheds to increase capture of precipitation and attenuate floods also has ramifications for growing human communities that rely on limited water supplies. In this arid state, the health of human communities may be closely linked to grassland health.

Reflections and Conclusion

Much of the rapid population growth in the United States and the world is occurring in semiarid areas. Scientists are now beginning to illustrate better the importance of healthy landscapes to sustaining water supplies, reducing soil loss, mitigating climate changes, and moderating effects of floods in semiarid areas. However, even with this new understanding about the importance of healthy landscapes, in Arizona these lands are now seen by many as speculative investments to be sold to the highest bidder for the development of homes.

For the most part, land use decisions drive water policy. By their nature, these land use decisions are often fragmented spatially and temporally, which can contribute to fragmented and unsustainable water policy decisions, particularly in rural areas and areas dependent on groundwater. The Arizona state legislature is reluctant to provide any direction or regulation on water use outside of active management areas. Many local governments are reluctant to use the few tools they have at their disposal to regulate water use. The pressure from private property rights groups and those who support growth and development defeat most water policy proposals that are raised.

The lessons that can be learned from attempts in Arizona to integrate water policy and environmental concerns include the following:

- protect important lands and sources of water before population pressure makes it too expensive or politically difficult;
- incentives are important to the success of conservation programs;
- involve those affected to ensure that they see the benefits and can gain ownership in the design of solutions;
- provide for water supplies to support key habitats during drought conditions; and
- use disincentives or regulatory approaches, such as the federal Endangered Species Act, to focus the attention of diverse interests to create local, sustainable solutions.

Incentives can include compensating landowners for their lost opportunity costs when directing growth to appropriate areas through density transfers, programs to purchase development rights, conservation reserve payments directed at long-term retirement and conservation of key agricultural lands, and others. However, many programs lack an overall plan or priority system to direct incentives to the most important lands to be conserved, such as along river corridors or over aquifers. Disincentives include moratoriums on new wells, moratoriums on new developments, and growth boundaries or other measures that focus attention on the need to balance a range of private interests with sustainability of land and water use.

Good information and science are both essential for decisionmakers, especially when groundwater is involved. Groundwater is treated as a shared resource, and it is commonly overused as a result. Also important is explaining the connection between a healthy environment and open space, and the benefits to people and communities. As long as this connection is apparent, people will take measures to protect their water supply, property values, and quality of life.

References

Arizona Revised Statutes. 2005. Sec. 11-821.03.

Brown, D.E., N.B. Carmony, and R.M. Turner. 1981. Drainage Map of Arizona Showing Perennial Streams and Some Important Wetlands. Phoenix, AZ: Arizona Game and Fish Department, 1 sheet (1:1,000,000).

Gori, D.F., and D. Backer. 2004. Watershed Improvement Using Prescribed Burns as a Way To Restore Aquatic Habitat for Native Fish. Proceedings of Biodiversity and Management of the Madrean Archipelago II and 5th Conference on the Research and Resource Management of the Southwestern Deserts. Tucson, AZ, May.

Schussman, H., and D. Gori. 2004. *An Ecological Assessment of the Bureau of Land Management's Current Fire Management Plans: Materials and Recommendations for Future Fire Planning.* Tucson, AZ: The Nature Conservancy.

Upper San Pedro Partnership (USPP). 2002. Upper San Pedro Partnership: About Us. http://www.usppartnership.com/about.html (accessed November 28, 2005).

———. 2005. Water Management and Conservation Plan. http://www.usppartnership.com/documents/Working%20Plan%202005%20(Final).pdf (accessed December 2, 2005).

U.S. Statutes at Large. 2003. National Defense Authorization Act for Fiscal Year 2004. Title 117, sec. 321.

Wirt, L., and H.W. Hjalmarson. 2000. Sources of Springs Supplying Base Flow to the Verde River Headwaters, Yavapai County, Arizona. U.S. Geological Survey Open-File Report 99–0378.

Yuma Desalting Plant/Cienega de Santa Clara Workgroup (YDP Workgroup). 2005. Balancing Water Needs on the Lower Colorado River: Recommendations of the Yuma Desalting Plant/Cienega de Santa Clara Workgroup. http://www.cap-az.com/images/newfinaldocument.pdf (accessed December 1, 2005).

8

The Disconnect between Water Law and Hydrology

Robert Glennon

Arizona, like many arid regions, faces the challenge of how to protect river ecosystems from environmental harm when water policies fail to consider the effect of groundwater pumping on streamflows. Quite simply, there is a disconnect between science and law: the science of hydrology instructs that surface water and groundwater are part of the same hydrologic cycle, but Arizona's legal rules treat groundwater and surface water as though they were unrelated. The failure to conform legal doctrine to hydrologic reality has profound and adverse consequences for river flows and riparian habitat in Arizona and throughout the United States. This chapter will first offer an overview of Arizona water law and principles of hydrology; then it will describe the environmental consequences of this failure to integrate law and science by examining in detail the San Pedro River in southeastern Arizona; and, finally, it will analyze efforts at reform aimed at protecting the remaining, but threatened, surface-water flows.

A Primer on Arizona Water Law and Principles of Hydrology

Like every other state in the western United States, Arizona uses the prior appropriation doctrine to govern rights to divert surface water. The essence of prior appropriation is "first in time, first in right," a system that rewarded the earliest entrepreneurs with the senior, most valuable rights. When shortages occur, the senior appropriators receive their full allotments while junior appropriators may go without water. This doctrine encourages economic development at the expense of treating all activities as equal in value. It creates perverse incentives to undertake intensive water diversions to support low-value activities because the government did not require appropriators to pay for the water, yet appropriators obtained rights to use it indefinitely. The prior appropriation doctrine was indifferent to the grave harm to rivers that came from diversions. In the nineteenth century when the doctrine developed, environmental consequences, such as drying up a river, seemed a reasonable price to pay for economic progress.

Some western states use a version of prior appropriation to determine rights to pump groundwater. Arizona, however, adopted the American reasonable-use doctrine. In the nineteenth century when American courts struggled to articulate principles that would govern groundwater use, the science of hydrology was rather primitive. Lacking guidance from scientists as to how water moved beneath the surface of the earth, judges decided that anyone who could get the water out of the ground could use it. The reasonable-use doctrine—an oxymoron, in this case—allows the pumping of groundwater in limitless quantities as long as the water is used on the land for a beneficial purpose, a loose concept that embraces practically all pumping. The reasonable-use doctrine seemed harmless during the nineteenth century when it was thought that groundwater existed in vast underground lakes and was as ubiquitous as the air we breathe.

In the late nineteenth century, some commentators argued for dividing water into more than groundwater and surface water. Clesson Kinney (1894) argued that some underground water moved in known channels in predictable ways—what he called "subflow"—and other water moved in unknown channels. For Kinney, subflow was connected to surface water and therefore was to be regulated as part of the prior appropriation system. The rest of the water, that flowing in unknown channels, would be governed by the reasonable-use doctrine. Kinney's basic hydrologic concept was that *some* groundwater was connected to surface flows, and other groundwater percolated, like water through a coffee pot, in unknown channels. Today, we know from the science of hydrology that groundwater, surface water, and subflow are not separate categories of water. The terms "groundwater" and "surface water" merely describe the physical location of water in the hydrologic cycle. Groundwater and surface water form a continuum, in which groundwater may become surface water in certain portions of a stream and vice versa.

The basin and range area of the southwestern United States generally has valleys bordered by steep mountain ranges. The valleys contain alluvial deposits that are quite permeable. To consider how water moves through aquifers in the basin and range region, imagine your bathtub filled with sand and the tap running for 15 minutes. Within a short time, the water will have made its way around all the grains of sand and arrived at a level steady-state situation. That is, the level of water at one end of the tub will be identical to the level of water at the other end of the tub. What is the relationship between your bathtub and a river?

Consider the following riddle: Where does water in a river come from if it has not recently rained and there is no melting snowpack upstream? The

A. Gaining stream

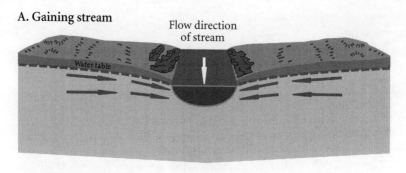

B. Losing stream

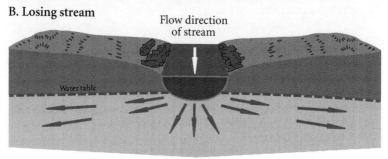

FIGURE 8-1. A Gaining Stream and a Losing Stream
Notes: In a gaining stream (A), water discharges from the surrounding soil into the stream, and in a losing stream (B), water infiltrates the ground.
Source: U.S. Geological Survey.

answer is that it comes from groundwater that has seeped from the aquifer into the river. If the surface level of the river is lower than the water table in the surrounding aquifer, then, by the force of gravity, water will flow from the aquifer into the river, a *gaining* stream (Figure 8-1A). However, if the water table were to drop below the level of the river, then gravity still applies, and the flow of water will be in the opposite direction, a *losing* stream (Figure 8-1B).

Groundwater pumping intercepts water that is moving beneath the surface of the earth toward the river. This water would have eventually arrived at the river, as shown in Figures 8-1 and 8-2. A groundwater well introduces a new demand on the system. When the well begins to operate, it first creates a cone of depression that lowers the water table in the immediate vicinity of the well in response to the extraction of water from the well. Solitary wells usually pose few problems for river systems. However, the cumulative effect of wells in a given region creates the most severe problem. That is one of the lessons of Figure 8-2. Pumping from wells eventually lowers the water table below the level of the stream and reverses the direction of the flow of water.

Even though the science of hydrology teaches that groundwater and surface water are intimately connected, Arizona water law treats them separately. In 1931, in *Maricopa County Municipal Water Conservation District v. Southwest*

A. Onset of groundwater pumping changes the flow of water

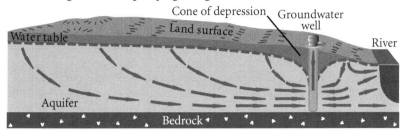

B. Pumping draws water from stream

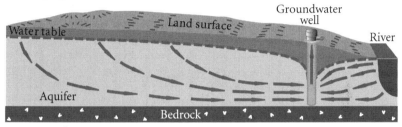

FIGURE 8-2. Groundwater Pumping and Streamflow
Notes: The onset of groundwater pumping changes the flow of water (A). In B, pumping draws water from the stream.
Source: U.S. Geological Survey.

Cotton Company, the Arizona Supreme Court adopted Clesson Kinney's "subflow" theory. Sixty-two years later, in *Gila River II* (1993), the Arizona Supreme Court reconsidered this question but, unfortunately, reaffirmed it. The result is that Arizona law governs surface water, including subflow, by the prior appropriation doctrine, and groundwater by the reasonable-use doctrine.

The reasonable-use doctrine encouraged unsustainable pumping, and the water levels in Arizona's aquifers began to plummet. Think of an aquifer as a giant milkshake glass, and think of each well as a straw in the glass. The reasonable-use doctrine permits a limitless number of straws in the single glass. This is a recipe for disaster, a classic example of the tragedy of the commons. Groundwater is a common-pool resource and a finite quantity, but access to it is limitless. By the 1970s, Arizona's farmers, miners, and cities were annually pumping 650 billion gallons more than nature recharged, and Arizona's rivers, riparian habitat, and wildlife paid the price.

In 1980, the Arizona legislature made a substantial advance in water policy by enacting the Arizona Groundwater Management Act. This progressive piece of legislation set sharp limits to drilling new groundwater wells in the heavily populated areas of the state. In active management areas, new irrigation is prohibited, and housing developers must sign up with an existing water provider, demonstrate an assured water supply themselves, or place their lands in the Central Arizona Groundwater Replenishment District, which then obligates the district to obtain renewable supplies to replenish the mined groundwater used by the developer.

In 2000, the Arizona Supreme Court revisited the subflow issue in *Gila River IV* and once again followed the Southwest Cotton Company case. This time, however, the court recognized that subflow is not a scientific term of hydrology but a legal concept too long ingrained in Arizona law to be disturbed. The court defined subflow as water pumped from wells located within the "saturated flood plain Holocene alluvium" or outside of this area if the well's cone of depression had extended into the Holocene alluvium. When a well pumps water, the withdrawal normally exceeds the rate at which groundwater flows toward the well. The pumping lowers the surrounding water table, which begins to slope toward the well, creating a cone of depression that looks like the vortex in a drain. The initial cone of depression is immediately adjacent to the well, but as the pumping continues, the cone expands. The *Gila River IV* decision determined subflow based on the location of the wells. Wells located in the saturated flood plain Holocene alluvium—and those outside whose cone of depression reaches into the younger alluvium—will be presumed to be pumping subflow. The *Gila River IV* court allowed a pumper to rebut this presumption by an analysis of the chemical composition of the water and other factors to demonstrate that the water being pumped was not related to the surface water.

In Arizona, most prior appropriation claims, including claims to pump subflow, are subject to the jurisdiction of the Gila River General Adjudication Court. This gargantuan proceeding, designed to require all surface-water users in a watershed to file claims in a single court proceeding, began in 1974. It now involves more than 65,000 claims of water rights filed by 24,000 parties. The process has been frustrating to all involved. Since 1974, the Arizona Supreme Court has issued decrees on a half dozen important issues of general application—questions that set the framework for the adjudication of particular water rights—but after 30 years has finally adjudicated only a handful of water rights.

The *Gila River IV* court's definition of subflow offers a measure of protection to riparian areas and to senior appropriators. It regulates those wells located close to the river and whose pumping is most likely to have the most pronounced effect on the river. However, it excludes all wells located outside this subflow region. The Arizona Supreme Court felt bound by the precedent of *Southwest Cotton Company* but recognized the absurdity of the disconnect between law and science and made a plea for the Arizona legislature to address this problem. To date, the Arizona legislature has not responded. Nor has there been any effective leadership by the Arizona Department of Water Resources to remedy this problem.

The Environmental Consequences of Groundwater Pumping

What has the disconnect between law and science meant for Arizona's rivers and riparian areas? A great deal. Let's start with the Santa Cruz River, now an expanse of dry sand that runs through Tucson. As Figure 8-3 demonstrates, the Santa Cruz once was a vibrant river with perennial flows and lush stands of cottonwood, willow, and mesquite trees bordering it.

Figure 8-3 illustrates dramatically the consequences of groundwater pumping. In 1942, the river was healthy, but by 1989, groundwater pumping had so lowered the water table that, first, the river dried up, and then, the trees and shrubs died once the groundwater pumping lowered the water table below the root zone of the trees. The Santa Cruz River is not alone. Diversions of surface water and groundwater pumping have contributed to the degradation of most of Arizona's Sonoran Desert streams, rivers, and riparian habitat.

What about the few healthy rivers in Arizona that continue to have perennial flows? Does the disconnect between water law and the science of hydrology threaten the remaining scarce rivers? Alas, it does.

The San Pedro River

Let us consider the San Pedro River in southeastern Arizona, which the novelist Barbara Kingsolver has described as "a sparkling anomaly for sunstruck eyes, a thread of blue-green relief" (Kingsolver 2000).

The last free-flowing river in southern Arizona, the San Pedro has an extraordinarily diverse riparian habitat, the largest surviving broadleaf riparian forest in the Southwest. Along either side of the river stretches a ribbon of cottonwood and willow trees, marshlands, and native Sacaton grasslands. This riparian habitat supports almost 400 species of birds—two-thirds of *all* species seen in North America. The American Bird Conservancy, Partners in Flight, and the National Audubon Society have bestowed honors on it. *Birder's Digest* named it the premier bird-watching site in the United States.

However, in July 2005, the San Pedro River went dry for the first time in recorded history. The nearby city of Sierra Vista and Cochise County are experiencing rapid growth. Supporters of this growth explain away the river drying up as the effect of a nine-year drought, the consumption of water by cottonwood and willow trees along the river, and the late arrival of the annual summer monsoon. However, droughts are hardly new to southern Arizona, and the river has never dried up before. Clearly, a contributing cause is unrestricted groundwater pumping to support municipal growth and agricultural irrigation. Many of the new wells being drilled in Cochise County and the town of Sierra Vista are located 8 or 10 miles west of the San Pedro River. These wells

FIGURE 8-3. The Santa Cruz River in 1942 (upper) and in 1989 (lower)
Source: U.S. Geological Survey.

intercept water that is moving subsurface, down gradient from the foothills of the Huachuca Mountains toward the river. But this water is not "subflow" and is not subject to the constraints of the prior appropriation system. Instead, under the reasonable-use doctrine, pumpers may pump this water to their heart's content.

Neither the city of Sierra Vista nor Cochise County has taken the steps necessary to protect the river. Local elected officials have observed that water problems stem more from legal matters, not from actual shortage, arguing that water to support population growth is adequate. However, growth will come at the cost of permanently drying up the river. Economic reality suggests that many people who would wistfully like to protect the San Pedro are moved by their own personal economic self-interest. In response to news that the San Pedro had dried up in July 2005, Jason Jackson, a 31-year-old plumber in San Pedro recognized that he is a beneficiary of the population growth in Sierra Vista. As for the San Pedro, he observed "It's nice; pretty trees. The business is more important to me" (Davis 2005).

Institutional Failure

In Arizona, the legislature has failed to give the Arizona Department of Water Resources (ADWR) significant authority to regulate groundwater pumping in the rural parts of the state or to protect riparian habitat. In areas outside of active management areas, even large-capacity wells are immune from regulations except to the extent that there must be a well registration certificate filed. In September 2005, Judge Eddward Ballinger, who presides over the Gila River General Adjudication Court, directed the Department of Water Resources to map the subflow zone in various watersheds. However, that map has not yet been completed by ADWR. If a well was located in the subflow region adjacent to a river, that well would require a prior appropriation permit.

Even when ADWR has authority and could act to protect surface flows and riparian habitats, it has moved timidly or has failed to act. In 1983, the Arizona legislature enacted Title 45, Section 598(A) of the Arizona Revised Statutes to instruct the director of ADWR to adopt rules governing new wells and replacement wells in active management areas "to prevent unreasonably increasing damage to surrounding land or other water users from the concentration of wells." After a long delay, the department finally began the official rulemaking process, which culminated in proposed rules in March 2006. During the stakeholder process, Pima County and the Pima County Regional Flood Control District urged that the rules consider damage to riparian habitat as part of the "damage to surrounding land" and that the rules should provide that "other water users" include not only groundwater pumpers but also surface-water diverters and those who pump "subflow" from wells. Ultimately, ADWR rejected this argument, taking the position that it had no authority to regulate surface-water users. The problem, of course, is that the statute requires that the department consider the impact on "other water users," not "other groundwater pumpers." The Groundwater Management Act includes multiple references to "groundwater users" when the legislature intended to limit the thrust of the statute only to groundwater users.

Strategies for Environmental Restoration

One potential bright spot is proposals for environmental restoration along the Santa Cruz River in Pima County. The U.S. Army Corps of Engineers, in partnership with the Pima County Regional Flood Control District, the city of Tucson, and the town of Marana, is studying the feasibility of ecosystem restoration for recreational uses, cultural resource preservation, and ground-water recharge and recovery projects. The ambitious aim of the project is to restore the Santa Cruz River to as close to a functional river system as is possible. The project has three discrete elements that cover almost 30 river miles of the river, stretching from the north boundary of the Tohono O'odham reservation south of Tucson to the town of Marana northwest of Tucson. The Army Corps and the local partners are conducting stakeholder hearings as a prelude to a final recommended plan that will be submitted to the Army Corps and the elected officials of the project's local sponsors for approval in late 2006. These are exciting projects that involve local storm-water harvesting and reuse of reclaimed municipal effluent to support cottonwood and willow galleries along the river and mesquite bosques and shrub communities on river terraces.

Federal Law

Even though Arizona law does not protect the San Pedro River from pumping groundwater outside the subflow region, federal law offers another alternative. In 2000, the U.S. Fish and Wildlife Service designated hundreds of miles of streams and rivers in Arizona and New Mexico as critical habitat for threatened species of minnows. This habitat included the San Pedro River. Under Section 404 of the Clean Water Act, a developer must obtain a permit from the Army Corps for the discharge of dredged or fill material into navigable waters, which include "intermittent streams" (i.e., dry washes). The U.S. Fish and Wildlife Service has taken the position that development adjacent to the San Pedro River requires a Section 404 permit because the completed homes would rely on groundwater to the detriment of the San Pedro, the listed species, and their critical habitat. Under Section 7 of the Endangered Species Act, the Army Corps must consult with the Fish and Wildlife Service to ensure that any permit issued will not jeopardize a listed species or adversely modify or destroy its habitat.

A second potential source of federal law that could protect the San Pedro River is the federal reserved-rights doctrine. In 1988, Congress created the San Pedro Riparian National Conservation Area (SPRNCA), which includes perennial reaches of the San Pedro River. The act created a federal water right for the SPRNCA. The act creating the SPRNCA expressly reserved sufficient water to protect the riparian area and the aquatic and wildlife resources. As the chair of the Senate subcommittee considering the bill put it, "There is no point in having this legislation unless we are going to protect ... the free flow of water year-round" (U.S. GPO 1987).

Congress charged the U.S. Bureau of Land Management (BLM) with managing the SPRNCA. BLM has acted aggressively to protect the SPRNCA by placing a moratorium on livestock grazing in the area and by retiring 12,000 acre-feet of agricultural water rights. BLM has also purchased conservation easements that offer additional protection. As of 2006, the SPRNCA includes 43 miles of the river and more than 55,000 acres of land.

The date of the federal reservation of land for the SPRNCA—1988—is critical. Anyone who initiated a water use before the creation of the SPRNCA may continue with their pumping. But newer pumpers stand in different shoes. In theory, federal law will protect the SPRNCA's water rights against interference by subsequent water users, whether these users are relying on groundwater or on surface water.

The Bureau of Land Management argues that post-1988 pumping that interferes with water rights for the SPRNCA must be halted. BLM has received support for its position from the Arizona Supreme Court, which in 1999 in *Gila River III* held that federal reserved rights extend to groundwater. The Gila River III court also held that federal reserved-rights holders are entitled to greater protection from groundwater pumping than are water users whose rights are based only in state law. This last critical point derives from a U.S. Supreme Court decision, *Cappaert v. United States* (1976). In this case, ranchers began pumping groundwater on their ranch approximately 2.5 miles from Devil's Hole National Monument. The pumping began to affect adversely the water level in the pool in the national monument. The U.S. Supreme Court held that the executive proclamation establishing Devil's Hole National Monument intended to reserve unappropriated water for the purposes of the reservation, which clearly included maintaining the water level in the pool to protect its scientific value. Ranchers, farmers, and municipal pumpers in the San Pedro River Valley are in a similar situation to the pumpers near Devil's Hole National Monument. Just because they are outside the parameters of the subflow doctrine does not mean that they can continue to pump with impunity to the detriment of the federally protected SPRNCA. Instead, federal law will, one hopes, eventually offer protection to the SPRNCA.

As early as 1999, the BLM and its lawyers from the Departments of Interior and Justice were urged to seek an injunction against irrigation pumping that commenced after 1988. However, BLM, which was then attempting to work cooperatively with local agencies and landowners, was reluctant to take a step that might be seen as confrontational. However, it is now seven years later, and the pumping has not only continued, it has expanded. In 2006, BLM intends to file a statement of claim in the Gila River General Adjudication Court for specific quantities of water to fulfill the federal reserved rights for the SPRNCA. These rights will include rights to the stream's base flows, flood flows, water for the evaporation and transpiration needs of the riparian habitat, and springs and seeps that are located within the SPRNCA.

Many individuals and organizations are earnestly committed to protecting the San Pedro River. Conservation and research efforts concerning the river have involved 4 agencies of the state of Arizona; 9 U.S. government agencies; 7 universities, colleges, and foundations; 11 environmental organizations; 2 international organizations; multiple consulting firms; 1 unit of local government; and 5 coordinating committees and task forces. The major player is the Upper San Pedro Partnership (USPP), a consortium of 21 federal, state, county, and city agencies and the Nature Conservancy, all of which own land, make land use policy, or have resource expertise in the upper San Pedro River basin.

The USPP has ambitious goals and has received substantial funding from the U.S. Department of Defense and other federal sources. The Department of Defense funds the USPP because Fort Huachuca, a federal military base, is located near the San Pedro River. Some people have blamed water use at Fort Huachuca as the culprit for the San Pedro's problems, but in fact, the fort has reduced its water use by 50% over the past 10 years. The real threat to the San Pedro comes from pumping outside Fort Huachuca to support the increasing population base in Cochise County.

The USPP hopes to achieve a number of changes, including conservation programs, recharge of municipal effluent, capturing storm-water runoff, and importing water from other basins. But no credible observer believes that conservation projects alone will eliminate the 10,000 acre-foot per year overdraft of the aquifer. As for water importation schemes, there is no readily available nearby source of water that would solve the overdraft problem. Water imported from farther away, such as Colorado River water through the Central Arizona Project, would be an expensive proposition, involving hundreds of millions of dollars, and would likely be opposed by other water users in the state. To date, no one has stepped forward to pay for an importation scheme.

In 2004, Congress passed legislation that limited Fort Huachuca's liability under the Endangered Species Act for actions outside the Fort's boundaries (National Defense Authorization Act for Fiscal Year 2004). Even though the fort was acting in a responsible fashion and had acted aggressively to conserve water, actions in the civilian sector beyond the base were undermining the effectiveness of the fort's actions. Congress decided that it did not want these actions in the civilian sector to be deemed the responsibility of Fort Huachuca. Although the environmental community criticized this legislation, an almost unnoticed section of the legislation required the Secretary of the Interior to prepare a report on water-use management and conservation measures that would be needed "to restore and maintain the sustainable yield of the regional aquifer" by the year 2011. The Secretary of the Interior submitted her report in March 2005.

The U.S. Geological Survey was the Department of the Interior agency that took the lead in preparing the draft report. One section of the report identified impediments in current laws that hinder efforts to maintain the sustainable yield of the aquifer. This section on legal impediments was a sensitive topic that the Geological Survey left to the USPP to draft as it wished. The USPP identified two pages of minor changes and slight modifications in state law, such as allowing for conservation easements, but they failed to mention the dichotomy in Arizona law between groundwater and surface water—the most serious legal impediment. What may ultimately doom the San Pedro River is the failure of Arizona to integrate laws relating to groundwater and surface water to prevent groundwater pumping from reducing flows in the river. Unless the state of Arizona comes to terms with that inescapable legal reality, the fate of the San Pedro River may be sealed.

Groundwater and Surface-Water Issues along the Colorado River

A third aspect of federal law that may curb groundwater pumping involves wells hydrologically connected to the Colorado River. One of the areas in Arizona experiencing surprisingly rapid growth is the western part of the state along the Colorado River. Developments from Yuma in the south to the area around Kingman in the north are sprouting up. Developers have proposed building more than 160,000 houses between Kingman and the Arizona border (Talton 2006). Some of these developments are close to the Colorado River, and others, though somewhat farther away, are most likely drawing water from the Colorado River. Under the 1928 Boulder Canyon Project Act, no one is allowed to take Colorado River water without a water-use contract with the Secretary of the Interior. Pursuant to the U.S. Supreme Court's decree in *Arizona v. California* (1964), the United States is required to account for diversions of water from the mainstream, return flow, and consumptive use of Colorado River water. The accounting of this water use, which is known as Article V accounting, also includes "water drawn from the mainstream by underground pumping." In the 1990s, the Bureau of Reclamation established an "accounting-surface method" to determine which wells would be deemed to be pumping Colorado River water (Wilson and Owen-Joyce 1994; Owen-Joyce et al. 2000). To understand the accounting-surface method, draw an imaginary line across the surface of Lake Mead and extend it into the earth adjacent to Lake Mead. Then draw another imaginary line across the surface of the river below Lake Mead and extend this line into the ground adjacent to the level of the river. This line is the accounting surface, and any wells that have a static water-level elevation that is at or below the accounting surface are presumed to yield water that will be replaced by water from the Colorado River (Owen-Joyce et al. 2000). The accounting-surface method has never been formally adopted, though the rules have been in place for more than 10 years. At some point, however, the Bureau of Reclamation will be required to report in the Article V accounting the amount of water pumped by wells in Arizona that are drawing water from beneath the static water level of the lake or the river.

In 2006, the Bureau of Reclamation implemented another system to regulate wells in the Yuma area. Irrigation in the Yuma area, particularly the Mesa District, has built up a groundwater mound beneath these lands. One side of the mound moves toward the river and the other side moves away from the river toward the Limitrophe section or into Mexico in the form of groundwater flow. The bureau has agreed not to include the latter wells located on the river in the accounting system to allow pumping of water that would otherwise flow into Mexico (U.S. BOR 2006).

One development will be interesting to follow. Mohave County has approved four or five large housing developments in the Kingman area. As discussed in Chapter 12, under state law, in rural nonactive management areas the only authority the Department of Water Resources has is to decide whether there is an adequate supply of water to serve the development. Even if the department finds that the water supply is inadequate—and that is what the state appears likely to do—the developer can still proceed with subdividing the land. The only consequence of being found to have an inadequate water supply is that the developer must notify potential purchasers that there may not be an adequate supply of water.

One housing development under consideration but not yet approved is the Retreat at Temple Bar, just south of Lake Mead. Because Hoover Dam was completed in the 1930s and Lake Mead was filled, water has been flowing laterally from the lake into the surrounding ground. The Retreat at Temple Bar project would likely tap into the supply of water that has been furnished by the ground becoming saturated by the elevation of water due to the filling of Lake Mead. Any water of this sort pumped by the Retreat at Temple Bar would in turn encourage additional infiltration of water from Lake Mead to replace the water now pumped from the wells. Thus far, there are no effective or enforceable rules that would prevent the developer from going ahead with this pumping. The question is whether the wells are located at or below the static water level pursuant to the bureau's accounting-surface method. If so, then, as a matter of federal law, they will eventually be deemed to be pumping Colorado River water, for which the developer would need a contract with the Secretary of the Interior.

Conclusion

Arizona law and institutions have been slow to respond to the environmental threats caused by pumping of groundwater hydrologically connected to surface flows. Federal law offers greater promise of reform and protection, but it applies intermittently throughout the state depending on the presence of endangered species or federal reserved-water rights. The problem is evident: wells located near rivers will harm rivers. But it will require considerable political will to tackle the machinery of housing development and population growth and to craft policy reforms that require new developments to live with a sustainable supply of water. If Arizona's past is any guide, there is no reason to be optimistic.

References

Arizona Revised Statutes, sec. 45–598(A). 1983.

Arizona v. California, 376 U.S. 340. 1964.

Boulder Canyon Project Act of 1928. U.S. Code. Vol. 43, sec. 617d.

Cappaert v. United States, 426 U.S. 128. 1976.

Davis, Tony. 2005. San Pedro River Is Running Dry. *Arizona Daily Star*, July 13.

Gila River II. 1993. In re the General Adjudication of All Rights To Use Water in the Gila River System and Source. 857 P.2d 1236.

Gila River III. 1999. In re the General Adjudication of All Rights To Use Water in the Gila River System and Source. 989 P.2d 739.

Gila River IV. 2000. In re the General Adjudication of All Rights To Use Water in the Gila River System and Source. 9 P.3d 1069.

Glennon, Robert. 2002. *Water Follies: Groundwater Pumping and the Fate of America's Freshwater*. Washington, DC: Island Press.

Glennon, Robert, and Thomas Maddock, III. 1994. In Search of Subflow: Arizona's Futile Effort To Separate Groundwater from Surface Water. *Arizona Law Review* 36: 567–610.

Groundwater Management Act of 1980. Arizona Revised Statutes, Title 45, Ch. 2, secs. 401, 403, 411, 461, 491, 452, 454, 511, 576, 591.

Kingsolver, Barbara. 2000. A Special Place: The Patience of a Saint San Pedro River. *National Geographic*, April.

Kinney, Clesson S. 1894. *A Treatise on the Law of Irrigation*. Washington, DC: W.H. Lowdermilk.

Maricopa County Municipal Water Conservation District v. Southwest Cotton Company. 4 P.2d 369 (1931).

National Defense Authorization Act for Fiscal Year 2004. U.S. Statutes at Large 117 (2003): 1392, sec. 321(a)(1).

Owen-Joyce, S.J., R.P. Wilson, M.C. Carpenter, and J.B. Fink. 2000. Method To Identify Wells That Yield Water That Will Be Replaced by Water from the Colorado River Downstream from Laguna Dam in Arizona and California. U.S. Geological Survey Water Resources Investigation Report 00–4085.

Talton, John. 2006. Tipping Point; Wake Up Arizona; Heed the Warnings of a Looming Water Crisis. *The Arizona Republic*, February 12.

U.S. Bureau of Reclamation (U.S. BOR). 2006. Summary Description of Accounting for Water Use in the Yuma Area Beginning with Calendar Year 2003.

U.S. Government Printing Office (U.S. GPO). 1987. San Pedro Riparian National Conservation Area: Hearing before the Subcommittee on Public Lands of the Committee on Interior and Insular Affairs, House of Representatives, Ninety-Ninth Congress, second session on H.R. 4811, held in Washington, DC, July 15,

1986. Washington, DC: U.S. GPO. Congressional Sales Office. OCLC: 15970821.

Wilson, R.P., and S.J. Owen-Joyce. 1994. Method To Identify Wells That Yield Water That Will Be Replaced by Colorado River Water in Arizona, California, Nevada, and Utah. U.S. Geological Survey Water Resources Investigations Report 94–4005.

9

Protecting the Supply

Arizona's Water Quality Challenges

Karen L. Smith and Charles G. Graf

Passage of the Clean Water Act in 1972 by the U.S. Congress marked a threshold event for Arizona's water quality. The Clean Water Act would provide a systematic, regulatory, data-driven framework to ensure that the water in Arizona's rivers and lakes was clean enough to drink, good enough for recreation, and safe for fish and wildlife. Before 1972, Arizona, through its state Water Quality Control Council and Department of Health Services, focused primarily on the public health aspects of drinking water. Arizona provided some attention to wastewater treatment and little attention to the new "fishable, swimmable" goals that Congress set forth in the Clean Water Act. Little fundamental data to determine water quality existed, and Arizona had no comprehensive program to monitor its surface water and groundwater. Fortunately for Arizonans, the population in 1972 was little more than 2 million people, and the pressures of growth on water quality, while evident, were not yet critical. Still, when Arizona completed its first assessment of Arizona's surface waters in 1976, the primary problems revolved around wastewater: from failing septic systems in the Colorado River communities of Bullhead City and the Parker Strip and areas near Pinetop–Lakeside and Prescott, to the discharges from the insufficiently treated wastewater from the state's largest city, Phoenix, at its regional 91st Avenue facility. Pathogenic bacteria, turbidity, and nutrients were the main surface-water quality problems then facing the state (AZDHS 1976).

That pathogens were Arizona's main surface-water quality problems in the 1970s is not surprising. Levels of wastewater treatment were primary: removal of solids followed by direct discharge of the remaining wastewater to watercourses. Disease-causing organisms remaining in the water—really barely treated sewage—posed a direct threat to Arizona's public health. Moreover, no regulatory framework was in place to set standards for wastewater dischargers to meet. The Clean Water Act established a new minimum standard of treatment, secondary treatment, which significantly reduced pathogens in wastewater. It also required National Pollutant Discharge Elimination System (NPDES) permits for wastewater dischargers, setting regulatory, numeric limits for the amounts of nutrients, biochemical oxygen demand, and total suspended solids that could be released into rivers and lakes. Hundreds of millions of federal, state, and local dollars have been invested through grants, loans, and local enterprise funds to raise the performance of wastewater treatment in Arizona. In 2004, the state's water quality assessment indicated that no river or lake was impaired due to pathogens. Infrastructure improvements, minimum standards of construction and treatment, advances in treatment technology, and a regulatory framework of permitting designed to maintain compliance with wastewater standards through inspection and monitoring have made Arizona's main surface-water quality problem in the 1970s a footnote in current water quality discussions (ASIWPCA 2004).

The federal Clean Water Act set new standards for water quality in Arizona's rivers and lakes and through its implementation, illuminated historic contamination of groundwater. Conventional wisdom had held that the soil overlying groundwater would effectively filter pollutants as water made its way from the surface to the underground aquifer. Arizona's aquifers are typically at a great depth, and potential for contamination was thought to be remote. As Priscilla Robinson noted in a 1989 article, that perception changed when our understanding of the toxic nature of synthetic chemicals, such as solvents and pesticides, became apparent in the 1960s and with the development, in the late 1970s and early 1980s, of methods for detecting small amounts of these toxic substances in water. "Contamination in Arizona's groundwater," Robinson wrote, "[is] revealed bit by bit as water testing programs are implemented" (1989).

These words were strikingly prescient. In 1979, a screening of wells for the nematicide dibromochloropropane (DBCP) in the citrus-growing regions of Arizona revealed large areas of contaminated groundwater. A 1984 follow-up study confirmed the presence of DBCP in groundwater beneath the citrus orchards and established the occurrence of another nematicide in groundwater, ethylene dibromide (EDB). In all, the two pesticides were detected in 90 wells, 49 of which were used for drinking water (Daniel et al. 1988).

At about the same time, concomitant with improved laboratory methods, industrial solvents began to be detected in Arizona's groundwater. By 1986, industrial solvents, most prominently the volatile organic compounds (VOCs) trichloroethane, trichloroethylene, and perchloroethylene (PCE), had been detected in 389 wells at 30 different sites in a total of 122 square-mile sections. Drinking water wells were contaminated by VOCs at 10 of the sites. Many of these locations later became federal and state Superfund sites; others have been discovered since then, and cleanup continues in most of them to the present day (Graf 1986). Federal Superfund sites are regulated under the Comprehensive Environmental Response, Compensation, and Liability Act (CERCLA), which makes landowners liable for the costs of cleanup of hazardous substances.

These detections of groundwater contamination, reported in the newspapers on a seemingly weekly basis, galvanized state policymakers. After intense discussions and the overcoming of many obstacles, they arrived at consensus and a solution in 1986, with passage of the Environmental Quality Act, the main purpose of which was to protect the quality of Arizona's groundwater resources for drinking water. It was, as the *Los Angeles Times* reported, "the nation's toughest law to protect underground water" (Derouin and Bartlett 1989). It established a new state agency focused solely on environmental protection, the Arizona Department of Environmental Quality (ADEQ) and a new groundwater quality permit program, the Aquifer Protection Permit program (APP), to regulate discharges to groundwater, much as the federal Clean Water Act regulated discharges to surface water. The APP program established numeric groundwater quality standards that mirror the Safe Drinking Water Act maximum contaminant levels. The program requires facilities discharging pollutants that have the potential to leak into groundwater to be designed, constructed, and operated to provide a high level of protection against contamination. Similar to the NPDES program, the APP program relies on monitoring and inspections to determine compliance. Since its inception in 1986, the APP program has permitted more than 2,000 facilities, ranging from mines to power plants to wastewater treatment plants, and has issued general permits to regulate discharges from tens of thousands of septic tanks.

The APP program analyzes the characteristics of the discharge from each facility and the discharge control technologies and then sets numeric effluent limits based on those specific discharges. Also, the APP program describes the point of compliance at the perimeter or boundary of the discharging facility and sets numeric aquifer quality limits at those points to protect groundwater for drinking water purposes. Finally, the APP program ensures that the permittee uses the best available demonstrated control technology. In summary, the APP program is one of the strongest groundwater protection programs in the country, and it substantially reduces the amount of pollutants entering the state's precious groundwater supplies.

Arizona's 1986 Environmental Quality Act also established a Pesticide Contamination Prevention program to prevent further contamination of soil and groundwater from pesticides and herbicides. Under this program, pesticides and herbicides that exceed threshold levels for mobility and persistence are placed on the Groundwater Protection List. Listed pesticides and herbicides are subject to strict application and reporting requirements. The Environmental Quality Act requires that the state monitor for these listed pesticides and herbicides in soil and groundwater. The preventive and corrective provisions of this program have been highly successful, virtually eliminating occurrences of groundwater contamination from pesticides and herbicides such as DBCP and EDB, which were prevalent in the late 1970s.

Despite these three water quality protection programs, NPDES for surface water, APP for groundwater, and the Pesticide Contamination Prevention program, contaminants enter Arizona's water supplies every day. These include pollutants discharged at levels below permitted limits, pollutants known to be in wastewater but for which no numeric standards exist, and pollutants not yet identified or quantified in waste streams. The implementation of permits regulating discharges, water quality standards to limit levels of contaminants entering Arizona's water sources, and compliance based on frequent monitoring and reporting have substantially eliminated the risk to public health and focused Arizona's public policy squarely on protecting valuable water supplies for future drinking water. Debate and discussion continue, however, over how much contamination is "acceptable" for humans and for fish and wildlife.

Regulation and Managing Risk

Arizonans are sometimes confused when they learn that some level of water contamination is acceptable. Both drinking water and surface water used for recreation and fishing are protected according to levels of risk to public health and fish survival. There is no single means to protect Arizona's water quality. Instead, ensuring clean and safe water is based on a multiple-barrier approach:

- developing risk-based standards, typically developed by the U.S. Environmental Protection Agency (EPA);
- establishing drinking water, wastewater, and on-site wastewater (septic tank and alternative system) technology and performance standards;
- using best management practices (BMPs) to reduce the amount of pollutants entering surface water and groundwater;
- certifying qualified operators of drinking water and wastewater facilities and;
- monitoring compliance and reporting by the permittee all supported by a regulatory enforcement program.

Although all elements of the multiple-barrier approach to protecting water quality are important, setting standards for drinking water and fishing and recreation is typically the main line of defense.

Water quality standards for drinking water are established for individual contaminants based on each one's occurrence in the environment; human exposure and risks of adverse health effects in the general population and sensitive subpopulations, such as pregnant women and infants; the existence and wide availability of analytical methods of detection; technical feasibility and availability of controls; and the effects of regulation of the particular contaminant on water systems, the economy, and public health. The EPA establishes maximum contaminant level goals (MCLGs) as the maximum level of a contaminant in drinking water at which no known or adverse effect on public health will occur. The MCLGs consider only public health and not any limitations posed by detection and treatment technology and can be set at levels that water systems cannot meet. MCLGs are nonenforceable public health goals, but they provide a known point where one can assume that public health is ensured when drinking water. The EPA sets MCLGs for noncarcinogens based on a reference dose, or the amount of a chemical to which one can be exposed on a daily basis over a person's lifetime without resulting harm. For carcinogen and microbial contaminants, EPA assumes that there is no dose that is safe, with some exceptions. If consumption of a known carcinogen in drinking water can have a safe dose, the MCLG is set above zero at that level.

The main enforceable regulatory standard established by the EPA, though, is the maximum contaminant level (MCL), the maximum permissible level of a contaminant in drinking water. Although the MCL is set as close to the MCLG as possible, importantly, federal and state regulators consider existence of best available technology and treatment techniques as well, always considering cost. Most, if not all MCLs, are set at higher levels than the MCLGs for these reasons. Risk to public health is managed, with an eye toward cost, to achieve acceptable levels of treatment of water. The EPA conducts an economic analysis to determine whether the benefits of establishing the standard justify the costs; if not, EPA may adjust an MCL to a level that maximizes health benefits at a cost justified by the benefits (U.S. EPA 2004). Under Arizona's Environmental Quality Act, groundwater is protected for drinking water purposes. To this end, the 1986 act established the federal MCLs in effect at that time as the state's aquifer water quality standards. For new pollutants, though, Arizona's APP program also uses the concept of managed risk in establishing the new standards, including an economic analysis evaluating costs and benefits to achieve aquifer water quality standards in certain situations, and provides for classifying an aquifer for other than drinking water purposes after a detailed economic evaluation, along with associated hydrological considerations.

Surface-water quality standards are designed to protect a variety of uses, in addition to drinking water. Recreational uses, such as swimming, must be protected. The main concern here is limiting pathogenic bacteria to protect public health. Other harmful contaminants must be limited, such as mercury, to allow safe fish consumption. Aquatic and wildlife standards must also consider the water quality effect on overall fish and wildlife health and propagation. Surface-water quality standards for fish and wildlife are often set at lower levels than those for humans because of bioaccumulative effects, but they are crafted in the same risk-based framework as drinking water MCLs. Contaminants that have bioaccumulative effects are of particular concern because these chemicals are concentrated through the food chain. Surface-water quality standards set for fish consumption vary from type of fish to region of the country. Mercury, a toxic persistent bioaccumulative pollutant that is both a public health threat and an environmental concern, is the single contaminant that typically drives fish consumption advisories. Mercury directly affects the nervous system; the organic form of mercury, methylmercury, is one of the most toxic contaminants known. Most at risk are babies and unborn children whose mothers consume fish during pregnancy or while nursing. Exposure to mercury at elevated levels can delay walking and talking and may cause learning disabilities in children.

ADEQ monitors Arizona's lakes and rivers for mercury and has found increasing evidence of contamination. More than a dozen water bodies throughout the state have fish consumption advisories in place, alerting consumers not to consume or to limit consumption of fish from those affected lakes or streams. To address this environmental problem, ADEQ developed a mercury strategy that combines three separate approaches: additional data collection and research to determine actual levels and sources of mercury in Arizona; development of education and outreach materials and workshops aimed at specific populations and industrial sectors; and development of regulatory and nonregulatory methods alike to reduce and eliminate the use of mercury and therefore stop its introduction to the environment. Whereas the immediate issue is water quality, mercury enters water through both air and land pathways. The Arizona mercury strategy focuses on how mercury gets into water and has both short- and long-term goals (ADEQ 2005a). In the near term, however, fish consumption advisories remain in effect at such popular lakes as Alamo, Lyman, Upper and Lower Lake Mary, and Parker Canyon.

Both the NPDES and APP programs craft permits to meet water quality standards and focus primarily on discharges from point sources: discrete pipes or conveyances of a discharge to surface water or groundwater. The pollutants can easily be measured and quantified and can be reduced, chiefly through technology. Both programs also provide for control of discharges from nonpoint sources: the everywhere, everyday pollution that runs off primarily from our streets and roads and from agricultural and grazing activities. These are not easily measured or controlled and are diffuse. As a result, Arizona's water quality protection framework focuses on BMPs to better manage the use of land and resulting runoff. These typically include voluntary measures and focus primarily on containing discharges on site, sometimes in lined impoundments, so that they do not flow into surface water or groundwater. Although the NPDES program, which applies to surface water, does not substantially regulate agricultural activities, Arizona's APP program attempts to balance regulatory and voluntary approaches to the important task of reducing the amount of nitrogen that is discharged to groundwater from those activities. Through its general permit for the application of nitrogen fertilizer, the APP program specifies BMPs for fertilizer application that will allow plants to consumptively use all that is applied. This approach provides for a regulatory permit structure yet allows the activity to continue, even if nitrogen continues to enter groundwater, if all economically feasible BMPs have been applied.

Discharges from septic tanks and alternative on-site sewage disposal systems are also considered nonpoint sources. In Arizona, an estimated 400,000–500,000 residential properties rely on septic tank systems for sewage treatment, about 18% of the population. About 12,000 new systems are approved for installation each year. ADEQ regulates the approval and installation of conventional septic tank and alternative on-site systems through general permits under the APP program. Because issuing individual aquifer protection permits requiring monitoring and reporting (such as for mines, power plants, and community sewage treatment facilities) would be impractical, ADEQ's general permits for on-site systems specify compliance with design, construction, operation, and maintenance requirements. Underlying these requirements is a set of performance standards established for biochemical oxygen demand, total suspended solids, pathogenic bacteria, and nitrate. A system designed, constructed, and operated in accordance with the terms of the general permit is deemed to meet the performance standards, thus minimizing potential adverse effects on groundwater quality. Arizona's performance-based approach for on-site wastewater treatment facilities, structured within a comprehensive statewide groundwater protection permitting program, is unique, or almost so, in the United States and more effectively protects public health and water quality than fragmented programs spread among multiple agencies.

Nitrate-contaminated groundwater underlying areas of historic agriculture and areas of densely located on-site wastewater systems continues to be a significant issue for Arizona's water quality management. As an acute contaminant with immediate public health effects for infants, nitrate levels in drinking water above the MCL of 10 milligrams per liter (mg/L, equivalent to parts per million) can result in death and must be monitored frequently in known areas of contamination. Nitrate levels exceed 10 mg/L in extensive and numerous areas in Arizona. For this reason, in changes to the APP regulations in 2005, ADEQ established additional nitrogen management measures, including nitrogen loading limits for new subdivisions using on-site systems for wastewater disposal and the ability to designate nitrogen management areas, within which special nitrogen discharge controls for on-site systems and agricultural activities may be required.

Managing nonpoint source pollution is still often more of an art than a science and typically requires several iterations of land and facility management before these practices have substantial effect on preventing water pollution. Though it is the number one cause of water quality degradation, Arizona's efforts to manage nonpoint source pollution reflects the same policy of managing risk as seen throughout the more regulatory wastewater permitting programs and the Safe Drinking Water Act program. State policymakers have determined to date that a voluntary, nonregulatory approach for many nonpoint source activities is the better way to address this trade-off between water quality benefits and the cost to achieve them in the world of nonpoint source pollution. Urban storm-water runoff remains the exception to the voluntary approach to managing nonpoint source pollution. Congress determined in the early 1990s that urban storm-water runoff must be managed and controlled through the NPDES permitting program. Communities with a population of 50,000 or greater that have storm-water runoff to surface waters must craft a storm-water pollution prevention plan, with BMPs, municipal ordinances, and other controls to reduce water pollution from storm-water runoff.

Arizona's regulatory framework for managing water quality risk, evaluating costs and benefits, applies as well to efforts to remediate, or clean up, groundwater and surface water that has already been contaminated. Two programs address this often Herculean task: the federal Superfund program, based on the Comprehensive Environmental Response, Compensation, and Liability Act (CERCLA), and the state analog, the Water Quality Assurance Revolving Fund (WQARF) program. Over the years, the programs have often emphasized liability issues and finding potentially responsible parties who contributed to the contamination, with real cleanup efforts lagging. In many ways, this is not surprising, given the near impossible tasks of identifying multiple sources at many sites, developing viable remediation strategies, and committing the substantial expense to implement them. Arizona policymakers attempted to shift focus, in 1997, with major changes to the liability aspect of the WQARF program: they eliminated the concept of joint and several liability, which meant that anyone responsible for any portion of the contamination could no longer be held liable for the total costs to remediate it, and they created an ongoing funding mechanism, through the state corporate income tax fund transfer, to finance what would then be "orphan" shares of groundwater remediation. The polluter still pays, under what is termed "new WQARF," but only for their proportionate share of contamination. Additionally, ADEQ offers different means for a polluter to settle, including through discounted methods. Unlike the federal CERCLA program, where joint and several liability still holds, "new WQARF" aims to spur cleanup by eliminating the argument over responsibility and using state funds to assist in cleanup efforts (Derouin and Bartlett 1989; ADEQ 2005b).

The 2005 WQARF registry showed 35 sites throughout the state in various stages of investigation or remediation, with an additional 9 federal Superfund sites and 12 Department of Defense sites, with state oversight of cleanup by Defense Department entities. Although Arizona has increased the number of early response actions for contaminated sites, actual groundwater cleanup has been slow, with a few treatment plants like the one in operation for the town of Payson, which actually removes PCE from the water supply, in use. Monitoring of known sites continues, as does debate over potential remediation strategies for some of the largest and most difficult contamination plumes. The most effective remediation for these difficult contamination plumes, such as the Phoenix West Van Buren plume, which stretches 10 miles, may be to do nothing and provide water treatment only when it is pumped for use. Time and advances in technology often dictate what will eventually be viable remediation strategies (ADEQ 2005c).

Arizona's regulatory efforts to manage risk center on aggressive water quality standard setting and permitting programs designed to prevent pollution from entering rivers, lakes, and groundwater in the first instance. These water quality protection programs are intended for the most part to maintain currently existing water quality and prevent further degradation. As areas of groundwater contamination are discovered, they are evaluated for risk to public health and then listed on the WQARF registry for further investigation and development of remediation strategies. All these programs use a cost–benefit analytical framework to drive results and are pragmatic in their implementation. This requires an often-iterative approach that accepts some level of pollution as an inevitable result of a modern industrial society and focuses on what is important to protect Arizona's waters for drinking, fishing, and recreation.

Arizona's Future Challenges

From the initial passage of the federal Clean Water Act and Arizona's own Environmental Quality Act, substantial gains have been made in developing regulatory programs, setting water quality standards, establishing standards of performance for water and wastewater treatment facilities, and improving water and wastewater infrastructure. The water quality problems of those early years, such as gross levels of pathogens in wastewater, unrestricted use of pesticides, and disposal of industrial solvents, have largely been solved. There has been no time for self-congratulation, however, as new threats to water quality emerge almost yearly.

In Arizona, recent concerns about emerging contaminants have focused on three threats: perchlorate, the pathogens *Norovirus* and *Naegleria fowleri,* and endocrine-disrupting compounds (EDCs). These contaminants have been the subject of considerable research in the state's universities because of potential adverse effects on human health, aquatic organisms, and wildlife.

Perchlorate salts are used in the manufacture of rocket fuels and may be present in some imported sodium nitrate fertilizers. Perchlorate is very soluble and mobile in aqueous systems and has been found in Colorado River water from lower Lake Mead to the Mexican border, originating from a former rocket fuel manufacturing plant in Henderson, Nevada, where historic releases into Las Vegas Wash carried it into Lake Mead (Hogue 2003). Perchlorate is present also in a few groundwater contamination sites in Arizona because of disposal of perchlorate-laden wastes. Perchlorate poses a health threat because it interferes with iodide uptake in the thyroid gland and accumulates in certain food crops. Due to the discharges into Lake Mead, perchlorate concentrations range from 5 to 9 parts per billion (ppb) in the lower Colorado River below Lake Mead (Sanchez et al. 2005). At Lake Havasu, the Central Arizona Project canal diverts Colorado River water for drinking water, agriculture, and recharge in the Phoenix and Tucson areas. Because of concerns that several years of direct and indirect use of Colorado River water in central and southern Arizona might have moved water with higher levels of perchlorate into Arizona groundwater, Governor Janet Napolitano asked the Departments of Environmental Quality, Health Services, Water Resources, and Agriculture to examine the impacts of perchlorate levels in surface and groundwater. The results of the perchlorate occurrence study revealed low to nondetectable levels of perchlorate in those areas served by the Central Arizona Project (Owens et al. 2004).

Much controversy has existed on the national level surrounding the setting of health-based criteria for perchlorate in drinking water, with levels between 1 ppb and 200 ppb debated, as policymakers, scientists, and regulators awaited a long-anticipated report from the National Academy of Sciences on an appropriate reference dose for perchlorate. In 2005, EPA established an official reference dose for perchlorate that was consistent with the reference dose recommended by the National Academy of Sciences. Although the EPA has not yet proposed a drinking water MCL for perchlorate based on the reference dose established by EPA, perchlorate levels in the lower Colorado River and associated Central Arizona Project canal diversions appear not to pose a threat to human health if present in a drinking water supply.

Federal Safe Drinking Water Act regulations have overwhelmingly succeeded in eliminating disease-causing organisms in public drinking water supplies in the United States. Still, troublesome pathogens emerge regularly as threats to drinking water supplies and in surface waters and reclaimed water as threats to human health, wildlife, and aquatic organisms. Of recent concern is *Norovirus* (Norwalk virus), which is implicated in outbreaks of gastrointestinal illness in the Grand Canyon, Flagstaff, Wahweep at Lake Powell, and elsewhere in Arizona. Outbreaks affecting hundreds of river rafters have been documented in the Grand Canyon during 1994 and in the 2001–2005 river-running seasons. In the Grand Canyon, the standard practice is to filter and disinfect water from the Colorado River for drinking and cooking, but *Norovirus* is noted for its resistance to disinfection.

Another emerging pathogen is *Naegleria fowleri*, a waterborne protozoan found in soil and water that exists in cyst, trophozoite (amoeboid), and flagellate forms. When the amoeboid or flagellate form is inhaled or forced into nasal passages, a fatal form of meningitis may result. The resistance of the cyst phase to disinfection complicates control measures. In October 2002, two young children in Peoria, Arizona, died of meningitis caused by *Naegleria fowleri*. Both cases were contracted at residences served by the same deep-well unchlorinated drinking water system. Both *Norovirus* and *Naegleria fowleri* are the subject of university research projects to develop efficient detection and control methods and to study their occurrence in the water environment. It is an easy prediction to expect the continuing emergence of new pathogens in the water supply needing study and regulatory attention.

As an arid state, Arizona's water resource portfolio consists of three kinds of water: surface water in rivers and lakes; groundwater in underlying aquifers; and reclaimed water, or water that is reused after it is initially treated. With finite amounts of both surface water and groundwater, Arizona's ability to grow and sustain ever-larger populations requires the ability to "produce" additional water from treated wastewater. This reclaimed water is reused directly on turf facilities or fiber crops; recharged into the underground aquifers for storage for later use; or recycled through industrial cooling towers for manufacturing or power generation. Although reclaimed wastewater reused for beneficial purposes has undergone tertiary treatment, which includes filtration and disinfection to eliminate pathogenic risk, an array of new contaminants detected in treated wastewater, including endocrine-disrupting compounds (EDCs), has prompted concern.

EDCs are hormonally active chemicals that include a variety of veterinary and human antibiotics; prescription and nonprescription drugs; steroids and hormones, including human-excreted estrogens from birth control pills; and other organic compounds such as pesticides, plasticizers, detergent metabolites, disinfectants, and fire retardants. These chemicals are present in sewage and can persist in treated wastewater and biosolids (sewage sludge). They enter the environment through disposal of wastewater into watercourses and soils or through use of reclaimed water and biosolids. Typically, the chemicals are detected at low parts-per-billion levels or in the parts-per-trillion range, using newly developed analytical methods. In addition, genetic-based testing methods have been developed to assess bulk estrogenic activity (estrogenicity) upon exposure of an environmental sample that may contain different chemicals at varying concentrations.

A paper published by Kolpin et al. (2002) provides the results of a U.S. Geological Survey pharmaceuticals study, a national reconnaissance of 95 emerging organic contaminants, including EDCs, in targeted streams likely to be affected by the chemicals. Data were included from four Arizona sites. These sites were located downstream of major municipal wastewater treatment plants in Phoenix, Tucson, and Nogales. Fifty of the ninety-five chemicals analyzed by the USGS were detected above reporting levels at one or more of the four Arizona sites. Sixteen chemicals were detected at the highest concentration in the United States at one of the Arizona sites, including the highest level in the United States of one of the EDCs found in birth control pills (Kolpin et al. 2002; USGS 2002).

Migration to groundwater of pharmaceuticals persisting in treated wastewater has been documented in Arizona. The antiepileptic drugs carbamazepine and primidone, which are resistant to conventional sewage treatment processes, were detected in groundwater in monitoring wells in Tucson along the Santa Cruz River downstream from a sewage treatment plant outfall. The two drugs also have been found in monitoring wells located down gradient from a facility recharging treated wastewater into the Salt River bed in Mesa, with detections in wells representing groundwater transit times from six months to more than eight years (Drewes et al. 2003).

The health and environmental impact of EDCs at these low concentrations is unclear. The EPA has established MCLs, health-based guidance levels, and aquatic-life criteria for a limited number of these chemicals. However, it is known that in humans and animals, human-excreted estrogen compounds from birth control pills, in the concentration range detected in wastewater, regulate body functions. There is still a lack of evidence linking ingestion of these chemicals at environmental levels to adverse health effects in humans. There is convincing evidence, though, that some aquatic organisms, such as frogs and fish, experience endocrine system disruption from environmental levels of these contaminants, which is manifested as sexual disruption and feminization of male individuals, among other effects.

Both nationally and in Arizona, much research is being conducted to better understand the occurrence of EDCs in the environment, their human health and environmental effects, and approaches to treatment and control. As this research is completed, it is expected to drive changes to Arizona's regulations on water quality standards, technology requirements for wastewater treatment plants, and practices for the use of reclaimed water.

Other emerging contaminants about which even less is known loom on the horizon, including nanoparticles and polybrominated diphenyl ether flame retardants. The occurrence in the environment and effects on human health and wildlife of these contaminants and others certain to be identified in the future will occupy researchers and regulators for years to come.

Arizona's "Curse" of Salinity

Salinity, one of Arizona's largest water quality issues, ironically is not well addressed by any regulatory program and has been an issue with Arizona's water supplies since prehistoric times. As Joe Gelt wrote in February 1992, "Salt with earth ... connotes an unaffected beneficence. Salt with water has less favorable implications, especially in Arizona and the West." Salinity is a small word that defies its constituents: primarily calcium, magnesium, sodium, bicarbonate, chloride, and sulfate. Measured as total dissolved solids, these constituents in excess characterize saline water and impart to it many deleterious effects. In drinking water, although not unhealthful, as levels increase above 500 mg/L, people increasingly do not drink it from the tap because of bad taste. Excessive salinity harms crop production because it affects water uptake by the plants, which limits crop yield. Left alone, salt will build up in the soil, resulting in soil toxicity. Anthropologists and archeologists believe that this was a key contributor to the prehistoric Hohokam leaving their villages in the Salt River Valley. To avoid this soil toxicity, farmers must leach the salt from the soil through flushing, either draining it to surface water or percolating it to groundwater, potentially contaminating those water bodies with salts. Flushing salt from soil also uses a substantial amount of water, which runs counter to the need to conserve water in an arid environment. Add to these issues the increased costs to industry and to cities, where salinity causes increased corrosion and early failure of metal pipes and fittings, water heaters, and other appliances and requires additional treatment for industrial processes that require purer water, and one has a sense of the negative effects of simple salt in water.

Saline water occurs throughout Arizona. Its presence depends on nature—geologic and climatic conditions—and human activities. For example, in Tucson, groundwater is generally low in salts, but in the metropolitan Phoenix area, higher salinity levels are the norm. In the Phoenix area, the salinity levels are due in large part to the major river that flows only sporadically through it, the Salt River, and from historic agricultural practices of the past 120 years. However, the largest salinity issue for Arizona is the Colorado River, as Gelt writes, "the largest and most managed and controlled of western rivers" (1992). The Colorado River also presents the most complicated salinity problems because it picks up about 9 million tons of salt in its journey from its headwaters in Colorado to its mouth in the Mexican delta. The unique plumbing of the Colorado River brings almost 2 million acre-feet of water each year into central and southern Arizona through the Central Arizona Project (CAP) canal for municipal, industrial, and agricultural purposes at salinity levels ranging from 500 to 800 mg/L. In some areas, this already saline supply exacerbates existing water conditions, but in other areas, such as Pinal County, a major agricultural center, it is an improvement.

Take the saline nature of the Colorado River, recycle it once or twice through a municipal water and wastewater system, and salinity levels increase even more. Estimates are that one cycle of municipal use increases the salt content of water by 200–400 mg/L. Yet wastewater treatment does not remove salts in the treatment process, and more and more of Arizona's treated wastewater is reused, recycled again, and often recharged into groundwater supplies. This growing salt content includes the concentrate left from water softeners, installed in more than 50% of all new homes in Arizona. Is there a looming groundwater crisis with salinity? No one knows for certain, but water and wastewater providers are not waiting to see if the problem occurs before they take action. A coalition has been formed, the Central Arizona Salinity Study (CASS), to evaluate salinity issues affecting central Arizona. With a mission focused on finding reliable, sustainable, and cost-effective alternatives, the CASS is evaluating ways to deal with the more than 1 million tons of salt that are added to the region each year. The group has completed phase one of its work and is exploring a combination of strategies, including development of local limits, adoption of a surcharge program, and BMPs. The overall management approach, however, is less a regulatory one than one based on partnerships and cooperative efforts in regional salinity planning and management (Gelt 1992; Smith 2005).

Conclusion

Arizona's water quality challenges are not unique to the desert Southwest, but its approaches toward managing them have been forward thinking. Arizona's policies toward water quality focus on protecting existing water quality and preventing further degradation, for both surface-water and groundwater supplies. Its regulatory approaches combine traditional permitting approaches, with numeric limits and established water quality standards, and less traditional performance-based approaches. Nonregulatory programs, such as those for nonpoint source pollution and for salinity, rely on best management practices and iterative applications to evaluate success. Underlying it all is an effort by federal and state policymakers to manage risk—the effects on humans, fish, and wildlife, and the associated costs to mitigate these risks. This fundamental framework for securing water quality for Arizona's citizens is comprehensive, focusing on what is practical and possible, and is a balanced and flexible approach to managing pollution. Its goal, after all, is to prevent further degradation of water quality from current levels, to protect against additional water contamination from known pollutants, and to clean up and remediate that water where it makes sense to do so.

Although it is a comprehensive framework, it is one, however, that is slow to keep pace with changes in science and technology. Development of enforceable water quality standards takes years, even decades, to complete, and the EPA has a long list of contaminants for which it must complete its risk-based analyses for safety in drinking water. Meanwhile, our abilities more precisely to measure and analyze contaminants in water far outpace our abilities to establish a standard. Hence, we know and are learning more every day about viruses, nanoparticles, and other emerging contaminants, but we are far from knowing what to do about them. Often, too, the unintended consequences of our water resource management efforts—to recycle water as many times as we can to take full advantage of every drop for our consumptive needs—can lead to water quality ramifications with the waste stream; thus, our added issues with total dissolved solids.

More can always be done. Arizona has done much, however, to meet its water quality problems, often much more than other states. Its water quality programs offer needed protection for its citizens and the environment from the adverse effects of domestic, industrial, and agricultural wastewater discharges. That protection is based on what we know today about contaminants, risk, and cost. The challenge for this decade and beyond is to move the program to a more proactive position, anticipating tomorrow's problems and ensuring that the necessary scientific research and risk-based analyses are completed in a more timely fashion.

References

Arizona Department of Environmental Quality (ADEQ). 2005a. Monitoring and Assessment: Ongoing Research, Mercury Strategy. www.azdeq.gov/environ/water/assessment/ongoing.html (accessed January 18, 2006).

————. 2005b. Superfund Programs: Liability and Real Estate Issues. www.azdeq.gov/environ/waste/sps/liability.html (accessed January 18, 2006).

————. 2005c. 2005 Water Quality Assurance Revolving Fund Registry. http://www.azdeq.gov/environ/waste/sps/download/wqarf.pdf (accessed January 18, 2006).

Arizona Department of Health Services (AZDHS). 1976. Bureau of Water Quality Control. 305(b) Report submitted to the Environmental Protection Agency, May.

Association of State and Interstate Water Pollution Control Administrators (ASIWP-CA). 2004. *Clean Water Act Thirty Year Retrospective: History and Documents Related to the Federal Statute*, Brian Van Wye, ed. Washington, DC: Association of State and Interstate Water Pollution Control Administrators.

Daniel, Debra L., Brian E. Munson, and Charles G. Graf. 1988. Groundwater Contamination by Pesticides in Arizona: An Overview. Proceedings of the Arizona Hydrological Society First Annual Symposium, Survival in the Desert: Water Quality and Quantity Issues into the 21st Century. Phoenix, AZ, 72–100, September 16.

Derouin, James G., and David Bartlett. 1989. New Arizona Act Designed To Assure Water Quality. In *Arizona Waterline*, edited by Althia L. Hardt. Phoenix, AZ: Salt River Project, 199–204.

Drewes, Jorg E., Thomas Heberer, Tanja Rauch, and Kirsten Reddersen. 2003. Fate of Pharmaceuticals during Groundwater Recharge. *Groundwater Monitoring and Remediation* 23(3): 64–72.

Gelt, Joe. 1992. Does Salinity Pose Problems to Arizona Water Users? *Arroyo* 5(4), February.

Graf, Charles G. 1986. VOCs in Arizona's Groundwater: A Status Report. Proceedings of the Conference on Southwestern Groundwater Issues, National Water Well Association. October 20–22, 1986, Tempe, AZ, 269–87.

Hogue, Cheryl. 2003. Rocket-Fueled River. *Chemical & Engineering News* 81(33): 37–46.

Kolpin, Dana W., Edward T. Furlong, Michael T. Meyer, E. Michael Thurman, Steven D. Zaugg, Larry B. Barber, and Herbert T. Buxton. 2002. Pharmaceuticals, Hormones and Other Organic Wastewater Contaminants in U.S. Streams, 1999–2000: A National Reconnaissance. *Environmental Science & Technology* 36(6): 1202–11.

Owens, Stephen, Catherine Eden, Herbert Guenther, and Donald Butler. 2004. Perchlorate in Arizona: Occurrence Study of 2004. http://www.azdeq.gov/function/about/download/perch1201.pdf (accessed January 18, 2006).

Robinson, Priscilla. 1989. Protecting Arizona's Groundwater. In *Arizona Waterline*, edited by Althia L. Hardt. Phoenix, AZ: Salt River Project, 213.

Sanchez, C.A., R.I. Krieger, N. Khandacker, R.C. Moore, K.C. Holts, and L.L. Neidel. 2005. Accumulation and Perchlorate Exposure Potential of Lettuce Produced in the Lower Colorado River Region. *Journal of Agricultural and Food Chemistry* 53(13): 5479–86.

Smith, Karen R. 2005. Central Arizona Salinity Study: Summary Reports and Conclusions. *Water Conditioning and Purification Magazine* 47(8): 21–22, August.

U.S. Environmental Protection Agency (U.S. EPA). 2004. Safe Drinking Water Act 30th Anniversary: Drinking Water Standards and Health Effects. http://www.epa.gov/

safewater/sdwa/30th/factsheets/standard.html#4 (accessed January 18, 2006).

U.S. Geological Survey (USGS). 2002. Open-File Report 02–94. Water-Quality Data for Pharmaceuticals, Hormones, and Other Organic Wastewater Contaminants in U.S. Streams, 1999–2000.

10

Implications of Federal Farm Policy and State Regulation on Agricultural Water Use

George B. Frisvold, Paul N. Wilson, and Robert Needham

Water use in the agricultural sector in Arizona is influenced by federal farm policy, but state water conservation requirements have had less impact than was anticipated by state regulators. This chapter explores trends over time in state and federal farm policy and the implications for water use.

Irrigation accounts for 80% of Arizona's freshwater withdrawals (Hutson et al. 2004). Despite its dominant role in state water use, agriculture faces growing competition for water from other sectors. Rapid population growth has increased household and industrial water demand, Native American tribes hold sizable claims to water currently used for irrigation, and there are also demands for water to protect riparian habitats and endangered species. Competition for water will only increase, with Arizona's population projected to increase by 2.4 million people (44%) between 2005 and 2025 (AZDES 2005).

Arizona's growing demand for water will be met primarily by shifting water from agriculture to other uses. Few potential sites exist for new water supply projects, and such projects now face far greater scrutiny of their environmental impacts. The marginal value product of water in agriculture is generally lower than in industrial or municipal uses. In times of water scarcity, industrial and municipal users often pay several times the marginal value product of water in agricultural use (Boggess et al. 1993).

Agricultural water use depends on four effects: scale effects (total acreage), crop mix effects (which crops are grown), location effects (where they are grown), and technology effects. The choice of irrigation technology affects the amount of water used per acre for a specific crop–location combination. Data from the U.S. Department of Agriculture's (USDA) Farm and Ranch Irrigation Survey (USDA 2003) illustrate the importance of crop mix and technology

TABLE 10-1. Arizona Irrigation Patterns by Crop, 2003

Crop	Irrigated acres harvested	Acre-feet applied per acre	Acre-feet applied	Percentage of water applied
Alfalfa	210,084	5.8	1,218,487	32.3
Cotton	231,296	4.2	971,443	25.8
Vegetables	132,799	3.6	478,076	12.7
Wheat	122,144	3.5	427,504	11.3
Orchards, nuts	31,450	5.2	163,540	4.3
Other hay	42,051	3.6	151,384	4.0
Corn for silage	15,564	4.6	71,594	1.9
Barley	23,564	2.7	63,623	1.7
Pasture	19,661	3.2	62,915	1.7
Other crops	43,769	varies	158,997	4.1
Total	872,382	4.3	3,767,564	

Source: USDA, Farm and Ranch Irrigation Survey, 2003.

effects. Application rates vary significantly by crop, from 1.8 acre-feet/acre for beans and 2.7 acre-feet/acre for barley to 5.2 acre-feet/acre for tree crops and 5.8 acre-feet/acre for alfalfa (Table 10-1). Sprinkler and drip systems can apply water more efficiently than gravity systems. In 2003, about 90% of Arizona's acres were irrigated with gravity systems, whereas farms relying solely on gravity systems operated 68% of acreage (USDA NASS 2003). Farms relying solely on gravity irrigation applied 4.5 acre-feet/acre. In contrast, farms relying solely on drip or sprinkler irrigation—which accounted for 10% of acreage—applied 3.4 acre-feet/acre.

Small changes in irrigation withdrawals translate into large percentage changes in water available for urban, tribal, or environmental uses. In Arizona, a 1% reduction of irrigation withdrawals would increase the amount of water available for other uses by 4%. A 10% reduction would increase water available for other uses by 40%. This phenomenon is found in arid regions worldwide that rely heavily on irrigated crop production. In 2003, Arizona had more than 870,000 acres irrigated, receiving applications of 4.3 acre-feet/acre (Table 10-1). By comparison, withdrawals for household and industrial use are about 0.25 acre-feet per person per year (Hutson et al. 2004).

Federal Farm Programs and Water Use

Water use by agriculture depends on farm production decisions that are heavily influenced by federal farm programs. In some years, more than 20% of the nation's cropland has been idled under federal programs. In Arizona, direct government payments to farmers exceeded $1.3 billion in 2003. Payments as a percentage of net farm income have ranged from a low of 1% in 1995 to a high of 50% in 1983. The median value from 1980 to 2004 was 11%.

U.S. farm policy includes a complex array of programs intended to support farm income, reduce agricultural pollution, or attempt to do both simultaneously. We divide farm programs into two broad categories: commodity programs and conservation programs. Commodity programs include policies designed to support farm income, such as direct payments and acreage controls, import controls, and export subsidies. Recent programs have their antecedents in New Deal legislation culminating in acts of Congress known as permanent law. Farm bills are temporary legislation superseding permanent law for five to six years. Farm bills include titles governing commodity, conservation, rural development, credit, nutrition, and other programs.

USDA conservation programs also date back to New Deal legislation. Early programs combined supply control and erosion control objectives and provided farmers assistance to adopt resource-conserving practices. Today, major USDA conservation programs include land retirement and technology adoption subsidies. The conservation titles of farm bills establish the operating parameters of these programs.

Basic Features of Commodity Programs

Historically, farm payments have been based on the difference between a government-set price and the actual market price (Lin et al. 2000; Westcott and Price 2001). Producers of corn, soybeans, cotton, rice, wheat, sorghum, and barley are eligible for direct government payments. Producers could receive marketing loan payments that act as a lower-tier price support. For these crops, except soybeans, they could also receive target price-deficiency payments, which act as an upper-tier price support. Because producers receive a high, stable effective price (market price plus government payment), they may continue to grow these crops even when market prices are low. Price supports, however, encourage overproduction, a greater divergence between market and government prices, and even greater program outlays.

From the 1930s until the 1996 farm bill (FAIR 1996), the federal government instituted acreage restrictions to control supply, raise market prices, and limit price support payments. Under the Acreage Reduction Program (ARP), farmers were required to set aside (fallow) a certain proportion of their acreage, determined annually, as a condition for receiving government payments. In the late 1980s, about one in seven acres were idled under annual set-aside programs (Daugherty 1997). Set-asides were "voluntary" in the sense that producers could forego some of their payments and withdraw land from USDA programs. In the late 1980s, land fallowing in Arizona under the ARP was quite substantial as 20% or more of base acres in major crops were often required to be idled (Table 10-2).

In the 1980s, farm legislation included planting restrictions that further limited producers' abilities to shift acreage between crops. A farmer's eligibility to

TABLE 10-2. Acreage Reduction Program (ARP) Land Idling Requirements for Major Program Crops, 1984–1996

	Percentage of crop acreage base to be idled			
	Cotton	Wheat	Corn	Barley
1984	25	20	10	10
1985	20	20	10	10
1986	25	22.5	17.5	17.5
1987	25	27.5	20	20
1988	12.5	27.5	20	20
1989	25	10	10	10
1990	12.5	2	10	10
1991	5	15	7.5	7.5
1992	10	5	5	5
1993	7.5	0	10	10
1994	11	0	0	0
1995	0	0	7.5	0
1996	0	0	0	0

Source: Daugherty 1997.

receive payments depended on establishing a history of planting program crops. Historical averages of plantings were used to compute a farm's base acres for each program crop. The size of deficiency payments a farm could receive depended on how many base acres a farm had established for each crop. Farmers who switched acreage between program crops or between program and non-program crops could forfeit some government payments. Because base acres were determined by historical averages, decisions to switch acreage in one year would affect payments a farm received over multiple years. This encouraged farmers to keep acreage in program crops even though the market might be signaling them to change. Farmers had an incentive to farm non-idled acreage more intensively because deficiency payments also depended on base yields, calculated as a historical average of a farm's yields. Farmers had an incentive to apply more water per acre to raise yields.

The government can encourage irrigated crop production, even without directly paying producers. The dairy program supports milk producers through direct payments, export subsidies, import controls, and regional marketing orders that limit interstate milk trade. The program affects water use indirectly through its impact on water-intensive alfalfa used as feed for dairy cows. Alfalfa accounts for 32% of irrigation water applied in Arizona (Table 10-1). A recent report to Congress suggested elimination of the dairy program, and combined with formation of regional compacts, this could reduce Arizona milk production 0.8–4.9% (USDA 2004).

Over the past 20 years, legislative changes have reduced many of the distorting effects of commodity programs. The 1985 farm bill (Food Security Act

1985) froze program yields at historic levels, so producers could not increase deficiency payments by increasing yields. The 1990 farm bill (Food Agricultural Conservation and Trade Act 1990) further decoupled deficiency payments from current production decisions and from base acreage calculations. This bill made it easier for growers to shift between crops without forfeiting deficiency payments and decreased incentives to alter plantings as a means of increasing payments (Thurman 1995; Gardner 2002). The 1996 farm bill eliminated acreage set-asides and replaced deficiency payments with fixed payments not tied to current production or prices. However, price supports under the marketing loan system were maintained. These payments are still tied to current production and in 2000 were estimated to increase production of wheat by 2.5% and cotton by 10% (Westcott and Price 2001; Gardner 2002). Furthermore, planting restrictions that would cause growers to lose payments if they planted fruits or vegetables on base acreage were maintained.

Conceptual and Measurement Issues for Commodity Programs and Water Use

How commodity programs ultimately alter water use depends on how they influence scale, crop-mix, location, and technology effects. Studies of the effects of farm programs using computable general equilibrium (CGE) models have found important scale effects, suggesting that the programs of the 1980s led to significant overproduction (Frisvold 2004).

For several reasons, it is more difficult to move from scale effects to overall effects on water use. First, there is the challenge of linking local-scale water demand models to national models designed to evaluate commodity programs. Large-scale policy models rarely include water as an input, and using them, one can only make indirect inferences based on changes in acreage between more and less water-intensive crops. Yet, to capture crop substitution and price effects of commodity programs, one needs a model that captures aggregate U.S. impacts. Water demand models, often developed at a watershed or river basin level, are not equipped to determine broad, multimarket effects of changes in farm policy.

Second, there is substitution between different crops. Policy changes can encourage shifts to either more or less water-intensive crops. Some non-program crops, such as vegetables or alfalfa, are relatively water-intensive, yet program changes affect acreage of these crops as well. For example, Konyar and Knapp (1990) estimated that cotton acreage set-asides reduced California cotton acreage but increased California alfalfa acreage 16%. Third, in the western United States, the price of surface water provided by the Bureau of Reclamation is sometimes so low that water demand is quantity- rather than price-rationed (Moore and Dinar 1995). With quantity rationing, demand for water may respond to only large changes in output price.

Studies conducted before the 1990 farm bill reforms have found that farm programs significantly increased water use but with great regional variation. Howitt (1991) used a multiregion, multimarket programming model of U.S. agriculture that explicitly included water as an input. He conducted a comprehensive analysis of the impact on farm programs (circa 1984) on water use. He considered a 50% across-the-board reduction in crop price supports. Nationally, the elasticity of water demand with respect to program support price was 0.47 but with significant regional variation. Elasticities were 0.74 in the Pacific region, 0.34 in the Plains, 0.30 in the East, and 0.0 in the Midwest and Mountain regions. In the Mountain region (which includes Arizona), growers could more easily shift to non-program crops such as alfalfa. Howitt, however, did not consider effects of reducing dairy support, which would affect demand for alfalfa. Horner et al. (1991) modeled the effects of a 20% reduction in cotton price supports linking an aggregate multimarket model with a localized one for California's Central Valley. Cotton acreage fell 19% nationally. Reductions ranged from 49% in Arizona and New Mexico and 41% in California to lows of 10% in Texas and Oklahoma.

The CGE and multimarket studies suggest first that, at least before reforms of the 1990 farm bill, commodity programs had significant impacts on production and national irrigation water use. Howitt's (1991) results suggest that cutting price supports 50% would have reduced water use by 20–25%. Second, there is great regional variation. In some regions, commodity programs appear to have relatively little impact. Here, crop-mix effects are particularly important. Third, assessing impacts of commodity programs in particular regions requires linkage of data on national markets and water demand on a smaller, more regional scale.

Federal Agricultural Conservation Programs

Since the New Deal, USDA has operated technical assistance, extension, and subsidy programs to promote adoption of resource-conserving technologies as well as long-term land retirement programs (Heimlich 2003). The Agricultural Conservation Program (ACP), initiated in 1936, provided partial subsidies, or cost-sharing, to encourage adoption of resource-conserving technologies and practices. The ACP and the Soil Bank (operating from 1958 to 1972) also encouraged land retirement. The primary goal of land retirement was to control supply (and support farm prices), with erosion control as a secondary objective. The Conservation Reserve Program (CRP), established in 1985, again had dual objectives of supply and erosion control but broadened the environmental objectives of land retirement. Under the CRP, farmers receive annual government payments for idling cropland under 10-year contracts. Landowners place bids to USDA that are ranked based on the land's potential for erosion control, migratory bird habitat, water pollution control, and other environmental benefits (Feather et al. 1999). More than 33 million acres are currently idled under the CRP, about 10% of U.S. cropland.

From 1985 to 2002, USDA conservation expenditures more than tripled in real terms. The CRP accounted for about two-thirds of this growth. Despite increased national funding, Arizona producers have had limited access to conservation payments. Conservation payments account for 9% of direct farm payments nationally but for less than 4% in Arizona. One reason for this discrepancy is that Arizona landowners have not been able to benefit from the CRP. This is because payments are based on local dry-land rental rates or productivity of the land. In irrigation-dependent Arizona, payment rates based on dry-land productivity provide little incentive for participation. In 2001, there was only one CRP contract in Arizona, covering 33 acres and paying only $9 per acre. In contrast, Arizona irrigated cropland rental rates—a measure of private returns to leasing out land—averaged $135 per acre.

USDA's technology adoption subsidies were often aimed at curbing water pollution but also provided subsidies to farmers to improve irrigation efficiency. One such program was the Colorado River Salinity Control Program (CRSCP), which provided payments to farmers who installed more efficient sprinklers and pipes and lined delivery canals (U.S. DOI 1990; USDA CFSA 1995). Irrigation is one of the main contributors to salinity problems (CAST 1992). Lohman et al. (1988) estimated that damages from salinity in the Colorado River basin ranged from $311 million to $835 million annually. The Department of the Interior (U.S. DOI 1999) reports that damages range from $500 million to $750 million per year, predicting damages could reach $1.25 billion per year by 2015 if no additional controls are put in place.

From 1984 to 1995, the CRSCP conserved 300,000 acre-feet of water. Salt loadings were reduced by more than 190,000 tons per year, at costs ranging from $38 to $70 per ton of salt removed (U.S. GAO 1995). The 1996 FAIR Act terminated this and other regional programs, instituting a single Environmental Quality Incentive Program (EQIP). One-third of EQIP funds have gone to encourage adoption of improved irrigation technology (Cattaneo 2003). In Arizona, Native American tribes have received about 40% of EQIP funds.

The Conservation Reserve Enhancement Program (CREP), first established under the 1996 farm bill, provides greater incentives for farmers engaged in irrigated agriculture to participate in the CRP. Like the regular CRP, the CREP provides farmers with federal rental payments for 10- to 15-year land retirement, but the CREP differs from the CRP in several respects (Smith 2000). First, CREP payments can be much larger than payments under the CRP and often include first-year signing bonuses. Federal funding has ranged from $1,300 to $2,500 per acre.

Second, states play a more active role in program design and implementation, allowing them to develop programs to target specific needs. Maryland's program addresses water pollution affecting the Chesapeake Bay and compliance with the Clean Water Act; New York's focuses on compliance with the Safe Drinking

Water Act; and Washington and Oregon's programs focus on protecting endangered fish habitat. Since 1996, 26 states have had CREP proposals approved, and 5 states are currently developing proposals. State enrollment targets range from 5,000 to 100,000 acres. Five states have large programs worth roughly $250 million, with the federal government paying 80% of the cost. Arizona currently does not operate a CREP, nor is one in the development stage. Both USDA and a state's governor must approve a CREP project, and states must provide 20% matching funds. States must develop proposals for submission by their governors to USDA based on comprehensive participation of state interests that include agricultural groups, conservation groups, watershed councils, and tribal governments, as well as state and federal agencies.

Third, CREP contract bidding and bid ranking are state-specific, rather than being conducted at a national level. Once an individual state's CREP is approved, farmers in that state may sign up any time without going through the nationally competitive bidding process of the regular CRP.

Fourth, states may tailor programs to encourage participation of irrigated agriculture. CREP programs in Oregon, California, and Nebraska provide federal payments for irrigated land retirement if saved water is applied toward approved environmental objectives. Payments based on local irrigated rental rates far exceed payments under the CRP. California's CREP is small, targeting 12,000 acres. Irrigated rice land would receive payments of about $165 per acre per year, whereas other irrigated land would receive payments of $100 per acre per year.

Oregon's CREP program, in contrast, is quite large, targeting 100,000 acres and budgeted for $250 million dollars, with $193 million coming from the federal government. The Oregon CREP seeks to restore riparian areas and to maintain in-stream flows for trout and salmon listed under the Endangered Species Act. Farmers are eligible for payments based on the rental value of irrigated land if they lease water to the state of Oregon. The leases require irrigators to divert less water to enhance in-stream flows. Farmers who idle their land and lease their water for in-stream flows have received annual rental payments ranging from $70 to $150 per acre.

CREP can provide states with substantial funds to pay for voluntary reallocation of water to meet obligations under federal environmental laws. It remains to be seen, however, how many farmers will enter into long-term water lease agreements with state agencies. The California program, approved in 2001, has 2,600 acres enrolled as of June 2003 (USDA FSA 2003). In the Oregon program, approved at the end of 1998, fewer than 9,000 acres have been enrolled as of June 2003. Participation in the state water lease and irrigated rental payment contracts has remained low. In both Oregon and California, landowners have raised questions about what happens to the water at the end of the 15-year contract period, especially if the water has been used to maintain habitat for threatened or endangered species. In California, USDA, state agencies, and the U.S. Fish and Wildlife Service have engaged in lengthy negotiations to clarify such questions for potential participants.

In 2005, USDA approved a $158 million CREP for the Platte and Republican River watersheds in Nebraska. Goals include a 125,000-acre-feet per year reduction in irrigation applications, increased surface and groundwater retention of 85,000 acre-feet, and reduction of fertilizer runoff to improve public water supplies. Irrigated cropland will be retired, and water is conserved through water contracts entered into between producers and the state of Nebraska.

Other CREP proposals in the development phase seek to retire irrigated land for water conservation. The Yakima tribe of Washington state has a $1.5 million CREP proposal pending that would provide incentives to convert irrigated cropland along the Yakima River to rangeland to conserve water for salmon recovery and protect wildlife habitat. In Colorado, a proposed CREP would reduce water use by 35,000 acre-feet annually through irrigated land retirement in the Republican River watershed.

In Idaho, a proposed CREP would seek to retire up to 50,000 acres of irrigated land, saving up to 100,000 acre-feet of water per year (Parsons 2004). The CREP is being developed in response to five consecutive years of drought. Junior water rights holders in the Eastern Snake Plain Aquifer see voluntary land retirement under CREP as an alternative to mandatory water-use reductions. In 2004, 1,300 junior water rights holders were notified that their pumps would be shut off (Idaho Ground Water Appropriators, Inc. 2004). According to the CREP proposal, irrigators would receive about $100 per acre through a combination of federal, state, and third-party payments. Implementing the CREP may require changes in state water law to prevent forfeiture of water rights. Water set aside under regular CRP contracts is not subject to forfeiture under the Idaho Code, but it is not clear that this currently applies to CREP. There has also been discussion of including dry-year leasing that would conserve water on a contingency basis.

The Central Arizona Project and State Conservation Programs

The Central Arizona Project (CAP) is a 335-mile aqueduct constructed and subsidized by the Bureau of Reclamation, with capacity to deliver 1.5 million acre-feet of Colorado River water to cities and agriculture in Maricopa, Pima, and Pinal Counties. Before its construction, Arizona could not use its full 2.8 million acre-foot entitlement of Colorado River water. Given beneficial-use doctrines of Western water law (see Chapter 3), this problem jeopardized Arizona's legal claim to the water. CAP water deliveries to Phoenix began in 1985 and to Tucson in 1992. Before CAP construction, central Arizona relied primarily on sizable groundwater reserves and on surface water from the Salt River Project. Lack of effective property rights determination and groundwater regulation, however, led to continued overdrafting of the region's aquifers.

Ex ante assessments of the CAP questioned its benefits relative to its costs. Economists warned that the costs of surface water from the CAP would far outweigh the costs of groundwater pumping (even with declining water tables) and that growers would not be able to afford the water supplied at cost (Young and Martin 1967; Kelso et al. 1973). This prediction proved correct. Some irrigation districts filed for bankruptcy, and others renegotiated contracts (Baker 1995; Wilson 2002). Water was eventually provided to agriculture at subsidized rates, the state tax burden was shifted to municipalities and property owners, and the state instituted programs for storage of CAP water in the ground to maintain Arizona's CAP allotment (Hanemann 2002; Wilson 2002).

The CAP has met certain state objectives. Parts of central Arizona most affected by groundwater overdrafting have increased their reliance on CAP-supplied surface water. Usage programs have allowed Arizona to lay a more solid claim on its Colorado River allotment. However, Holland and Moore (2003) estimate that although CAP construction has been economically beneficial to Arizona, its costs borne nationally outweigh the benefits. They estimate that CAP's construction costs of $5 billion are subsidized by the Bureau of Reclamation at a rate of 52%, whereas operating costs (about $275/acre-foot) are subsidized at a rate of 61%.

The CAP also spurred changes in Arizona groundwater management law. As has been described in previous chapters, threatened by the Carter administration with a withdrawal of federal support for CAP construction, Arizona was pressured into adopting the Groundwater Management Act of 1980 (GMA) Title 45, Arizona Revised Statutes, which was designed to regulate groundwater pumping and eliminate overdrafting by the year 2025 (Hanemann 2002; Holland and Moore 2003). Along with the threatened cutoff of CAP funding, a series of legal decisions contributed to the GMA's passage, including *Jarvis v. State Land Department* (1969, 1970, 1976) and *Farmers Investment Company v. Bettwy* (1976) (see Chapter 3).

The GMA regulated agricultural water use within active management areas (AMAs) by not allowing the development of new agricultural land and by requiring a series of management plans intended gradually to reduce the quantity of water available to the grower in a given year. Annual water allotments represented the amount of water a grower could use from wells, surface supplies (unless 100% CAP water was used), or both. The Arizona Department of Water Resources (ADWR) requires the measurement and reporting of actual water use with flow meters on all wells and irrigation district-managed turnouts in all AMAs. Allotments were calculated for farms based on water-use records and the crops grown from 1975 to 1979. If a grower used less water than his allotment in a given year, that grower could bank the difference in a flexibility account (known as flex credits). In a year when a grower had greater demand for water than his annual allotment, the grower could use his accumulated flex credits to use more water. Starting in 1991, growers could buy flex credits from other growers.

Individual farms adopted water conservation technologies in the late 1970s and throughout the 1980s. The passage of the GMA created a perception of an impending water constraint. Fear that the GMA could hurt future agricultural operations induced some growers to line ditches and laser level fields. Simultaneously, the impending arrival of CAP water in central Arizona encouraged some farmers to level fields, create level basins, and construct high-volume turnouts. Yet, based on extensive interviews with state water experts, there is wide agreement that these decisions had little to do with requirements in the first and second management plans for the AMAs (Needham 2005; Needham and Wilson 2005). The only legislated policy that "conserved" water was the requirement that irrigated acreage could not be expanded in the AMAs beyond the acreage irrigated from 1975 to 1979. Quantitative, econometric results are consistent with these overall findings (Needham 2005). Water prices, crop prices, weather, and acreage cropped explain almost all the variation in water purchased and pumped over the study period. Tightened conservation provisions in the second and third management plans for the AMAs had no apparent effect on the quantity of water used by growers.

The GMA has had little effect on agricultural water use because management plans did not establish a binding water-use constraint for most farms. The GMA used the highest number of acres irrigated from 1975 to 1979 as the benchmark to determine water duty acres authorized to receive a water allocation. This period was the all-time peak of irrigated acreage in central Arizona (Figure 10-1). To compound matters, for the first management plan, ADWR calculated a generous water duty based on average crop needs during 1975–1979. As a result, most growers felt no constraint on their irrigation water use.

The flex account program, initiated in 1986–1987, further weakened the water constraint. Accumulated flex credits have grown to tens of thousands of acre-feet of water for individual farms. During the 1980s, the agricultural economy went through a period of low commodity prices and high interest rates that discouraged planting. High, federally mandated acreage set-asides for program crops further reduced acreage (Table 10-2). Set-aside acres (and other fallowed acreage) earned flex credits. The average flex credit account in the three AMAs represents six years of irrigation water for the average grower (Figure 10-2).

AMA agricultural water use has declined slightly due to urbanization in some of the irrigation districts (Figure 10-2). Fluctuations in water use over this period are explained largely by changing crop prices, input costs, weather, and macroeconomic conditions (e.g., interest rates, urbanization). The trend in per-acre water use has remained relatively constant over the life of the GMA (Figure 10-3).

In sum, generous initial water allotments, federal acreage restrictions, and generous flex credit provisions combined to render GMA water allotments as nonbinding constraints on agricultural water use. The GMA has raised the visibility of state water issues, and the required record keeping, reports, planning, and negotiation sensitized agriculture to its important role in the management

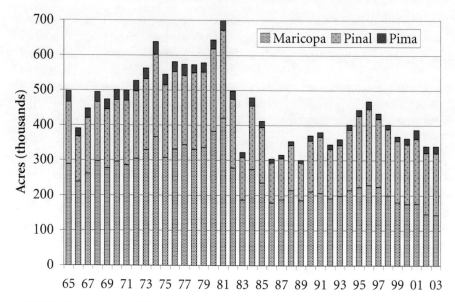

FIGURE 10-1. Acreage of Principal Field Crops in Maricopa, Pinal, and Pima Counties, 1965–2003
Source: Arizona Agricultural Statistical Service.

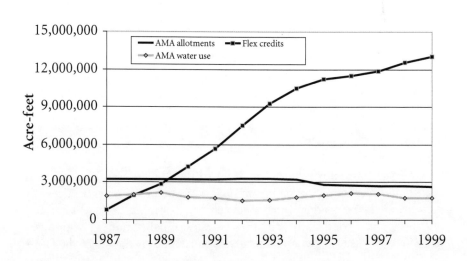

FIGURE 10-2. Allotments, Water Use, and Flex Credit Accumulation in the Phoenix, Pinal, and Tucson AMAs, 1987–1999
Source: Arizona Department of Water Resources.

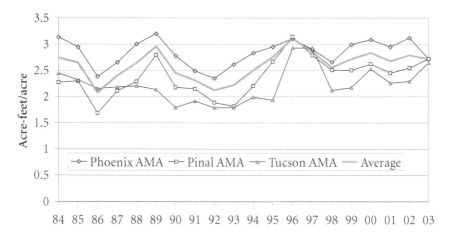

FIGURE 10-3. Water Use per Acre in the Phoenix, Pinal, and Tucson AMAs, 1984–2003
Source: Arizona Department of Water Resources.

of water resources. However, the agricultural water conservation provisions under GMA management plans have not created significant incentives for on-farm water conservation practices and technologies. Many growers have adopted water conservation practices and technologies over the past 25 years, but factors other than the AMA management plans have been largely responsible (Needham 2005; Needham and Wilson 2005).

Current Trends: The 2002 Farm Bill and the Role of Conservation

The 2002 farm bill, known as the Farm Security and Rural Investment (FSRI) Act (2002), which expires in 2007, reintroduced target price-deficiency payments (now called countercyclical payments) while maintaining fixed payments based on historic production. This change guaranteed that farmers would receive payments both when market prices were low and when they were high.

The FSRI Act also significantly increased authorization for technology adoption subsidies. The 1996 farm bill authorized EQIP funding of $1.3 billion, and the FSRI Act increased this funding to $5.8 billion from 2002 to 2007. However, actual funding levels depend on annual congressional appropriations. EQIP payments are budgeted to improve irrigation efficiency on almost 25 million acres, with projected reduction of agricultural water applications of 5.4 inches per acre. Measures include switching to dry-land production, to less water-intensive crops, and to more water-efficient practices. According to the USDA's Natural Resources Conservation Service, "Any water saved would be available for alternative uses such as by municipalities, utility generation, and wildlife habitat restoration" (USDA NRCS 2003a, 56). Assuming 20% loss in storage and transmission, the program would free 8.9 million acre-feet of water per year over 10 years. This is sizable, considering that total water withdrawals by public suppliers in the entire United States are about 50 million acre-feet per year (Hutson et al. 2004).

These ambitious objectives lead to the question: does improving irrigation efficiency actually conserve water? Economists have long recognized that improving irrigation efficiency need not reduce agricultural consumptive use of water (Caswell and Zilberman 1986; Boggess et al. 1993; Huffaker and Whittlesey 1995, 2000, 2003; Jaeger and Mikesell 2002; Peterson and Ding 2005). By definition, improved efficiency means that consumptive use as a percent of total water withdrawals increases. If crop choice, acreage, and yields are held fixed, less water needs to be withdrawn to maintain a constant level of production. Yet, new irrigation technology can lead to changes in all these variables so that reductions in diversion need not mean reductions in consumptive use. In systems relying on surface water and where return flows are an important source of water supply, irrigators may reduce withdrawals but increase consumptive use at the expense of return flows (Huffaker and Whittlesey 1995, 2000, 2003; Jaeger and Mikesell 2002). Given beneficial-use doctrines, irrigators may simply withdraw the same amount of water and consume a higher percent of it (for example, by planting more acres or more water-intensive crops) (Huffaker and Whittlesey 2003). In surface-water systems with negligible return flows, improved technology may be less effective at conserving water in low-flow years (when conservation is needed most) than in normal years (Huffaker and Whittlesey 2000). In the case of groundwater, withdrawals may be a better measure of conservation than consumptive use because return flows are limited or slow (Peterson and Ding 2005). Improved efficiency reduces the cost of consumptive use, but the effect of this cost reduction on withdrawals is ambiguous (Caswell and Zilberman 1986; Peterson and Ding 2005). Caswell and Zilberman's (1986) theoretical model suggests that irrigation improvements tend to conserve groundwater except in cases where water costs are high (for example, when wells are extremely deep).

Some economists have attempted to identify conditions under which subsidizing irrigation technology adoption can backfire, working counter to water conservation goals (Huffaker and Whittelesy 1995, 2000, 2003; Peterson and Ding 2005). Subsidizing more efficient technologies affects application rates, total acreage planted, crop choice, and return flows. It is possible that the net effect of all these changes is to increase consumptive water use by agriculture.

Peterson and Ding (2005) estimate that subsidies to encourage a switch from flood to drip or sprinkler irrigation in the Kansas high plains conserve water, but there is anecdotal evidence that improved irrigation efficiency has increased consumptive use in Idaho (Idaho Ground Water Appropriators, Inc. 2004). Huffaker and Whittelesy (2000, 58) suggest that to truly conserve water,

"Encourage only those private investments in on-farm irrigation efficiency that do not decrease the return flows relied upon by downstream appropriators and instream users." They discuss how the California water code is consistent with this approach, but the Oregon code and proposals in other states are not (Huffaker and Whittelesy 1995, 2000).

Other, far-reaching proposals for water conservation were discussed but ultimately abandoned during 2002 farm bill negotiations. Senators Harry Reid (Nevada) and Patrick Leahy (Vermont) introduced two interesting provisions for water conservation to the conservation title of the Senate version of the farm bill. A water conservation reserve enhancement program would have provided for 500,000 acres to be retired specifically for water conservation under the CREP. Farm owners or operators could receive payments based on the irrigated rental rates for retiring land if water was allocated to in-stream flows to protect endangered species. Water or water rights appurtenant to land would be leased or sold to state water agencies or state-designated water trusts. Preferences would be given to states that provided 20% or more matching funds.

A second water benefits program would have provided payments to farm owners or operators who invested in more efficient irrigation technology, switched to less water-intensive crops, or entered into dry-year option contracts (see Chapter 6 for a discussion of dry-year options). Dry-year options have been pursued and explored by some state governments but were new to USDA programs. Under the proposed dry-year program, producers would fallow land in drought years, allowing water to be reallocated to in-stream flows to protect endangered aquatic species. In wetter years, farmers would retain their rights to water and agricultural production.

Provisions for irrigated land retirement and dry-year options were eventually stripped from the final farm bill. Some states whose congressional delegations opposed the irrigated land retirement proposals (Idaho, Nebraska, and Colorado) are now pursuing irrigated land retirement under CREP. In Idaho, there is also discussion about including dry-year options within its CREP proposal (Idaho Ground Water Appropriators, Inc. 2004).

Opportunities and Challenges for Arizona in the 2007 Farm Bill

In 2002, Brazil filed a complaint with the World Trade Organization (WTO) alleging that the U.S. cotton program violated international trade agreements. In March 2005 an appellate panel upheld Brazil's main complaints (Schnepf 2004; Hudson et al. 2005). Brazil argued that the Step 2 Program and U.S. export credit guarantees were prohibited export subsidies and that coupled payments such as marketing loan payments caused "serious prejudice" to Brazilian (and other) producers by depressing the world cotton price. Furthermore, Brazil argued that fixed and countercyclical payments were not truly decoupled (and therefore not exempt from trade agreement limits) because they restricted planting of fruits and vegetables on base acres. The panel ruled that the United States should withdraw the prohibited export subsidies. In October 2005, Brazil requested WTO permission to retaliate with more than $1 billion in sanctions. The United States has since eliminated Step 2 and modified its export credit guarantee program. Brazil has temporarily suspended seeking retaliatory sanctions, but awaits further U.S. reforms. Design of 2007 farm bill programs will be influenced by a desire to comply with the WTO and avoid trade sanctions.

The WTO cotton case calls into question the entire structure of U.S. farm policy, with important implications for Arizona agriculture. Coupled marketing loan payments have increased the effective price Arizona cotton producers receive from 10% to 45% in recent years. Changes in planting restrictions for fruits and vegetables may alter the mix of crops grown (and water demand) in the state. A decrease in cotton and wheat acreage could be offset by an increase in alfalfa, vegetable, and melon acreage. Net impacts on agricultural water demand are uncertain.

The WTO dispute may also cause conservation programs to play a more prominent role in the 2007 farm bill. The WTO ruling places virtually all U.S. commodity programs in a category requiring reduction over time, but the WTO exempts conservation payments from international commitments to reduce agricultural subsidies. Environmental groups have already begun to press for a shift in emphasis from traditional farm payments to conservation payments. Proposals for USDA funding of dry-year leasing options may also resurface. In the western United States, environmental groups such as Environmental Defense and Trout Unlimited are interested in restructuring EQIP payments to better ensure actual water conservation and increases in in-stream flows.

Conclusions

The agricultural water-use issues in Arizona illustrate the types of problems other regions may face. Because agriculture accounts for such a large share of Arizona's overall water consumption, changes in agricultural policy have profound implications for the state's task of balancing water supply and demand. In response to the WTO cotton dispute, the 2007 farm bill may significantly change the structure and scope of farm income support and conservation programs. The impact of farm program changes on agricultural water use will depend on total acreage, the mix of crops grown, where they are grown, and growers' irrigation management practices. Evidence suggests that farm programs have significantly stimulated agricultural demand for water overall, but effects vary greatly by region.

The Conservation Reserve Enhancement Program (CREP) has emerged as an important policy tool to help states ease conflicts over water between agricultural and environmental interests, with some states receiving federal funding of more than $200 million. However, to start a CREP program, a state's governor must develop and submit a CREP proposal to USDA, and the state must provide 20% matching funds. Half the states either have an ongoing CREP or are in the proposal-writing stage. Although CREPs initially focused on water pollution issues, some western states have developed or are developing CREPs as voluntary irrigated land fallowing programs. Idaho is considering provisions for dry-year leasing options in its CREP proposal. Arizona currently does not operate a CREP, nor is one in the development stage. It may, however, be a way of leveraging sizable federal funds to ease state water allocation conflicts.

References

Arizona Department of Economic Security (AZDES). 2005. *Projections for State and Counties.* ADES Population Statistics Unit. Phoenix, AZ: ADES.

Baker, W.D. 1995. Chapter 9 Bankruptcy: A Haven for Central Arizona Project Irrigation Districts? *Arizona State Law Journal* 27: 663–75.

Boggess, W., R. Lacewell, and D. Zilberman. 1993. Economics of Water Use in Agriculture. In *Agricultural and Environmental Resource Economics*, edited by G.A. Carlson, D. Zilberman, and J.A. Miranowski. Oxford, U.K.: Oxford University Press, 319–91.

Caswell, M., and D. Zilberman. 1986. The Effects of Well Depth and Land Quality on the Choice of Irrigation Technology. *American Journal of Agricultural Economics* 68: 798–811.

Cattaneo, A. 2003. The Pursuit of Efficiency and Its Unintended Consequences: Contract Withdrawals in the Environmental Quality Incentives Program. *Review of Agricultural Economics* 25: 449–69.

Council for Agricultural Science and Technology (CAST). 1992. *Water Quality: Agriculture's Role.* Task Force Report No. 120. Ames, IA: CAST.

Daugherty, A. 1997. *Land Use.* Agricultural Resources and Environmental Indicators, 1996–1997. AHS–705. Economic Research Service. Washington, DC: USDA.

Farm Security and Rural Investment (FSRI) Act. 2002. P.L. 107–171.

Farmers Investment Company v. Bettwy. 1976. 558 P.2d 14 (Ariz.).

Feather, P., D. Hellerstein, and L. Hansen. 1999. *Economic Valuation of Environmental Benefits and the Targeting of Conservation Programs: The Case of the CRP.* Agricultural Economic Report No. 778. Economic Research Service. Washington, DC: USDA.

Federal Agricultural Improvement and Reform (FAIR) Act. 1996. P.L. 104–127.

Food Agricultural Conservation and Trade Act. 1990. P.L. 101–624.

Food Security Act. 1985. P.L. 99–198.

Frisvold, G. 2004. How Federal Farm Programs Affect Water Use, Quality, and Allocation among Sectors. *Water Resources Research* 40. Art. No. W12S05.

Gardner, B.L. 2002. *Agricultural Policy: Pre- and Post-FAIR Act Comparisons.* Policy

Analysis Report 01–02. Center for Agricultural and Natural Resource Policy. College Park, MD: University of Maryland, College Park.

Groundwater Management Act of 1980. Arizona Revised Statutes, Title 45, Ch. 2, secs. 401, 403, 411, 461, 491, 452, 454, 511, 576, 591.

Hanemann, M. 2002. *The Central Arizona Project.* CUDARE Working Papers, Number 937. Department of Agricultural and Resource Economics and Policy. Berkeley, CA: University of California, Berkeley.

Heimlich, R. 2003. Conservation and Environmental Program Overview. In *Agricultural Resources and Environmental Indicators, 2003.* Agricultural Handbook 722. Washington, DC: Economic Research Service, 1–28.

Holland, S.P., and M.R. Moore. 2003. Cadillac Desert Revisited: Property Rights, Public Policy, and Water-Resource Depletion. *Journal of Environmental Economics and Management* 40: 131–55.

Horner, G.L., S.A. Hatchett, R.M. House, and R.E. Howitt. 1991. Impacts of San Joaquin Valley Drainage-Related Policies on State and National Agricultural Production. In *The Economics and Management of Water and Drainage in Agriculture,* edited by A. Dinar and D. Zilberman. Norwell, MA: Kluwer Academic Press, 557–73.

Howitt, R.E. 1991. Water Policy Effects on Crop Production and Vice Versa: An Empirical Approach. In *Commodity and Resource Policies in Agricultural Systems,* edited by R.E. Just and N. Bockstael. New York: Springer, 234–53.

Hudson, D., C.P. Rosson, III, J. Robinson, and J. Malaga. 2005. The WTO Cotton Case and U.S. Domestic Policy. *Choices* 20: 143–47.

Huffaker, R., and N. Whittlesey. 1995. Agricultural Conservation Legislation: Will It Save Water? *Choices* 10: 24–28.

———. 2000. The Allocative Efficiency and Conservation Potential of Water Laws Encouraging Investments in On-Farm Irrigation Technology. *Agricultural Economics* 24: 47–60.

———. 2003. A Theoretical Analysis of Economic Incentive Policies Encouraging Agricultural Water Conservation. *Water Resources Development* 19: 37–53.

Hutson, S., N. Barber, J. Kenny, K. Linsey, D. Lumia, and M. Maupin. 2004. *Estimated Use of Water in the United States in 2000.* USGS Circular 1268. Reston, VA: USGS.

Idaho Ground Water Appropriators, Inc. 2004. *Idaho Proposal for Idaho Irrigated Conservation Reserve Enhancement Program.* Boise, ID: Idaho Ground Water Appropriators, Inc.

Jaeger, W.K., and R. Mikesell. 2002. Increasing Streamflow To Sustain Salmon and other Native Fish in the Pacific Northwest. *Contemporary Economic Policy* 20: 366–80.

Jarvis v. State Land Department. 1969, 1970, 1976. City of Tucson I, II, III, 456 P.2d 385 (Ariz. 1969); mod. 479 P.2d 169 (Ariz. 1970); injunction mod. 550 P.2d 227 (Ariz. 1976).

Kelso, M., W.E. Martin, and L. Mack. 1973. *Water Supplies and Economic Growth in an Arid Environment: An Arizona Case Study.* Tucson, AZ: University of Arizona Press.

Konyar, K., and K. Knapp. 1990. Dynamic Regional Analysis of the California Alfalfa Market with Government Policy Impacts. *Western Journal of Agricultural Economics* 15: 22–32.

Lin, W., P. Westcott, R. Skinner, S. Sanford, and D. De La Torre Ugarte. 2000. *Supply*

Response under the 1996 Farm Act and Implications for the U.S. Field Crops Sector. Technical Bulletin No. 1888. Economic Research Service. Washington, DC: USDA.

Lohman, L.C., J.G. Miliken, and W.S. Dorn. 1988. *Estimating Economic Impacts of Salinity of the Colorado River.* Denver, CO: U.S. Bureau of Reclamation.

Moore, M.R., and A. Dinar. 1995. Water and Land as Quantity-Rationed Inputs in California Agriculture: Empirical Tests and Water Policy Implications. *Land Economics* 71: 445–61.

Needham, R. 2005. An Econometric Evaluation of Water Conservation Programs: The Case of Arizona's Groundwater Management Act. M.S. Thesis. Department of Agricultural and Resource Economics. University of Arizona, Tucson.

Needham, R., and P.N. Wilson. 2005. Water Conservation Policies in Arizona Agriculture: Assessing the Groundwater Management Act of 1980. *Arizona Review* Spring, 13–15.

Parsons, R.M. 2004. USDA Officials To Get First Hand Look at Water Problems. *South Idaho Press*, August 13, 1.

Peterson, J.M., and Y. Ding. 2005. Economic Adjustments to Groundwater Depletion in the High Plains: Do Water-Saving Irrigation Systems Save Water? *American Journal of Agricultural Economics* 87: 147–59.

Schnepf, R. 2004. *U.S.–Brazil WTO Cotton Subsidy Dispute.* CRS Report for Congress Order Code RL32571. Washington, DC: Congressional Research Service, Library of Congress.

Smith, M. 2000. Conservation Reserve Enhancement Program: Early Results from a Federal–State Partnership. *Agricultural Outlook* AO–277, 16–20.

Thurman, W.N. 1995. *Assessing the Environmental Impact of Farm Policies.* Washington, DC: American Enterprise Institute Press.

U.S. Department of Agriculture (USDA). 2003. Farm and Ranch Irrigation Survey. Washington, DC: USDA.

_____. 2004. *Economic Effects of U.S. Dairy Policy and Alternative Approaches to Milk Pricing: Report to Congress.* Washington, DC: USDA.

U.S. Department of Agriculture, Consolidated Farm Services Agency (USDA CFSA). 1995. *Colorado River Salinity Control Program: From Inception of Program through 1994 Fiscal Year.* Washington, DC: USDA.

U.S. Department of Agriculture, Farm Service Agency (USDA FSA). 2003. *Conservation Reserve Monthly Summary.* June. Washington, DC: USDA.

U.S. Department of Agriculture, National Agricultural Statistics Service (USDA NASS). 2003. *Farm and Ranch Irrigation Survey, 2003.* Washington, DC: U.S. Government Printing Office.

U.S. Department of Agriculture, Natural Resources Conservation Service (USDA NRCS). 2003a. *Environmental Quality Incentives Program Benefit Cost Analysis: Final Report May 21, 2003.* Washington, DC: Natural Resources Conservation Service.

———. 2003b. *EQIP Benefit Cost Analysis: Final Report.* Washington, DC: Natural Resources Conservation Service.

U.S. Department of the Interior (U.S. DOI). 1990. *Colorado River Damage Estimate Program.* Analysis, Contracts and Lands Division. Denver, CO: U.S. Bureau of Reclamation.

———. 1999. *Quality of Water Colorado River Basin: Progress Report No. 19.* Denver, CO: U.S. Bureau of Reclamation.

U.S. General Accounting Office (U.S. GAO). 1995. *Information on Salinity Control Projects in the Colorado River Basin.* GAO/RCED–95–58.

Westcott, P.C., and J.M. Price. 2001. *Analysis of the U.S. Commodity Loan Program with Marketing Loan Provisions.* ERS Agricultural Economic Report No. 801. Economic Research Service. Washington, DC: USDA.

Wilson, P.N. 2002. Economic Science and the Central Arizona Project: Lessons Learned. *Water Resources Update* 123: 30–37.

Young, R.A., and W.E. Martin. 1967. The Economics of Arizona's Water Problem. *Arizona Review* 16: 9–18.

11

Urban Growth
and Water Supply

James M. Holway

The sustainability of urban growth in central Arizona, including the Phoenix and Tucson metropolitan areas, is a key issue for Arizona's future, as well as for urbanizing arid regions worldwide. To secure this future, huge investments have been made in water management, particularly in the development of renewable supplies. Arizona, as it grows, will have to continue to address challenges to the availability and management of long-term supplies.

Arizona's municipal water management programs have been shaped by the nature of available supplies in a semiarid state; the economics and technology of acquiring, treating, and distributing those supplies; the legal framework of land ownership and water rights; the growth and pattern of water demands; and the political nature of Arizona and its major historic water users. Earlier chapters have presented many of the key elements of this context. This chapter examines growth and water quantity management in Arizona's urban areas, focusing on the central Arizona active management areas and the processes, regulations, and analytic tools used by the state to address these issues.

Growth, Growth, and More Growth

Central Arizona, one of the fastest growing areas of the country since the 1970s, is projected to continue growing rapidly well into the future. The region, currently home to 4.7 million people, is projected to reach 11 million residents by 2050 (Figure 11-1). As a result, rural and agricultural Pinal County, which lies between Phoenix and Tucson, is urbanizing, and the separate Phoenix and Tucson areas will likely become one continuous metropolitan region. The water management implications of the location and magnitude of this growth will be discussed later in this chapter.

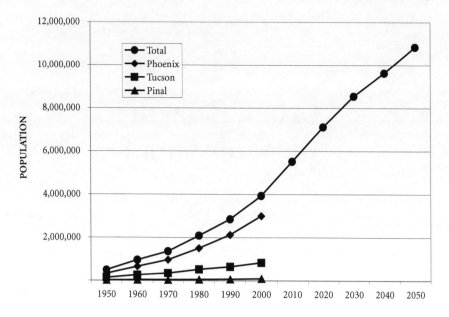

FIGURE 11-1. Central Arizona Historic and Projected AMA Populations
Sources: ADWR 1994, 1999; Morrison Institute for Public Policy 2005.

Current and Projected Water Demand and Supply

Significant changes in the pattern of water use in central Arizona include increasing municipal use, decreasing agricultural water use, and a shift to greater use of surface water and effluent. Municipal water demand has increased with population; historically, however, this increase has been more than offset by declining agricultural use, and total water use in central Arizona has declined from its peak in the 1970s (Figure 11-2). Agricultural water use varies from year to year but has declined because of both the urbanization of agricultural land and a decline in the agricultural economy since the late 1970s.

Population, household consumption patterns, and the nature of nonresidential water uses are the principal factors driving municipal water use. For central Arizona, 60–70% of municipal water deliveries go to residential uses, with the remainder going to nonresidential purposes (e.g., commercial, industrial, public buildings, and parks). Exterior uses, principally turf and other landscape watering, include approximately 60% of municipal water deliveries across both residential and nonresidential users. Per capita use rates have generally declined since the mid-1980s. However, population growth outstrips conservation savings, and municipal demand continues to increase.

Figure 11-3 illustrates the changes that have occurred since the mid-1980s in the use of renewable supplies in the central Arizona active management areas (AMAs). These changes in the mix of water supplies have resulted from

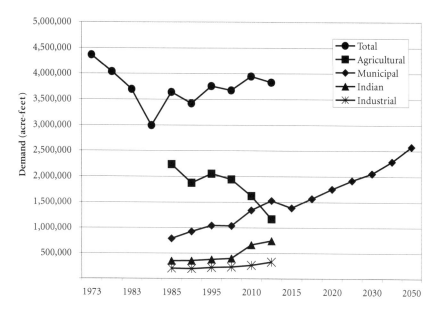

FIGURE 11-2. Historic and Projected Sector Water Demands in Central Arizona AMAs
Sources: ADWR 1994, 1999; Morrison Institute for Public Policy 2005.

the completion of the Central Arizona Project (CAP) aqueduct to Phoenix in 1987 and to Tucson in 1993, investments in treatment plants to deliver CAP water, urbanization of groundwater-irrigated agriculture, the use of subsidized CAP water by agriculture, the assured water supply requirement to use renewable or imported supplies for new growth, and the tightening effluent discharge standards, which further encouraged reuse. The investments in water and wastewater treatment required for this transition were facilitated as the rapidly growing communities achieved the necessary levels of population to finance the investments.

Future projections assume that these demand and supply trends will continue. However, it is difficult to predict the degree to which increases in urban water use will be offset by decreases in agricultural water use. Although the conventional wisdom is that urban development uses less water than agriculture, this is not necessarily the case. A medium-density residential development (four to six houses per acre) with a moderate level of landscaping and a golf course for every 2,000–3,000 homes would use approximately the same quantity of water as the cotton farm it replaced. The architects of the 1980 Groundwater Management Act (GMA) (Connall 1982) believed that water supplies for new growth and a reduction in groundwater mining would come in part from urbanization of previously irrigated agricultural lands. To some degree, this change has occurred. However, new development is generally not allowed to use mined groundwater, so there is limited incentive to develop overirrigated land and retire the grandfathered irrigation rights. Urban development relies primarily on renewable or imported water supplies to meet the requirements of Arizona's assured water supply program. Therefore, even if overall water use remains relatively constant, municipal providers will need to acquire significant volumes of new renewable and imported supplies.

Potential Future Supply Issues

The potential future supplies to serve municipal growth include Central Arizona Project (CAP) water, Colorado River water, other surface waters, groundwater, and reclaimed effluent. Each of these supplies has different costs and infrastructure requirements as well as unique institutional, legal, and political issues described in Chapter 2 of this book, which complicate the ability of the urban areas to develop a firm long-term portfolio.

Colorado River, Central Arizona Project, and surface-water supplies are for the most part fully allocated, though approximately 100,000 acre-feet of non-Indian agricultural (low priority) CAP water is available for reallocation. (Note: "Indian" and "non-Indian" in this context are specific terms used to designate a particular category of water.) Rights to some of these supplies can be purchased outright; others (such as Native American water rights) can only be leased and in some cases may require congressional authorization for transfers.

Acquiring supplies from existing users or pumping groundwater for importation into central Arizona may raise economic concerns and lead to political efforts to limit such transfers by areas of origin (those communities that would transfer their supplies). The Central Arizona Project aqueduct, designed to import 1.5–1.8 million acre-feet of water into central Arizona, would also need to be expanded at some point to allow additional imports. The volume of new supplies potentially available to central Arizona is more than sufficient to cover additional growth, even beyond the projections shown in this chapter. However, long-range infrastructure and water management planning and a statewide consensus on future water supply strategies would make a major contribution toward reducing uncertainty regarding the ability to acquire and import these supplies.

Water Management in Arizona's Active Management Areas

Arizona chose, through the 1980 Groundwater Management Act (GMA), to establish a strong regulatory water management and conservation program within five active management areas (AMAs) (Figure 1-2 in Chapter 1). The 1980 GMA set in place requirements for state-directed management within the AMAs, established management goals for each AMA, and created a rights system that grandfathered in many existing users. The GMA includes four broad areas of state authority and tools to regulate municipal water management: groundwater withdrawal authorities, water measurement and reporting requirements, demand management programs, and supply management programs. This section provides an overview of this regulatory framework for municipal water supplies with a focus on active management areas and the assured water supply requirements linking urban growth to available water supplies.

Active Management Areas' Water Supply Regulations

Management Goals

The Groundwater Management Act established a management goal for each AMA and set in place a framework to accomplish the goals through a series of five management plans from 1980 through 2025. The goal for the Phoenix, Prescott, and Tucson AMAs is to achieve safe yield by 2025. The Pinal AMA, established in a predominantly agricultural area that is now rapidly urbanizing, was given the goal of protecting the agricultural economy for as long as feasible and preserving water supplies for future nonagricultural purposes. The Santa Cruz AMA, separated from the Tucson AMA in 1994, has the dual goal of maintaining safe yield and preventing local water tables from experiencing long-term declines. Programs are currently under development for achieving the Santa Cruz AMA goal, and local stakeholders are discussing the possibility of modifying certain programs for the Pinal AMA because of its rapid urbanization.

Withdrawal Authorities and Measurement and Reporting

Water users must have a withdrawal right or permit to use groundwater within an AMA. For example, municipal water providers hold a service-area right, which allows them an unquantified right to pump groundwater within their service area to serve their customers. A permit is also required to drill new water supply wells, and a municipal provider must demonstrate that they will not create an unreasonable burden on surrounding land or water users. Well spacing requirements prevent new wells from creating a drawdown of more than two feet per year on any surrounding well without obtaining a waiver from the owner of the affected well. Finally, water users must measure and report all water uses annually and pay a groundwater withdrawal fee (ranging from $2 to $3 per acre-foot) to the Arizona Department of Water Resources (ADWR). Wells with a pumping capacity of less than 35 gallons per minute that are not irrigating more than two acres, are exempt from most provisions of the groundwater code and do not need permits.

Demand Management for Municipal Users

Water-use efficiency is a key component of Arizona's strategy for achieving safe yield and ensuring a sustainable supply. Additional investments in conservation may also be the cheapest source of supply to meet new demands or to deal with shortages caused by drought. The GMA required implementation of mandatory conservation requirements within AMAs for all large water users through a series of management plans adopted every 10 years. In addition, certain high-level water uses are deemed unacceptable and banned, such as private subdivision lakes filled with groundwater or surface water.

Most AMA municipal providers are regulated by the state based on per capita water-use targets. However, alternative programs based on the adoption of prescribed best management practices are used by a few providers. For the first management plan (1985 to 1990), water providers were required to reduce their per capita use by a fixed percentage (0–11%) based on the size of their current per capita use rate. The GMA required additional reductions in per capita use rates for both the second and third management periods. The AMAs are currently in the middle of the third management plan (2000 to 2010). For the third management plan, individual per capita use targets were calculated for each water provider based on their historic uses, conservation potential of existing uses, and assigned model use rates for new development that assume a high level of efficiency. For the Phoenix AMA, new households are expected to meet an interior use rate of 57 gallons per capita per day and an exterior use rate for single-family homes of 178 gallons per housing unit per day (77 gallons per housing unit per day for multifamily housing). Nonresidential uses are restricted to the per capita levels in a base year, generally 1985, and for the Phoenix AMA are expected to be reduced by 7% per capita from the 1985 levels.

Finally, lost and unaccounted for water must be less than 10% of total deliveries. Based on a formula that includes these use rates multiplied by actual housing unit types and population in each service area, per capita water-use targets are calculated annually for each service area.

Table 11-1 shows the actual average per capita use rates for the central Arizona AMAs. Per capita use rates in the Phoenix AMA have decreased significantly, and rates have been relatively stable in the Pinal and Tucson AMAs. Conservation efforts by existing users account for some of the decrease in the Phoenix AMA, but the major factor is lower per capita use rates in areas of new construction. In the Tucson AMA, per capita use rates were already among the lowest in the southwest United States. Ongoing conservation efforts of some areas in Tucson have been more than offset by new developments with greater use of landscaping that uses more water. The GMA provides significant penalties for noncompliance (up to $200 per acre-foot and $10,000 per day of violation); however, such penalties are rarely used, and in recent years the state has not had the resources to pursue actively compliance actions for conservation program violations.

TABLE 11-1. Gallons per Capita per Day Rates for Central Arizona AMAs

AMA	1985	1990	1995
Phoenix	308	301	282
Pinal	220	227	225
Tucson	176	169	172

Source: ADWR 1999.

A non-per capita conservation program was implemented in 1995 to provide a prescriptive best management practices (BMP) program for municipal providers. This program is only available to providers who have largely eliminated dependence on mined groundwater. Providers in this program implement BMPs that are specified through a negotiated agreement between the water provider and the Arizona Department of Water Resources.

Cities, municipal water providers, and the state have all gained considerable experience in developing and implementing conservation programs. There likely is additional conservation potential in Arizona's urban areas. However, a key role of the regulatory conservation programs has been to achieve a moderate level of water-use efficiency and to "keep the lid on" by helping to prevent increases in per capita use rates with increasing affluence and new development.

One key component of Arizona's approach to conservation was the quantification of grandfathered groundwater rights. These rights allow existing groundwater users to pursue conservation opportunities aggressively without fearing that they will forfeit water rights because of the "use it or lose it" standard that applies in many prior appropriation systems. Another distinction of importance in designing conservation efforts is recognizing the difference between permanent conservation practices and those that are needed during the short or medium-length shortages that always occur in arid and semiarid environments (see Jacobs and Holway 2004 for additional details on Arizona's regulatory conservation programs).

For the first decade after the 1980 GMA, state water management efforts focused on development of conservation programs, but implementing supply management programs has been the principal activity since the mid-1990s.

Supply Management for Urban Users

Achieving safe yield within the Phoenix and Tucson AMAs will require alternative water supplies to serve new growth and to substitute for the groundwater currently used by existing customers. Conversion of agricultural land to urban development and requirements that new development use renewable supplies are key components of the 1980 GMA approach to reaching safe yield. Arizona's supply management programs include the Assured Water Supply Rules (Arizona Revised Statutes 45–576 and Arizona Administrative Code R12–15–701 through 725, adopted in 1995), requiring all new subdivision approvals in the safe-yield AMAs to be based on renewable or imported supplies; the recharge and recovery program (Arizona Revised Statutes 45–801 through 898, adopted in 1986 and substantially revised in 1994), facilitating conjunctive management of surface water, groundwater, and effluent; the Central Arizona Groundwater Replenishment District (CAGRD, created in 1994), facilitating replenishment of mined groundwater to comply with assured water supply requirements; and the Arizona Water Banking Authority (created in 1996) to store excess water for recovery during shortages. Each of these activities is described in more detail in other chapters, particularly Chapters 3 and 13. In addition, incentives to use renewable supplies are incorporated into the conservation requirements. For example, effluent use is not counted against a water provider's allowable per capita water use. These programs have been important in motivating and facilitating the changes in water supplies since 1985 that are illustrated by Figure 11-3.

The remainder of this section focuses on the assured water supply program. Although issues related to groundwater storage and recovery, in particular the CAGRD, are touched on below, they and the other programs listed above are covered in depth in Chapter 13.

Assured Water Supply Program History

Arizona adopted Adequate Water Supply Rules in 1973 (Arizona Administrative Code R12–15–701). This consumer protection program was a response to large-scale marketing of lands without access to water in Arizona. The adequate water supply program, which still operates outside AMAs, requires a demonstration of whether a 100-year water supply exists. The subdivision can proceed whether the supply is adequate or not, but if a 100-year supply is not demonstrated, the seller is required to notify the first buyer of any lot or house that the Arizona Department of Water Resources has determined that a 100-year supply has not been demonstrated.

Assured Water Supply Rules were adopted in 1995, as required by the 1980 Groundwater Management Act, to ensure that new growth would be consistent with each AMA's goal (safe yield for most of them) and management plans (conservation requirements). Discussions over the nature of this assured supply requirement were a subject of significant controversy in the negotiations that led up to the GMA (Connall 1982). The ADWR first proposed rules in 1988 that were withdrawn four months later after significant opposition. Formulating rules to move the AMAs toward safe yield, while also allowing development of lands outside the urban core and existing water supply infrastructure, was a key challenge that had to be overcome before any rules became politically acceptable.

Development industry interests designed and gained legislative approval in 1993 for a multicounty voluntary replenishment district, the Central Arizona

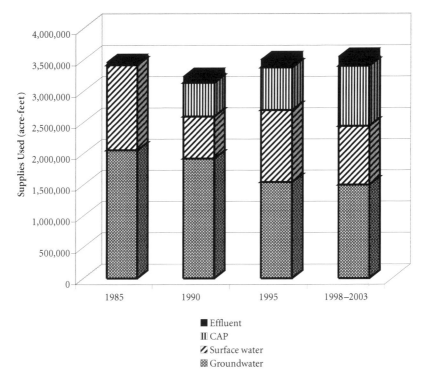

FIGURE 11-3. Water Supplies in Central Arizona AMAs
Sources: ADWR 1999, 2001, 2003.

Groundwater Replenishment District (CAGRD). With the CAGRD in place as a mechanism allowing new subdivisions without access to renewable supplies to prove an assured water supply, the way was cleared politically for adoption of Assured Water Supply Rules.

Assured Water Supply Rules

The assured water supply (AWS) requirement for renewable water supplies as a condition of new municipal growth forms the cornerstone of Arizona's effort to reduce groundwater overdraft in the AMAs. The rules prohibit the subdivision of land until an applicant meets five criteria:

- physical, legal, and continuous availability of water for 100 years;
- water quality that meets state and federal drinking water standards;
- sufficient financial capability to build and operate the necessary infrastructure;
- consistency with the AMA management plan (effect on conservation requirements); and
- consistency with the AMA management goal (typically safe yield).

The key criteria are consistency with the safe-yield goal and physical availability. Essentially, the subdivision needs to be supplied with a renewable or imported water supply. If the subdivision relies on groundwater, then any mined groundwater must be replenished, typically by joining the CAGRD. Subdivisions relying on groundwater and CAGRD membership must demonstrate that after 100 years of pumping, the depth to groundwater will not exceed 1,000 feet below land surface, or 1,200 feet in the Pinal AMA.

The assured water supply requirement can be met through either a designation or a certificate. Water providers can obtain a designation of assured water supply for their entire service area by demonstrating a firm portfolio of supplies to meet the five criteria for their entire current and committed demand (approved but not yet occupied subdivision lots) plus at least two years of estimated new subdivision approvals. Most of the cities in the Phoenix and Tucson metropolitan area are designated, but few of the private water companies and smaller communities are. The principal advantages of a designation are that it gives a water provider additional control over its service area, facilitates development, and ensures that the water provider or city is planning for its future water supply needs on an ongoing basis. Providers who choose not to be designated usually do so because they lack sufficient access to long-term water supplies, lack the financial resources to treat and deliver renewable supplies, or choose to reduce water supply costs by continuing to serve groundwater to the customers who existed before the 1995 rules were adopted.

Developers of subdivisions not served by a designated provider must apply individually to the Arizona Department of Water Resources for a certificate of assured water supply. Individual certificate holders can acquire their own assured water supply, but most often they pump groundwater and join the CAGRD for replenishment services to meet the consistency with management goal criteria of the AWS rules.

Current Assured Water Supply Issues

Arizona's assured water supply (AWS) program is arguably the most stringent program that links available water supplies to urban growth in the United States. During the program's first 10 years, a number of significant policy and administrative issues have arisen. This section briefly discusses a few of the issues arising from the unique goals or hydrologic conditions in three of the five AMAs, future challenges from changes in available water supplies, and the role of the Central Arizona Groundwater Replenishment District (CAGRD) and its effect on the increasing competition for water supplies.

The Prescott and Santa Cruz AMAs' AWS issues are mentioned here because of their potential relevance to the transferability of Arizona's experience to other locations. The 1999 determination that the Prescott AMA was no longer at safe yield is one of the most politically contentious issues addressed to date by the ADWR. This decision resulted in a significant rush of development applications to beat any changes in rules, a legislative effort to halt or slow any rule changes, and preparation of an alternative groundwater model to dispute the findings of the state agency (ADWR 1998).

The unique goal of the Santa Cruz AMA, preventing long-term local water table declines, will necessitate a modification of the rules to facilitate the conjunctive management of surface water, effluent, and groundwater. Unlike the other AMAs, where safe yield only requires basinwide accounting and management, the Santa Cruz AMA's programs require water tables to be stabilized throughout the AMA. The Santa Cruz AMA is also unique in that it depends on the flow of the Santa Cruz River and contains relatively shallow aquifers that are rapidly depleted (ADWR 1997, 2004).

In the Pinal AMA, where 97% of water use is for agriculture and the goal in part is to protect the agricultural economy, potential AWS rule changes have been under discussion for several years. Unlike the safe-yield AMAs, new subdivisions are allocated either 60 or 120 gallons per capita per day of allowable groundwater use, and they require little if any renewable supplies to obtain their assured water supply. However, both the Phoenix and Tucson metropolitan areas have expanded into the Pinal AMA, leading to increasingly rapid population growth. Water interests in the Pinal AMA are looking to modify their Assured Water Supply Rules to reduce the groundwater allowance for new development so that renewable or imported supplies will be acquired and that future groundwater overdraft will not be further increased.

One future challenge for the AWS program will be its need to evolve over time with changes in the types of supplies available to water providers. Water providers receiving designations of AWS today are mostly relying on subcontracts for Central Arizona Project (CAP) water, senior surface-water rights, and reuse of their effluent. The available CAP water and surface-water rights are nearly all allocated, and future supplies will come largely from leased water. Many of these future supplies will not meet the current AWS criteria (for example the requirement of a 100-year lease). This is one of the major factors pushing providers to join the Central Arizona Groundwater Replenishment District, thereby increasing reliance on groundwater pumping and replenishment instead of investing in direct delivery of renewable supplies.

The role and operations of the CAGRD are covered in Chapter 13, and this section discusses a few CAGRD issues that are central to municipal water management. The CAGRD is projecting that by 2015 they will have accepted obligations ultimately to replenish 227,000 acre-feet each year for their members. This amount represents approximately 15% of the estimated 2015 demand for the central Arizona AMAs. The CAGRD, when established, was not expected to assume such a large role, and every indication is that under current policies the CAGRD will continue to absorb a larger and larger share of new growth. The difficulty of securing long-term firm supplies that satisfy the requirements of the Assured Water Supply Rules, as discussed above, is a key factor in this growth. Although the water supply portfolio requirements of the

CAGRD were revised recently to require a 20-year supply plan and a 100-year assessment showing likely available supplies, this is still much weaker than the 100-year firm supply requirement to receive an AWS designation or certificate for non-CAGRD members.

The CAGRD recently completed a plan of operation for the 2006–2015 period. This planning process illustrated the increasing competition for future water supplies. In the initial draft plan of operation, the staff of the CAGRD proposed to build a portfolio relying 80% on firm water supply contracts, purchases, and allocations. The remainder of supply would be made up of excess CAP water and use of other short-term surpluses and temporary transfers. This draft plan of operation met considerable opposition from both the cities and the development community. The cities viewed the CAGRD as competing for the same firm supplies that the cities would need to meet their AWS requirements. The cities believed that it was better for the CAGRD, with its supply mechanism of groundwater pumping and replenishment, to rely on short-term and less firm supplies. The development community was particularly opposed to the CAGRD's proposals for financing the increased costs to acquire firm supplies, which would have put more up-front costs on the developer instead of the eventual homeowner.

After an extensive stakeholder negotiation process, a compromise was reached. Cities, private water companies, state agencies, and the development industry all participated in lengthy negotiations. As part of the process, the staff of CAGRD took the most comprehensive look to date at regional population and water demand growth, potentially available supplies, and acquisition and infrastructure costs for importing new water supplies into central Arizona (CAGRD 2004). Essentially, the CAGRD agreed to target a lower portion of firm supplies (approximately 50%); to pursue contracts for transferring water supplies from main-stem Colorado River water users, which the cities were not yet pursuing; to seek legislation lowering the volume of extra replenishment reserve the CAGRD would be required to store; and to alter the financing scheme, thereby reducing and delaying the CAGRD fees paid up front by developers.

Data and Technical Tools
Used to Assist Water Management

Information about water resources, improved access to data, long-range regional planning, and education efforts targeted at decisionmakers and the public are all critical to good water management. Arizona has compiled extensive data on local hydrology, water demands, and water supplies within the AMAs, but much less is known in most of the rural non-AMA portions of the state (see Chapter 12).

Water-Use Reporting and Hydrologic Information

Arizona and other parties within the state invest significant resources in tracking water levels, monitoring surface-water flows, measuring snowpack in the watersheds, and monitoring land subsidence. Groundwater levels are measured at approximately 1,500 index wells throughout the state annually. In addition, comprehensive basinwide measurements of multiple wells are typically conducted every 5–10 years for most of the basins in the state. This water level information is used for basin characterizations, as input for groundwater modeling efforts, and for administering programs such as the assured and adequate water supply and well impact regulations. In the latest technology to be applied, the Arizona Department of Water Resources has been conducting detailed land elevation and gravimetry surveys to closely monitor current and potential land subsidence and earth fissure zones and attempt to determine changes in water storage.

Hydrologic Modeling and Regional Planning Efforts

Numerical computer models of the aquifer systems in the AMAs are used for planning and regulatory purposes. Though developed initially to improve understanding of hydrologic conditions and available supplies, these models are increasingly being used for Assured Water Supply Rule implementation and to facilitate regional planning efforts. Groundwater models were the primary tools used to demonstrate that the Prescott AMA was no longer at safe yield, and they have also been used for regional-scale preliminary evaluations of the 100-year physical availability for the Assured Water Supply Rules. Models currently under development will be essential for implementing the Assured Water Supply Rules in the Santa Cruz AMA to determine how new demands may affect local water levels. Perhaps the most effective uses of the models have been the efforts to develop future water supply and demand scenarios and use the groundwater models to project resulting groundwater conditions. The results of such efforts have influenced decisionmakers and public opinion to support significant investments in infrastructure for securing, treating, and delivering renewable supplies in the Phoenix and Prescott AMAs.

Conclusions

Arizona's water managers, particularly since the adoption of the 1980 Groundwater Management Act, have been at the forefront of innovations for managing municipal water supplies to accommodate rapid urban growth. These conclusions focus on lessons learned from Arizona's experience. Historically, throughout the United States, there has been a disconnect between water supply considerations and urban land use or growth management planning.

Reasons for this disconnect range from the relative roles of federal, state, and local government, to the character of growth, to the differing nature of land use and water resources planning (Lucero and Tarlock 2003; Arnold 2005; Coulson 2005; Holway and Jacobs 2006).

Lessons from Arizona on Efforts to Link Water and Growth

Arizona's innovations to ensure sustainable water supplies sufficient for continued urban growth include

- adoption of conservation programs and investments in the use of renewable supplies by cities and water providers;
- the conservation and assured water supply provisions of the Groundwater Management Act (discussed above);
- the recharge and recovery program, groundwater replenishment district, and Arizona Water Banking Authority (discussed in Chapter 13);
- water rights settlements with Native American communities (discussed in Chapter 14);
- new requirements for a water resources element in local government comprehensive plans; and
- recent legislation that requires water supply, drought, and conservation planning by water providers throughout the state.

Arizona is in a unique position relative to the linkages between water and population growth. Within the AMAs, new development is subject to the rigorous AWS requirements. In the primarily rural non-AMA areas, however, Arizona has one of the weakest programs in the country.

Adoption of Arizona's AWS approach in other arid regions will likely be politically acceptable only where alternative supplies are available to meet the requirements. However, requiring investments in renewable supplies for new growth is much more likely to be accepted than using such requirements to halt growth. In addition, given the intensely political nature of local land use decisions, placing the authority for requiring adequate water supplies at a level of government higher than that responsible for approving subdivisions may be critical to a successful program. Conservation programs, on the other hand, may be most effective when managed by the local level of government, which both oversees land use decisions and is closest to the water provider and the water users.

Additional Reflections on Arizona's Future Directions and Water Politics

Arizona's water managers have an excellent track record of working together and developing innovative programs to address the state's water management challenges. The collaborative process on the most recent CAGRD plan of operation is only one recent example. Other examples include the recently enacted

Arizona Water Rights Settlement Act and discussions with the other Colorado River basin states to develop shortage-sharing criteria. Major current and future challenges for central Arizona's urban water users include the need to do the following:

- work cooperatively with water users and interested parties throughout the state and the Colorado River basin to secure future supplies for urban growth;
- forge regional partnerships within urban areas to develop coordinated long-range aquifer management strategies that incorporate conjunctive use and both water quantity and water quality needs;
- modify the CAGRD as necessary to facilitate an appropriate balance between direct delivery and groundwater pumping and replenishment and an appropriate balance between reliance on long-term and short-term water supplies;
- improve the understanding of climatic variability and future global climate change and incorporate this knowledge into long-range water management planning;
- modify the state's regulatory framework to facilitate the necessary water management programs and investments (particularly the AWS and conservation programs);
- look beyond the 2025 AMA safe-yield goals and commit to longer term objectives; and
- address environmental quality, ecosystem health, and quality of life concerns as they relate to water management.

The continued rapid growth of Arizona's urban areas requires that we build on past water management successes and further invest in our infrastructure and water management capacity to ensure long-term sustainability.

References

Arizona Department of Water Resources (ADWR). 1994. Arizona Water Resources Assessment: Vol. 1 Inventory and Analysis. Phoenix: Arizona Department of Water Resources.

———. 1997. Santa Cruz Active Management Area: Management Goal and Program Implementation Concept Paper. Phoenix: Arizona Department of Water Resources, July 11.

———. 1998. ADWR Preliminary Determination on the Safe-Yield Status of the Prescott Active Management Area. August 28. Phoenix: Arizona Department of Water Resources.

———. 1999. Third Management Plans for the Phoenix, Pinal, and Tucson Active Management Areas. Phoenix: Arizona Department of Water Resources.

———. 2001. Governor's Water Management Commission Final Report; CD Version 1.0. Phoenix: Arizona Department of Water Resources.

———. 2003. Pinal AMA Virtual Tour. http://www.azwater.gov/WaterManagement_2005/Content/AMAs/PinalAMA/default.htm (accessed January 20, 2006).

———. 2004. Santa Cruz Active Management Area: Assured Water Supply Program Implementation Concepts. Phoenix: Arizona Department of Water Resources, April.

Arnold, Craig Anthony. 2005. *Wet Growth: Should Water Law Control Growth?* Washington, DC: Environmental Law Institute.

Central Arizona Groundwater Replenishment District (CAGRD). 2004. *Plan of Operation.* Phoenix: Central Arizona Groundwater Replenishment District.

Connall, D., Jr. 1982. A History of the Arizona Groundwater Management Act. *Arizona State Law Journal* 2: 313–43.

Coulson, Scott E. 2005. Locally Integrated Management of Land-Use and Water Supply: Can Water Continue To Follow the Plow? Master's Thesis. University of Colorado, Denver.

Groundwater Management Act of 1980. Arizona Revised Statutes, Title 45, Ch. 2, secs. 401, 403, 411, 461, 491, 452, 454, 511, 576, 591.

Holway, Jim, and Katherine Jacobs. 2006. Managing for Sustainability in Arizona, USA: Linking Climate, Water Management and Growth. In *Water Resources Sustainability*, edited by Larry Mays. Forthcoming. New York: McGraw-Hill.

Jacobs, K.L., and J.M. Holway. 2004. Managing for Sustainability in an Arid Climate: Lessons Learned from 20 Years of Groundwater Management in Arizona, USA. *Hydrogeology Journal* 12: 52–65.

Lucero, L., and A.D. Tarlock. 2003. Water Supply and Urban Growth in New Mexico: Same Old, Same Old or a New Era? *Natural Resources Journal* 43: 803–5.

Morrison Institute for Public Policy. 2005. *Superstition Vistas: Water Matters.* Tempe: Arizona State University.

12

Water Supply and Management in Rural Arizona

Katharine L. Jacobs and Linda S. Stitzer

The rural portions of Arizona and the cities and towns outside of the active management areas (AMAs) have water-related challenges that are different from those within the AMAs. There has been significantly less investment in water management outside of AMAs, and water supply options are limited. Furthermore, outside the AMAs, the regulations of the Groundwater Management Act (1980) have minimal impact. The result is that there is substantially less information about water availability, less effort focused on long-term water supply planning, and few options for access to alternative water supplies. The impacts of drought are felt most strongly in these areas, and the implications of continued growth are of great concern. There are essentially two Arizonas: the major metropolitan areas and irrigation districts, with multiple reliable sources of water, and the rest of the state, which has limited water supply alternatives and limited planning information.

The non-AMA portions of the state encompass 87% of the land area and almost 1 million people. The population in these areas is expected to more than double in the next 50 years. High population growth rates, in the context of water supplies that often are susceptible to drought, increase the likelihood that there will be water supply shortages in rural communities. In addition, increased demand for groundwater and drought impacts are likely to affect important springs and surface-water flows that support riparian areas and recreation.

From a water supply perspective, access to imported surface water is the major characteristic that distinguishes the central Arizona AMAs (Phoenix, Pinal, and Tucson) from the rest of the state, including the Prescott and Santa Cruz AMAs. There are two major surface-water supply distribution systems in the state: the Salt River Project (SRP) and the Central Arizona Project (CAP).

The watershed of the SRP system extends significantly beyond the AMAs, but the benefits accrue primarily within the Phoenix AMA. The CAP system has delivery capacity of more than 1.5 million acre-feet, making the Colorado River the major new renewable water supply source for central and southern Arizona. The CAP is interconnected with the SRP system, providing maximum flexibility for conjunctive management. This management option has proven to be extremely beneficial in the context of the recent drought but does not result in enhanced water supplies outside the AMAs.

Many communities and tribes along the Colorado River in western Arizona have Colorado River water contracts and, consequently, their water supply circumstances differ markedly from other parts of the state. However, despite their proximity, some communities along the river do not have legal access to Colorado River water rights.

Water Supplies in Rural Arizona

Groundwater is the primary water source used for domestic supply in rural Arizona. It is generally considered to be a nonrenewable resource because the rate of natural replenishment is so slow. Groundwater is withdrawn from aquifers that vary dramatically in terms of water yield based on local geology (see Chapter 4).

Although effluent use is expanding in the major municipalities, it is relatively rarely used in the rest of the state. Outside the AMAs, effluent is now a significant source of supply only for Flagstaff, Payson, Sierra Vista (where it is recharged to replenish the aquifer), and a few smaller communities, such as Tusayan.

Water supply availability has multiple components. Physical access to water is the limiting factor in many places where there is no surface water and where groundwater may be either limited or difficult and expensive to withdraw. Reliability of the supply is also important because some supplies are subject to seasonal or drought-related shortages. In some cases, physical availability is not a problem, but there are legal impediments to the use of the water, such as objections to a proposed use from a senior water right holder with a court-decreed right to a particular supply. Financial access is the third major challenge. If water supplies are available and water rights issues are resolved, there may still be inadequate financial resources to build the required distribution or storage system. The rural parts of Arizona have a limited tax base, and development of new infrastructure is challenging in those circumstances.

If major new pipelines or canals are constructed in the future to transfer water supplies within the state, financial constraints may require that there be a federal partner in the project. In some cases, partnerships may develop as a component of Native American water settlements. Among the options that have been evaluated is the piping of Colorado River water from Lake Powell south to Flagstaff and then west to Williams and also east to the Navajo and Hopi reservations. Many other water transfer, storage, and exchange options are under consideration, including some that focus on moving groundwater from one location to another. Water transfers generally entail multiple legal, economic, and political issues that may prove difficult to overcome. With some specific exceptions, transfers of groundwater between basins are currently prohibited by statute (Groundwater Transportation Act of 1991).

Assured vs. Adequate Water Supply Rules

The water adequacy program is the only regulatory mechanism addressing water supplies for new housing subdivisions outside of AMAs. A statewide water adequacy program has been in place since 1973 as a consumer protection measure. The water adequacy program, described in Arizona Revised Statutes (1980) and in rules adopted by the Arizona Department of Water Resources (ADWR) in 1995, requires subdivision developers to obtain a determination from the state regarding the availability of water supplies before marketing lots. Subdivisions are defined as six or more lots (with additional lot size considerations). Developers are required to disclose any inadequacy of supply to potential initial lot buyers, but subdivisions can be and frequently are approved in areas where the water supply is inadequate.

In the AMAs, a more restrictive assured water supply (AWS) program is in effect (see Chapter 13). The AWS requirements do not allow new subdivisions if the water supply is inadequate to serve the proposed use for 100 years. The AWS program has proved to be a major incentive for investment in renewable water supplies in the AMAs.

Water Supply and Growth

The connection among water supply problems, drought, and growth is complex. A traditional perspective is that water supply availability is an incentive for growth and that lack of supplies is a significant disincentive. Yet, water is being hauled from standpipes (water supply valves used for filling tanks) and from larger communities as a regular business practice in many parts of rural northern Arizona even in the absence of drought. The willingness to haul water may mean that the theory that inadequate local water supplies will limit growth does not apply.

Many communities, especially in northern Arizona and on the Mogollon Rim, already have hit a threshold relative to their ability to serve new customers. However, the absence of an enforceable water availability requirement for new subdivisions outside of AMAs means that most of these communities continue to grow even though their water supplies do not. There clearly are health and welfare implications, and state and federal agencies already have been involved in bail-out activities, e.g., water hauling, that do not increase the likelihood of a more sustainable long-term solution.

Data and Resources for Planning

A basic inflow–outflow calculation for a basin is key to understanding whether additional growth can be sustained in an area. By evaluating the amount of water that is available to a basin on an average annual basis as surface flows or as recharge to an aquifer and subtracting the amount that leaves the basin as outflow, it is possible to identify a "sustainable yield" that can support human communities without affecting long-term water supply availability in that basin. The concept of sustainable yield typically includes a presumption that riparian vegetation and surface flows that support them will be protected. This concept is discussed further in Chapter 4.

Virtually all watershed groups and communities outside the AMAs are hampered by inadequate hydrologic information to develop a water budget, although some basins, such as the Upper San Pedro, have been extensively modeled. Most counties and jurisdictions also have indicated that they have inadequate information with which to plan for future water needs. The AMAs have a great advantage over areas of the state outside the AMAs regarding the availability, amount, and quality of information. Since 1984, all water pumped from wells with a capacity over 35 gallons per minute in AMAs has been required to be measured and reported to the state by the well owners. This has resulted in high-quality water-use data. There is virtually no annual pumpage information outside of AMAs, with the exception of private water companies regulated by the Arizona Corporation Commission (ACC). Without measured pumpage data, it is difficult to correlate changes in water levels with inflows and outflows to an aquifer.

Though rural areas generally lack sufficient hydrologic and water demand information on which to base water resource management decisions, some general information is typically available, including water-level measurements and water quality data for some wells and basic hydrogeologic information. If there are public or private water providers in an area, pumpage or delivery data and the number of total delivery connections are also usually available. These data can be requested either from the public utility itself or through ACC reports for private water providers. However, long-term consistent data, detailed water demand information, total groundwater in storage, net natural recharge, riparian demand, incidental recharge, water demand from private domestic wells, agricultural and industrial pumpage, water-level trends, depth of the aquifer, and other critical water resource assessment information are often not available. The Community Water System Planning and Reporting Act of 2005, which requires annual reports from water providers outside of

AMAs starting in 2007, will result in significantly more data becoming available regarding water use of municipal providers outside of AMAs.

The U.S. Geological Survey (USGS) produces reports of annual water use for groundwater basins outside the AMAs (Tadayon 2005). The reports include groundwater withdrawals and surface-water use for which there is reported information. Where metered data are not available, irrigation estimates are based on a variety of methods, including old power records, Arizona Agricultural Statistics Service reports, and digitized satellite images or aerial photos.

In 1994, ADWR produced a broad overview of water supply and demand conditions and an analysis of water resource management issues statewide in the Arizona Statewide Water Resources Assessment (ADWR 1994). ADWR has more recently compiled a water atlas for rural Arizona that contains water resource information for each of the 46 groundwater basins, organized into six planning areas. The purpose of the atlas is to provide water resource information to assist water management efforts in rural Arizona, to help identify the needs of growing communities, and to identify data gaps. Information includes, where available, data and location of geographic features, land ownership, precipitation and meteorological stations, springs, perennial and intermittent streams, stream and flood gages, runoff contours, reservoirs, current depth to water, groundwater level changes since 1991, general groundwater flow direction, hydrographs, groundwater in storage, natural recharge, measured and reported well yields, water quality conditions, cultural water demand, and water adequacy and inadequacy determinations. The long-term objective is that the information compiled for the atlas will be updated and improved in a systematic way.

Current Rural Planning Efforts

Regional Watershed Partnerships

The Rural Watershed Initiative was established in 1999 to assist watershed groups outside AMAs with development of information to support water resource planning in their areas. The initiative is focused on local efforts to manage water supplies. The key advantage to this approach is empowering local citizens to find solutions that match the specific problems in their own regions. The main projects funded by the initiative are USGS hydrologic studies in the Coconino Plateau, Upper and Middle Verde, Mogollon Highlands, and Upper San Pedro areas.

A handful of rural partnerships in Arizona are extensively involved with water management or planning. The most active of these is the Upper San Pedro Partnership (USPP), a consortium of 21 land and water management agencies and organizations in the Upper San Pedro basin that was formed in

1998 under a memorandum of understanding. The USPP and its members have agreed to pursue a variety of water management and conservation actions, including codes, incentives, water conservation surcharges, public conservation awareness, irrigated agriculture restrictions, and water demand management tools. Recently, they have also been considering water supply augmentation options.

In addition, the USPP is required, under Section 321 of the National Defense Authorization Act for Fiscal Year 2004, to submit annually to Congress a report on water-use management and conservation measures that have been implemented and are needed to restore and maintain the sustainable yield of the regional aquifer by and after September 30, 2011 (U.S. Statutes at Large 2003). This federal requirement to implement water management actions is unique to the USPP; there are no other similar voluntary partnerships in the country that are directed by the federal government to achieve a water quantity-related water management objective. However, a similar approach has been initiated through federal legislation in the Verde River basin.

Issues for the watershed groups are the following:

- most are entirely volunteer groups, with no paid staff, and thus are severely constrained in their ability to accomplish a cohesive planning effort;
- most have inadequate hydrologic data;
- in some areas, the multiple water management entities involved have little incentive or ability to forge regional cooperative efforts;
- in some cases, the absence of key players makes planning difficult; and
- given the strong private property rights sentiment in rural Arizona, it is not clear that all of the watersheds can find meaningful solutions that are generally acceptable to the residents.

Table 12-1 summarizes water-related issues, sorted by watershed.

Drought Plan Implementation

The impacts of the recent (post-1998) drought on the rural parts of Arizona have been substantial, including effects on ranchers, who have reduced herd size by two-thirds statewide over the past five years; severe wildfires in the mountains; widespread bark beetle infestations and die-off of up to 2 million ponderosa and pinyon pines; forest closures limiting recreation opportunities; and health and safety concerns in many municipal supply systems because of inadequate water supplies. The visibility of this issue resulted in strong interest in developing a state drought plan to limit such impacts in the future, with particular focus on rural areas. Earlier state drought response efforts focused entirely on short-term reactive mechanisms, such as hauling water, which do not reduce risk in the longer term.

The recently completed Arizona Drought Preparedness Plan (Governor's Drought Task Force 2004) focuses on the need for drought planning within

TABLE 12-1. Issues Faced by Watershed Partnerships and Advisory Councils

Watershed partnership or water advisory council	Limited groundwater supplies	Lack of data	Water quality	Unresolved general adjudication	Endangered species protection	Tribal water rights
Upper San Pedro				X	X	
Yavapai County/Verde	X		X	X	X	X
Coconino Plateau	X		X	X	X	X
Gila			X	X	X	X
Mogollon Rim/Highlands	X	X				X
Upper Little Colorado River	X		X		X	
Silver Creek		X	X	X		X
Upper Bill Williams River	X	X				
Northwest Arizona	X	X	X			
Upper Agua Fria River	X	X	X			
Community Watershed Alliance (formerly Middle San Pedro)		X	X		X	
Reddington Natural Resources Conservation District (Lower San Pedro)				X		X
Little Colorado		X	X	X	X	X
Arizona Strip Partnership		X	X			
Show Low Creek				X		X
Eagle Creek		X				X
Northern Arizona Municipal Water Users Association	X		X		X	
Navajo Nation	X	X	X	X	X	X

Source: ADWR 2005.

rural communities, which have fewer water supply options available. The drought plan depends heavily on ongoing monitoring of conditions statewide, with major participation of local area impact assessment groups (see Chapter 5). These groups will be composed of local governments and resource managers and will be triggered into active status depending on the drought level. Assessment of vulnerabilities and development of mitigation strategies are expected to be ongoing processes, with the intent to minimize the impacts of future droughts.

Legal limitations on the ability to transfer groundwater across basin boundaries also pose some unique challenges in the context of drought. The 1991 Groundwater Transportation Act was intended to protect rural areas' water supplies from being exported to the AMAs to meet assured water supply requirements. The act, along with 1993 amendments, prohibits moving groundwater from one basin to another, with certain specified exceptions. Ironically, it is now the rural areas that seek to move groundwater from one basin to another to alleviate severe shortages outside the AMAs. Exceptions to this prohibition have been allowed by ADWR permit, pursuant to annually readopted emergency legislation over the past few years, during severe drought conditions.

Enhancing the reliability of municipal supply systems is a key objective of the drought plan. However, individual wells in shallow and fractured rock aquifers, where productivity may be low, are often affected by drought. High densities of domestic wells exacerbate the drought impacts in some areas, and although the ADWR is monitoring public reports of individual well problems, finding solutions is more difficult than addressing issues for larger water systems. The drought plan currently is in the implementation phase. (See Figure 12-1 for the drought plan's organizational structure.)

Before adoption by the Arizona state legislature of the drought preparedness plan in 2004 and the community water system planning and reporting requirements in 2005, few water companies in rural Arizona had adopted drought plans. However, curtailment plans existed for roughly 30 private water providers regulated by the Arizona Corporation Commission. Some of these plans were put in place in response to emergency conditions, and others were adopted as part of a revised ACC standard procedure that requires these plans as part of the application for a new rate structure. Curtailment plans are not focused specifically on drought, but once they are in place, they provide the water company with authority to restrict water deliveries to their customers to avoid more serious consequences.

The community water system planning and reporting requirements call for all community water systems to adopt a water supply plan that includes a conservation plan and a drought preparedness plan. This requirement is phased in earlier for larger water companies (January 1, 2007), and small water companies and water systems that are developing joint plans have an extra year to comply (January 1, 2008).

Conservation Efforts

Most potable water conservation efforts to date have occurred within AMAs, though there are notable exceptions, such as in the town of Payson, the Upper San Pedro Partnership, and the city of Flagstaff. Statewide conservation efforts have been limited. Governor Janet Napolitano's executive order 2003–12 on March 20, 2003, establishing the Arizona Drought Task Force, contains a requirement to "develop and implement a statewide conservation education strategy that emphasizes educational advertising for good water habit development." The statewide conservation strategy was submitted to the governor at the same time as the Arizona Drought Preparedness Plan in October 2004. Although education and demonstration activities are under way, the strategy itself has not yet been fully implemented.

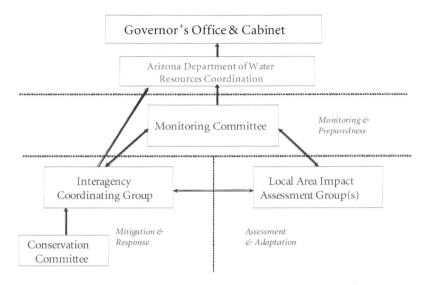

FIGURE 12-1. Arizona Drought Plan Organizational Structure

Several rural communities have developed strong conservation programs in response to serious water supply limitations. Payson's program involves distribution of conservation literature, a rebate program for conservation investments, and conservation-oriented ordinances that (1) restrict turf, (2) require low-water-use landscaping, and (3) provide for waterless urinals in public restrooms, and short-term water restrictions in response to drought. There is also a program for wastewater reuse for recharge and irrigation. Flagstaff uses most of the same methods and has significantly restricted outdoor watering year-round in response to drought (City of Flagstaff n.d.).

Many municipal delivery systems outside the AMAs do not fully meter their pumpage or their deliveries. In such systems, losses due to system leaks and high-water-use customers may go undetected. Conservation potential in such circumstances may be substantial. However, potable water use on a per capita basis in the rural parts of the state is usually relatively low by comparison to the larger urban areas. This is in part because of the differences in temperature and precipitation that result in higher demand for landscape water in the lower desert areas. In addition, some parts of the state lack adequate water-delivery infrastructure. For example, water users on the Navajo reservation, where up to 50% of the rural residents haul their own water, use as little as 10 gallons per person per day (Navajo Nation 2002). Many rural communities resist the idea of conservation regulations because they witness the higher per capita water use rates within the AMAs.

Climate and socioeconomic factors need to be taken into account when assessing water-use efficiency. Demand reduction is an option in some rural areas, but conservation yields are limited in cases where there is already little discretionary water use. Many rural water users are interested in ensuring that scarce supplies are used wisely, but they may not have the information needed to evaluate the efficiency of their own households and businesses. Only half of the rural water company respondents in the 2003 ADWR survey (ADWR 2003) reported having a conservation program, consisting primarily of conservation literature; the majority indicated that they would welcome more assistance with developing their programs.

Basic conservation opportunities in the non-AMA portions of the state include the following:

- system improvements to reduce leaks;
- expansion of the use of pumpage and delivery meters;
- price-related conservation signals, such as rate structures that charge more for higher volumes of water use;
- ordinances limiting high-water-use landscaping and encouraging appropriate landscape irrigation design and scheduling;
- financial or other incentives for replacing high-water-use fixtures with conserving appliances, removing high-water-use landscaping, incorporating water harvesting (collection of rain water), gray water (water from sinks and washing machines), and effluent for landscape applications in new developments; and
- conservation-oriented hookup policies and building code provisions.

Government Roles in Rural Water Management

The state of Arizona has primary responsibility for management of water rights within its boundaries. The Arizona Department of Water Resources is the lead agency for management of the surface water and groundwater of the state. Under the McCarran Amendment, federal water rights are determined in state courts through the state's general stream adjudication process, which determines the water rights of all users to a particular water source. In contrast, water quality standards are generally established by the federal government (see Chapter 9), with delegation of authority in Arizona's case to the Arizona Department of Environmental Quality.

A number of federal agencies have water supply and management authorities in rural Arizona, in part because federal land makes up a large portion of the state. The Bureau of Reclamation administers the Colorado River reservoirs and contractual arrangements for the use of Colorado River water. Management of the Colorado River involves a complex array of management authorities, determined over the years by federal laws and court cases collectively called "The Law of the River" (see Chapter 3). These laws have resulted in dam construction, apportionment of Colorado River water to the basin states and to Mexico, salinity reduction requirements, and other actions that have affected water management in Arizona. The Bureau of Reclamation is also involved with regional planning activities, water conservation programs, and water augmentation feasibility studies. One such study is evaluating the potential to extend the Central Arizona Project to Sierra Vista in the San Pedro watershed.

The U.S. Geological Survey gages streamflows, conducts scientific analyses of hydrologic resources, and produces reports on Arizona water use by sector and source. The U.S. Forest Service develops plans that include watershed management criteria to protect and enhance runoff and holds many surface-water rights for various uses. Because the national forests tend to be in the mountains, the source of in-state surface-water supplies, the Forest Service holds many rights. The Bureau of Land Management is a major land steward in the state and has responsibility for some key water management areas, such as the San Pedro Riparian National Conservation Area. The U.S. Environmental Protection Agency implements national programs that include watershed management, groundwater protection, water quality standards, toxic waste cleanup, and border-region environmental programs.

Native American Nations

The role of Native American nations in water supply and management in rural Arizona is becoming increasingly important. With approximately 28% of Arizona land held in trust by the federal government for the benefit of Native Americans, water demand by Native American communities and the determination of Native American water rights has a significant effect on water supplies and water management in the state. Rural areas affected by Native American water rights issues include the Coconino Plateau, the Little Colorado River basin, the Lower San Pedro basin, the Upper Gila River, the Verde River basin, the Mogollon Rim, and northwestern Arizona south of the Colorado River in the rapidly developing greater Kingman area.

Native American nations are not subject to state water rights and management systems or to state regulations. Tribal claims to water are based on the federal reserved-water rights doctrine (the "Winters Doctrine" discussed in Chapters 3 and 14). The priority date for tribal water rights is the date the Indian reservation was established. Because most reservation land in Arizona was dedicated before non-Indians began using water, tribal water rights are senior to most state-law based water rights (see Chapter 14). However, many tribes have not had their water rights quantified.

Since 1980, there have been multiple efforts to determine the quantity of water reserved for tribal lands in Arizona. Passage of the Arizona Water Settlements Act of 2004 , the largest settlement in terms of dollars and volume of water in the western United States, represents a major milestone in providing certainty about water supplies in much of central and parts of southeastern Arizona. The settlement involves 40 parties in six counties and provides 653,500 acre-feet of water to the Gila River Indian Community and 76,000 acre-feet to the Tohono O'odham Nation (see Chapter 14). The substantial quantity of water allocated in the Arizona Water Settlements Act changes the role of Native American nations relative to water management statewide. A key issue will be how much of the settlement water will be used on reservations and how much will be available for leasing to off-reservation users.

The Arizona Water Settlements Act of 2004 and its side agreements have significant implications for water management and access to water in parts of rural Arizona. These side agreements include limits on access to water, restriction of agricultural irrigation to historic acreage, caps on water use that may affect municipal and industrial use, and limits on the number of new wells in certain areas. In southeastern Arizona, there is a prohibition against the construction of new large reservoirs in the Upper San Pedro basin, and in Cochise County there is a blanket waiver from future lawsuits in exchange for no limits on agriculture. Whereas the settlement creates limitations on non-Indians, it does not adjudicate their rights nor does it restrict groundwater use except in designated impact zones. Passage of the Arizona Water Settlements Act required substantive changes to Arizona state law.

The water rights claims of the Navajo nation, the Hopi tribe, and the San Juan Southern Paiute within the Little Colorado River (LCR) basin are still unresolved. These claims involve both the Little Colorado River and the Colorado River. Claims to the Colorado River are complicated by provisions of the Law of the River that restrict transfers between the upper basin and the lower basin states. Discussions have included proposed pipelines to move water from various sources to areas within the LCR basin, including partnerships with non-Indian entities. Talks also continue with the San Carlos Apaches about uses in the upper Gila River.

Counties, Cities, and Towns

The authority of the ADWR is relatively limited in ensuring adequacy of water supplies for new housing subdivisions outside AMAs, and other jurisdictions have even more limited authority to address the connections among land use, population growth, and water supply. This situation is particularly frustrating to county land use jurisdictions, which have more limited powers than cities and towns to deny approval of or to limit the size and density of new subdivisions. Results from the ADWR survey conducted in 2003 found that of the 10 responding counties (out of a total of 15), 8 cited frustration with the state's water adequacy program, which allows new subdivisions even if the water supply is found to be inadequate by ADWR (ADWR 2004).

Counties are also faced with an inability to control lot splitting. The Adequate Water Supply rules require subdivision developers to obtain a determination from the state regarding the availability of water supplies before marketing lots. Lots may be split into up to six parcels before subdivision rules apply, which creates a major loophole in the assured and adequate water supply programs. Lot splitting leads to multiple other infrastructure and service problems, for example, with road and school capacity and public safety. All the counties that responded to the 2003 ADWR survey reported that lot splitting was a concern.

Unlike counties, rural cities and towns are better positioned to play a role in local water management. Municipally owned water systems are common, and cities have the authority to enact water conservation ordinances, set water rates, and restrict water-intensive uses. They are also more likely to have the financial resources to implement conservation and other water management programs than are privately owned water companies.

Many communities in rural Arizona are served by private water companies that are regulated by the Arizona Corporation Commission. These companies lack the water management tools available to public utilities and are generally required to keep the cost of service low and provide service on demand. However, the ACC is increasingly considering allowing private water companies to increase their rates to allow the companies to use renewable supplies and to implement modest water conservation programs.

Growing Smarter

The state Growing Smarter Plus Act of 2000 (Arizona Revised Statutes 2000) requires that counties with a population of more than 125,000 people include planning for water resources in their comprehensive plans. Mohave and Yuma Counties are the only two counties entirely outside AMAs that fit the population criteria. In addition, Yavapai and Pinal Counties meet the population criteria and have substantial land area outside the AMAs located within county boundaries. The legislation requires identification (based on existing data) of known legally and physically available supplies, future demand for water, and how demand will be served by currently available supplies, or if current supplies are not sufficient, a plan to obtain the necessary supplies.

Given the lack of hydrologic and other data, counties have found preparing the water resources element to be difficult (AZDOC 2002). Beyond requirements for the counties, the Growing Smarter Plus Act of 2000 also requires that 23 communities outside AMAs include a water resource element in their general plans. An overall assessment of these requirements concludes that they have not been consistently applied and have not contributed substantially to water supply management solutions.

Future Management Options for Rural Arizona

There is strong interest in improved water availability data as well as information for building planning scenarios to support water management decisions outside AMAs. Long-term planning is hard to do in the context of significant uncertainty, so developing alternative scenarios of plausible futures is one way to frame the context for decisionmakers. Clearly, the demand side of the equation is critical because communities are growing rapidly and the supplies are relatively finite. Though importation options are frequently referenced, financing and water supply availability are limited. The recent severe drought adds a touch of reality to our view of what the future may be like. Severe, sustained drought is now widely recognized as a component of Arizona's future, especially in the context of increasing temperatures (see Chapter 5).

Given the likely continuation of strong population growth in the southwestern United States, what are the future management options? There is interest in several non-AMA areas in establishing regional water management entities to oversee the planning and management of water resources within watersheds. Many rural entities are concerned that state-level regulatory entities will not develop appropriate solutions to local problems and that local management would be more acceptable and effective because there would be local buy-in and commitment. However, significant legal, financial, and representational issues need to be resolved if effective regional entities with the legal and financial capability to implement water management solutions are to be established. Experience with one such district, the Santa Cruz Valley Water Authority within the Tucson AMA, demonstrated that such issues can undermine the structure of the regional management entity, despite good intentions. The Santa Cruz Valley Water Authority began under provisional authority but was unable to resolve taxation and representation issues and dissolved before being officially established.

Some people believe that enhancing local land use planners' authority to say no to new subdivisions if the water supply is inadequate would make a big difference. However, in some counties, elected officials do not want to be forced to make those hard decisions. Having a more rigorous water adequacy program, enforcing subdivision laws, putting limits on new agriculture, and establishing locally designed but state-enforced well-spacing criteria in areas that are considered sensitive would go a long way toward a more rational water management policy outside the AMAs. Another option is to establish new AMAs or AMA-like areas with alternative management goals (other than safe yield) that still implement many of the existing AMA programs, such as metering, annual reporting, groundwater pumping limits, and mandatory conservation. Support for new AMAs is limited, yet a growing number of citizens are concerned about effects of growth on their quality of life as well as on their water supplies. AMAs do not provide a solution to the problem of increasing demand in the context of limited supplies, but they do provide a planning framework that is focused, goal-oriented, and enforceable.

It is curious, given the widely acknowledged success of the assured water supply program and the Groundwater Management Act, that the rural parts of Arizona have generally concluded that those solutions are inappropriate for their region. The strong antiregulatory perspective of rural Arizonans is only part of the explanation; there is a clear perspective that the "one size fits all" regulatory structure is inappropriate and that local solutions are inherently better than state solutions. It should be acknowledged that the goals of the act within the safe-yield AMAs would not be achievable in the absence of the Central Arizona Project, some degree of flexibility relative to the ability to retire agricultural water use, and significant financial resources and political support. Will resources of this magnitude be available for subsequent AMAs or regional management districts? Time will tell whether local solutions can be effective in the face of serious economic pressures and limited resources. In the meantime, pressures on Arizona's water supplies are increasing daily, and solutions are much easier to come by now than they will be in the future.

References

Arizona Department of Commerce (AZDOC). 2002. Growing Smarter/Plus 2002 Questionnaire. Phoenix: Growing Smarter Plus Oversight Committee.

Arizona Department of Water Resources (ADWR). 1994. Arizona Water Resources Assessment, Vol. 1 Inventory and Analysis. Phoenix: Arizona Department of Water Resources, August.

———. 2003. Rural Water Resources Study (unpublished report). October.

———. 2004. Rural Water Resources 2003 Questionnaire Report. Phoenix: Arizona Department of Water Resources, October.

———. 2005. Upper San Pedro Basin Active Management Area Review Report. Phoenix: Arizona Department of Water Resources, March.

Arizona Revised Statutes. 1980. Title 45, sec. 108 (1980 Groundwater Management Act).

———. 2000. Growing Smarter Plus Act of 2000.

Arizona Water Settlements Act of 2004. P.L. 108–451, 118 Stat. 3478.

City of Flagstaff. n.d. City Code, Section 7–03–001–0015 Water Conservation.

Community Water System Planning and Reporting Act of 2005. Arizona Revised Statutes, sec. 45–342.

Governor's Drought Task Force. 2004. Arizona Drought Preparedness Plan, October 8.

Groundwater Management Act of 1980. Arizona Revised Statutes, Title 45, Ch. 2, secs. 401, 403, 411, 461, 491, 452, 454, 511, 576, 591.

Groundwater Transportation Act of 1991. Arizona Revised Statutes, sec. 45–544.

Navajo Nation. 2002. Navajo Nation Drought Contingency Plan.

Tadayon, Saeid. 2005. Water Withdrawals for Irrigation, Municipal, Mining, Thermoelectric-Power, and Drainage Uses in Arizona Outside of Active Management Areas, 1991–2000. U.S. Geological Survey Scientific Investigations Report 2004–5293, 28 pp. http://pubs.usgs.gov/sir/2004/5293/ (accessed January 13, 2006).

Upper San Pedro Partnership (USPP). 2005. Upper San Pedro Water Management and Conservation Plan. Sierra Vista: Upper San Pedro Partnership, March 9.

U.S. Statutes at Large. 2003. Vol. 117, 1392. National Defense Authorization Act for Fiscal Year 2004, sec. 321.

13

Arizona's Recharge and Recovery Programs

Sharon B. Megdal

Overdraft of Arizona groundwater aquifers led to adoption of the 1980 Groundwater Management Act (Arizona Revised Statutes, Title 45). The desire to replenish underground aquifers, coupled with the availability of surface-water supplies, resulted in the development of an active groundwater recharge and recovery program in Arizona. This program, which began in 1986 when the Arizona legislature amended the Groundwater Management Act to authorize recharge and recovery, has emerged as an important water management tool for the state. This program allows for the replenishment of groundwater with surface water or effluent. Since its adoption, Arizona has refined this multifaceted legislation several times. The program provides a flexible, cost-effective approach to renewable water supply usage.

The 1995 adoption of the Assured and Adequate Water Supply Rules, as well as the desire by Arizona to use fully its Colorado River entitlement, highlighted the role of water storage in furthering near- and long-term water supply and management objectives. In the mid-1990s, two innovative government agencies, the Central Arizona Groundwater Replenishment District and the Arizona Water Banking Authority, became operational. They rely on Arizona's water storage program to achieve important state and regional water management and supply reliability goals.

This chapter explains the fundamentals of Arizona's storage and recovery program and describes how it is central to furthering important water management policies.

The Regulatory Framework for Water Storage and Recovery

The Arizona Department of Water Resources (ADWR) assumes primary responsibility for implementing and enforcing the laws governing water storage and recovery through a system of permits and accounts. The system is designed to allow for groundwater augmentation through recharge while protecting other water users and ensuring sufficient monitoring. Three types of permits are used. The facility at which the storage occurs must be permitted, and then each entity or individual storing water at the facility must hold a storage permit. Finally, to recover stored water, a permit must be issued before using a well to recover the water. Credits are accrued depending on the type of storage facility and the timing of recovery. Credits are recorded in accounts maintained by ADWR under the name of the storing entity.

Other regulatory considerations may come into play when permits are issued or credits are used. For example, the Arizona Department of Environmental Quality is involved in issuing permits for facilities involving recharge of effluent and reviews facility permits involving Central Arizona Project (CAP) water. How the recovered water affects compliance with ADWR active management area conservation requirements may depend on the location of the recovery well. The specific criteria for permitting and recovery are established by statute and other regulations.

Types of Storage Facilities and Permits

Storage occurs either at underground storage facilities (USFs) or groundwater savings facilities (GSFs). USFs typically are constructed basins, such as those pictured in Figures 13-1 and 13-2. Figure 13-1 shows the Granite Reef Underground Storage Project, whose six basins cover 210 acres. Built by the Salt River Project in Maricopa County, which is home to more than half of the state's population, it is permitted to store up to 200,000 acre-feet of water annually. Operation of this facility began in 1994. Figure 13-2 shows the Lower Santa Cruz Replenishment Project in Marana, which is near Tucson. Operated since 2000 as a state demonstration recharge project, this 33-acre facility has been efficient at recharging water. Its annual permitted capacity is 51,000 acre-feet. Central Arizona Project water is delivered to both of those facilities and is allowed to infiltrate the groundwater aquifer.

Both facilities were granted full-scale permits at the time of initial permitting. Full-scale permits require submission of a significant amount of hydrologic information, including information about expected infiltration rates, possible perching (mounding of water above a confining layer in the aquifer), and rises in the water table affecting other wells. Sometimes facilities are granted limited or pilot permits so that sufficient information can be gathered to justify a full-scale permit. Once a facility is operational, monitoring of water quality and groundwater levels is required on an ongoing basis.

Storage at USFs is commonly called direct recharge because the water is directly delivered to the groundwater aquifer through infiltration or injection. Stream beds may be permitted as USFs. When recharge is accomplished without any construction in the stream, it is considered "managed" recharge. The

FIGURE 13-1. Granite Reef Underground Storage Project in Maricopa County
Source: Salt River Project.

Agua Fria Recharge Project in Maricopa County, for example, combines stream-bed recharge with basin recharge. Well injection is also an acceptable method of underground storage, but this option has been used sparingly to date in Arizona. USFs have also been built to store effluent or surface water other than CAP water.

Groundwater savings facilities (GSFs) are used for indirect recharge. At a GSF, a water source other than groundwater is used, thereby "saving" the groundwater for future use. The groundwater aquifer is recharged indirectly by not removing water from the aquifer. GSF recharge is sometimes called in-lieu recharge because surface water or effluent is used in lieu of groundwater. The typical GSF in Arizona is operated by an agricultural entity that has demonstrated to the Department of Water Resources that it has the ability to use groundwater but instead will use surface water. The actual facility consists of farm fields and surface-water or effluent delivery systems.

FIGURE 13-2. Lower Santa Cruz Replenishment Project in Pima County
Source: Central Arizona Project.

GSF permit requirements differ from USFs. With a USF, the facility permitting process is distinct from the storage permitting process, and the holders of
the different types of permits may or may not be the same. For USFs, often the
holder of the facility permit—the entity that actually operates the project—has
a permit to store water there as well. However, several entities may have permits
to store water at a given facility. Each facility has a maximum amount of water
that can be stored there for accrual of credits, and it is up to the operator to
ensure that the permitted maximum is not exceeded in a given year.

For GSFs, on the other hand, the agricultural entity that holds the facility permit is not expected to be the storing entity. The benefit the agricultural entity receives for participating in this voluntary arrangement is access to water that is less expensive than the water it would otherwise be using. The storer, or the entity that is accruing credits for the stored water, pays some portion of the per acre-foot cost, thereby buying down the cost of the water for the farmer. Because there is usually no operational cost assessed on the storer per acre-foot for GSFs because the farming entities have already invested in the infrastructure to deliver the surface water to their fields, the economics work for the storer and the farmer. It is a mutually beneficial partnership. The cost per credit accrued is less for the storing entity than if it had stored at a USF, and the cost for the farmer of the water is reduced by the amount of the buy-down offered by the storer. In contrast, at USFs, the storer does not have a party with which to share the cost of the water stored. The storer pays the full cost of the water plus an assessment covering the operational cost of storing the water at the facility.

In most cases, a permit to store water is essentially a permit to accrue credits for that storage. The accrual of credits for the stored water is also under the purview of ADWR, as accounts are maintained by storage permit. Credits may be held in accounts indefinitely and, with some conditions, may be assigned or sold.

Recovering Water

To recover the stored water, a recovery well permit must be issued by ADWR. Recovery of water stored in an active management area (AMA) must occur within that AMA. Wells used for recovery usually are also municipal production wells. The wells do not need to be located within the area of hydrologic impact of the storage facility, but it can be easier to have a well qualify as a recovery well if it is in the area of hydrologic impact. If outside the area of hydrologic impact, well recovery permits are required to look at the rate at which the groundwater level is declining in the vicinity of the well. If the rate of decline exceeds the rate established in the respective AMA management plan, ADWR will not allow the well to be used as a recovery well. Several water providers in the Tucson AMA, for example, have experienced the specified rate of decline, especially in recent years because of the drought. ADWR is in the process of modifying its regulations governing the permitting of recovery wells.

A stored credit provides the holder of the credit the ability to recover an acre-foot of water. Exactly when the recovery occurs and where it occurs, however, may affect the amount of recovery. For example, in most cases, if water is recovered in the same calendar year in which it was stored or if effluent is stored at a constructed facility, full recovery is allowed and there is no "cut" to the aquifer. If the recovery does not occur until some future year, the storer is required to leave 5% of the water stored underground as a benefit or "cut" to the aquifer.

These requirements make sense because depletion of groundwater aquifers is the reason for the establishment of the Groundwater Management Act, and there is a desire to have these storage facilities do more than serve as holding basins and actually provide a benefit to the aquifers even after recovery of the stored water.

Although the recovered water is pumped from the ground, legally it is not considered groundwater at the time of recovery. Instead, it is considered to be the type of water that was stored. The legal characteristic of the water is important when showing compliance with the Assured and Adequate Water Supply Rules and can be of significance for showing compliance with active management area conservation requirements.

Although the ability to recover outside the area of hydrologic impact provides flexibility and is consistent with basinwide water management goals, location of recovery relative to storage has been a source of concern to many. Recharge facilities are not necessarily located near portions of the aquifer that have experienced the most significant decline in groundwater levels. And, as discussed below, the assured water supply system allows for replenishment of groundwater pumping anywhere in the AMA. This issue is well recognized but difficult to resolve.

This brief coverage of the storage and recovery regulatory system provides a backdrop to the next section, which looks at Arizona's use of groundwater recharge as a means of meeting water policy objectives.

Storage and Recovery in Practice

To date, more than 4 million acre-feet of water have been recharged in Arizona, and the amount of water in storage is growing. This section discusses the innovative financial and institutional mechanisms that contributed to this vast amount of recharge activity.

State Demonstration Recharge Projects and Incentive Recharge

The State Demonstration Recharge Program was designed to provide a source of revenues to support construction and use of demonstration USFs. It was funded through a property tax assessed by the Central Arizona Water Conservation District, the operators of the Central Arizona Project (CAP). The CAP is governed by a 15-person elected board, which has the authority to levy property taxes in its three-county service area. The tax to fund the demonstration project was assessed for 1991–1995 in Pima and Maricopa Counties at the rate of 4 cents per $100 secondary assessed valuation. Collected funds were to be used by the CAP board in the county of origin. Funds were targeted primarily toward construction of demonstration USFs as well as to store water at those facilities and at the Granite Reef Underground Storage Project. Figure 13-3

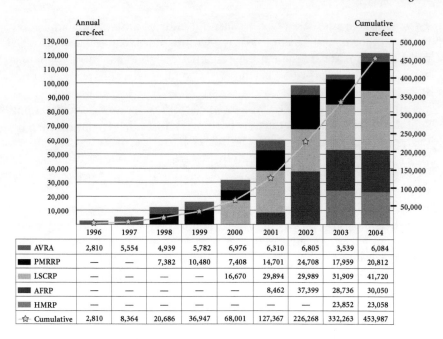

FIGURE 13-3. Annual and Cumulative Storage at Demonstration Recharge Facilities, 1996–2004
Source: Central Arizona Project.

shows annual and cumulative storage for the period 1996–2004 at the facilities constructed using demonstration recharge tax funds.

The beginning year of operation of the USFs reflects the time involved in planning, gaining approval, and then building large-scale USFs. Conceptual planning for the Lower Santa Cruz Replenishment Project, for example, was begun by the Pima County Flood Control District in 1994; the project, which was constructed by CAP in conjunction with a flood control levy, became operational in 2000. The Pima Mine Road Recharge Project, also located in the Tucson metropolitan area, operated first as a pilot facility. The basins for full-scale operation were constructed in two phases. As shown in Figure 13-3, the temporary demonstration recharge project tax was instrumental in jump-starting underground storage in the two most populous counties in Arizona (Maricopa and Pima Counties), where groundwater mining or overdraft was of greatest concern.

In addition to facilitating storage project construction through investment of the special tax revenues, in the latter half of the 1990s, CAP adopted a special incentive pricing program for excess CAP water. Excess CAP water is available because demand by subcontractors has not yet grown to meet the full CAP allocation. This pricing program is designed so that the price charged for the water is high enough to cover CAP's operation and maintenance expenses but low enough to encourage water providers to invest in accumulating long-term storage credits. For many water providers, the use of credits to offset future groundwater pumping is an important component to satisfying the requirements of the Assured and Adequate Water Supply Rules. In addition, the Arizona Water Banking Authority (AWBA) has benefited from the incentive pricing program. The AWBA and the Central Arizona Groundwater Replenishment District have used the storage capacity at several of the demonstration recharge facilities.

Storage and Recovery as a Surface-Water Delivery Mechanism

Commonly, municipal use of Colorado River or surface water involves treating the water at a centralized treatment facility before delivery of the water into the potable water system. Some communities in Arizona use this approach. However, others have found that using storage and recovery of CAP water is an attractive alternative to operating a treatment plant at a centralized point of delivery. These communities rely on the portion of Arizona's recharge program known as annual storage and recovery. Under this program, if water is recovered in the same year that it is stored, the ADWR treats that usage as if it were direct use of the renewable supply, and no cut to the aquifer is required. If a water provider stores more water than it recovers in a given year, long-term credits are accrued and the cut to the aquifer is assessed before the posting of credits to the storer's long-term storage account. The water provider can then use the credits to offset groundwater pumping so that future water use is considered CAP water rather than groundwater, which is important for showing compliance with the Assured and Adequate Water Supply Rules.

Tucson Water, the utility serving approximately 80% of the municipal water demand in metropolitan Tucson, relies on both the use of the annual storage and recovery program and the accrual and later use of long-term storage credits as the indirect means of using surface water. This departure from its plans for direct delivery of CAP water resulted from difficulties the water utility had in the early 1990s with direct delivery after treatment of CAP water. Concerns regarding this problem led to a citizen-initiated limitation on the manner in which Tucson Water could use its CAP allocation. (See Pulwarty et al. 2005 for more detail.) Tucson Water currently uses large-scale storage and recovery for integrating CAP water into what had been a totally groundwater-based potable water system. Their program involves simultaneously recharging the aquifer with CAP water and recovering that water in the area of hydrologic impact.

Tucson's Central Avra Valley Storage and Recovery Project, which includes a series of basins covering 80 acres, is an important component of its Clearwater Renewable Resource Facility. On-site recovery wells deliver water into a large 11-mile water main that takes the water from the northwest part of the Tucson basin to Tucson Water's potable delivery system. The process used to deliver a blend of groundwater and CAP water is depicted in the schematic shown in Figure 13-4. Because the recovery wells are deep, the recovered water

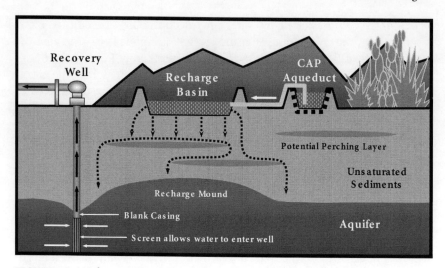

FIGURE 13-4. Schematic Depicting Tucson Water's Annual Storage and Recovery Program
Source: Tucson Water.

in the early years resembles groundwater, but it will assume more of the characteristics of CAP water over time.

This approach to delivering CAP water, although not Tucson Water's first choice, has some advantages to it. It is an example of the old adage that "every cloud has a silver lining." Tucson Water does not depend on a single large-scale treatment facility for meeting its potable water needs, as it had originally intended, but instead depends on this program and a series of groundwater wells to meet system demands. This process makes the system less vulnerable to planned or unplanned canal outages, which is an advantage since this large community is located near the terminus of the canal where there are no surface-water reservoirs. It also makes the system less vulnerable to problems at a large treatment plant. The end result may be a more reliable water-delivery system.

This indirect approach to using a water supply is also available to water providers wishing to integrate effluent water into their potable water portfolio. Long-range plans for many utilities include increased reliance on wastewater through storage and recovery. The water quality implications, however, are quite different, and water providers and customers alike are working on developing an understanding of the cost and other implications of using effluent to meet potable water needs.

The Central Arizona Groundwater Replenishment District

The Assured and Adequate Water Supply Rules limit the extent to which growing water demands in active management areas may rely on mined groundwater. For the three AMAs in central Arizona, this limit necessitates increased reliance on Colorado River water delivered through the Central Arizona Project. Completed in 1993, the CAP canal was built to deliver 1.5 million acre-feet of water annually to central Arizona. The 336-mile system cost approximately $4 billion to build.

Water providers throughout the three-county service area—Maricopa, Pinal, and Pima Counties—have signed subcontracts for CAP water. However, not all providers are located near the backbone CAP canal. Additionally, not all providers who are required to use renewable water supplies under the assured water supply (AWS) provisions have CAP allocations. Lack of proximity to the canal generally means that expensive infrastructure must be constructed to deliver CAP water directly to a municipal water supplier's service area. Without a CAP subcontract, a municipal water provider does not have legal, long-term access to this renewable water supply.

Although the 1980 Groundwater Management Act mandated adoption of an AWS program, it was not until the early 1990s that ADWR began in earnest a rulemaking process. For those without CAP subcontracts or without physical access to water under subcontract, it was essential that there be a mechanism to enable compliance with the Assured and Adequate Water Supply Rules' requirement that municipal growth use renewable water supplies. Without such a mechanism, there could be no growth outside service areas with the demonstrated means of using CAP water or other non-groundwater supplies. The requirement that the state adopt Assured and Adequate Water Supply Rules, coupled with the need for a means of complying with the rules, resulted in the 1993 legislative establishment of the Central Arizona Groundwater Replenishment District (CAGRD) as a subsidiary of the Central Arizona Project.

The CAGRD represents an innovative way of facilitating compliance with the Assured and Adequate Water Supply Rules. Like the rules themselves, the CAGRD has many complexities associated with it. However, the CAGRD concept itself is simple. If a water provider or housing development is a member of the CAGRD and certain conditions are met, groundwater can be used to meet the needs of municipal growth. The CAGRD in turn has the responsibility to replenish (replace) what is calculated annually by ADWR to be the member's "excess groundwater use" (the use in excess of allowable amounts under the rules). The CAGRD must find water and perform the replenishment within three years of the excess groundwater use. The CAGRD currently is the only organization that has the ability to perform this after-the-fact replenishment function for a water provider or housing development to show compliance with the renewable water supply use requirement of the Assured and Adequate Water Supply Rules.

The replenishment may occur at any location within the AMA in which the groundwater is pumped. For most members, the replenishment obligation must be met in perpetuity. The CAGRD assesses charges for its services, with the type of charge depending on whether the member is a housing development (member land) or a water company (member service area).

Although envisioned as a mechanism for those without CAP subcontracts, membership in the CAGRD has exceeded all expectations. The 2004 plan of operation, which projects membership through the year 2015 only, estimates the 2035 annual replenishment obligation to exceed 225,000 acre-feet (CAGRD 2004). When that number is compared to the 2003 replenishment obligation of 19,500 acre-feet, the growth in the obligation is remarkable. With virtually no access to firm supplies of water, the CAGRD has a daunting task ahead of it. Its approach to meeting its replenishment obligations going forward is outlined in the 2004 plan of operation.

As reported in the plan of operation, most of the CAGRD's obligation has been met through recharge at underground storage facilities (9,195 acre-feet), recharge at groundwater savings facilities (2,724 acre-feet), and through the purchase and extinguishment of recharge credits (5,787 acre-feet). Storage credits can be sold or assigned. The CAGRD can perform its replenishment through the acquisition and extinguishment of credits that have been accrued. *Extinguishment* means that the credits are no longer available to be used to offset future pumping.

CAGRD's policy states that replenishment "will be accomplished at reasonably priced facilities in consideration of water resource management goals, with preference for use of state demonstration projects when appropriate." This statement has been interpreted to mean that the CAGRD will strive to perform its replenishment in a hydrologically sound manner, although much replenishment occurs at quite a distance and down gradient of the earlier pumping (CAGRD 2004). To date, surplus CAP water has been used for replenishment, although the CAGRD identifies in its plan of operation many other sources for meeting future replenishment obligations. Because it does not currently have a firm, long-term source of supply, finding cost-effective methods of securing water supplies is of utmost importance to the CAGRD and its members. In 2002, the CAGRD was authorized to establish a replenishment reserve that allows CAGRD to store water before the time when CAP water is expected to be fully used by those with subcontracts. This action will help the CAGRD manage the costs of meeting future replenishment obligations.

The CAGRD's replenishment obligation has grown from under 500 acre-feet in 2000 to almost 20,000 acre-feet in 2004 and is expected to grow to more than 225,000 acre-feet by 2035. Unless membership is restricted at some time in the future—an option that would require the legislature to change the statutes—or members themselves assume greater responsibility for finding alternatives to using groundwater, the replenishment obligation will continue to grow. This requirement means that use of recharge facilities by the CAGRD will be expected to grow as well. The use of the CAGRD to provide water for compliance with Assured and Adequate Water Supply Rules means that Arizona's recharge program is essential to central Arizona's ability to grow.

The Arizona Water Banking Authority

Like the CAGRD, the Arizona Water Banking Authority (AWBA) is a legislatively created government entity that uses Arizona's storage and recovery program to meet important water policy and management objectives. And like the CAGRD, it was created as a result of a need, in this case, the need to make full use of Arizona's share of the Colorado River. Water allocated to Arizona but not used by Arizona flows to California, where it is available for its use at no charge. Southern California's use of Colorado River water already exceeded its 4.4 million acre-foot allocation by several hundred thousand acre-feet, and Nevada was approaching full use of its 300,000 acre-foot allocation. If not used, Arizona water officials, users, and others worried that Arizona's allocation of Colorado River water delivered through the CAP could be in jeopardy. This concern galvanized the water community and led to the creation of the AWBA in 1996.

Lower than expected usage of CAP water became evident in the early 1990s. The CAP was predicated on substantial early use of CAP water by agriculture, with increasing conversion of agricultural water use to municipal water use as central Arizona's population grew. As CAP construction neared completion and repayment to the federal government was to begin, economic considerations led most agricultural entities to conclude that use of CAP water, according to the terms of their subcontracts, was too costly. Absent some adjustment to the pricing formula, CAP water costs would substantially exceed the cost of using groundwater. At the same time, repayment of federal loans, which enabled the construction of infrastructure from the backbone CAP canal to the irrigation districts, was to begin. Although several large irrigation districts signed "take or pay" contracts for a percentage of the CAP supply not used by subcontractors for municipal, industrial, and Indian water, they were unable to pay the water costs associated with their non-Indian agricultural subcontracts. It was, in fact, partly in response to the deficiency in usage by agriculture relative to expectations that the groundwater savings recharge program was developed. According to the complex formula for CAP repayment, which has since been changed, the federal repayment interest rate varied inversely with the proportion of CAP water used by agriculture.

In addition, the junior status of the Central Arizona Project and of certain other uses of Colorado River water was also of concern. In times of shortage, due to Arizona's junior priority status, the entire 1.5 million acre-foot allocation that is delivered to central Arizona through the CAP canal would be among the first uses to be cut (other post-1968 on-river users have the same low priority). There was also recognition that CAP water would likely be a component of future Native American water rights settlements and that storage of water could assist in meeting water management objectives. The AWBA was therefore created to use Arizona's share of Colorado River water and to meet four primary objectives:

- store CAP water to lessen the impact of drought or canal outages on municipal and industrial subcontractors, also called firming;
- support the management goals of the active management areas;
- support settlement of Native American water claims; and
- provide for interstate banking of Colorado River water to assist Nevada and California, while simultaneously protecting Arizona's entitlement (Colby et al. 2004).

The AWBA, authorized for a 20-year period, is governed by a five-person board, appointed by the governor. It is chaired by the director of the Arizona Department of Water Resources, and the president of the CAP Board (or his or her designee) serves on the board. A representative from the municipal sector, one from Colorado River cities, and a person generally knowledgeable about water fill out the board.

The AWBA is funded by three sources of revenues. The first source is related to the temporary revenue source for the state demonstration projects for construction of underground storage facilities. Expiration of that temporary tax was to occur at the end of 1995, at the very time the proposal for the AWBA was being formulated. At the same time, there was uncertainty regarding Arizona's repayment obligation for the federal investment in the CAP. The CAP had in fact filed suit against the federal government over disputes regarding this amount. Because enacting new taxes has become difficult in Arizona, it was agreed that the four-cent "temporary" tax would be extended in Pima and Maricopa Counties and instituted for the third county in CAP's service area: Pinal County. As before, the tax would be levied by the CAP Board but, if not needed to meet repayment obligations, the revenues would be made available to the AWBA to meet its firming goals. These revenues would be used to benefit the county of origin.

The second revenue source was a substantial portion of the groundwater withdrawal fees paid by those entities pumping groundwater in the three central Arizona active management areas—the Phoenix, Pinal, and Tucson AMAs. The funds would be used for the benefit of the AMA of origin. The final authorized revenue source was general revenues. These funds could be used in several ways, including meeting the firming needs of municipal users along the Colorado River whose allocations of Colorado River water were of priority like that of the CAP. Although general fund revenues were appropriated by the Arizona legislature in the early years of the AWBA, budget constraints have caused the legislature to zero out this appropriation. Although some additional types of banking activities have been authorized for the AWBA, its primary functions relate to the four purposes delineated above.

Like the CAGRD, there are many complexities associated with the AWBA's operations. The AWBA relies on multiple sources of funding, with some constraints on how certain funds are used. The AWBA stores water on behalf of cities along the Colorado River and in the central part of Arizona to ensure that their future water deliveries are secure in the context of shortages on the Colorado River. The expectation is that at some future time, the Colorado River cities will take water off the Colorado River that otherwise would have flowed into central Arizona. The central Arizona users will at that time recover and use water that was stored underground. This is also roughly how the AWBA will accomplish interstate banking, particularly on behalf of Nevada. Targets for how much water should be stored for firming purposes have been established, but recent drought conditions have raised concerns about whether the targets, which are based on river operation models based on the hydrology of the past 100 years, are sufficient. In addition, the revenues available over the 20-year life of the AWBA may not be sufficient to fund the targeted storage, presuming sufficient excess CAP water is available.

AWBA storage activities have been significant. The AWBA has stored more than 2.2 million acre-feet of water through 2004 (AWBA 2005). The AWBA has stored water at both groundwater savings facilities (GSFs) and at underground storage facilities (USFs), with more than 60% of historical storage occurring at GSFs. This distribution reflects the economics of storage, in that a given amount of money buys more storage at GSFs than at USFs because of the lower cost per acre-foot of storage at GSFs, as well as the availability of storage capacity. The AWBA was not meant to compete with others for use of storage facilities; it is not authorized to own and operate storage facilities. The AWBA generally uses capacity at storage facilities that is made available to it after determining the need for capacity of other storers. The distribution of credits by type of facility, which varies considerably across the three geographic regions in which the AWBA has stored water, reflects variation in available storage capacity.

A large proportion of the AWBA storage to date is for firming purposes. The AWBA is the major storing entity, but the CAP is responsible for recovery during times of shortage or outage of the CAP canal. Even though the vast majority of storage to date has been for intrastate purposes, the AWBA has committed to store—and recover—water on behalf of Nevada (Gelt 2004). Although a crucial element of Arizona's water management strategy, limited effort has gone into planning for recovery of water stored by the AWBA. A program of recovery, including estimation of its cost, has yet to be established.

Storage and Recovery outside Central Arizona

Most of this discussion has focused on storage and recovery in the three-county CAP service area, but water storage also occurs elsewhere in Arizona. In the Upper San Pedro watershed, where there are considerable concerns about use of groundwater, the director of ADWR concluded that continuation of local efforts to recharge water has important benefits to reducing groundwater overdraft and recommended continuation of recharge projects throughout the basin (ADWR 2005). The city of Sierra Vista currently operates an effluent recharge facility that is permitted to store a little more than 4,000 acre-feet of effluent annually. A program of storage and recovery of effluent is likewise important to the Prescott active management area, as they work to achieve their water management goal of safe yield. A large, full-scale facility to store CAP water has been constructed by a private company west of the Phoenix AMA. Vidler Water Company operates a recharge project in the Harquahala Valley in La Paz County, which is west of Maricopa County and not in an active management area. Permitted to store 100,000 acre-feet of water annually, the project covers 464 acres and consists of 35 basins. In recent years, Vidler Water Company has purchased roughly 25,000–30,000 acre-feet of excess CAP water annually to store at the facility (CAP 2002–2004). These credits can be used for future recovery of the CAP water, which could be transported into central Arizona through the CAP canal.

As other parts of Arizona develop water management strategies, additional storage and recovery projects are likely.

Summary

Arizona has developed several innovative programs that are designed to facilitate optimal use of surface-water supplies. Use of Arizona's storage and recovery programs has been both reactive and opportunistic. Infrastructure, treatment, and cost considerations associated with use of Central Arizona Project water have resulted in reliance on water storage and recovery as a water treatment, blending, and delivery mechanism. The CAGRD was formed to avoid difficulties in gaining approval for the Assured Water Supply Rules by providing a mechanism to enable compliance with the renewable water supply requirement applicable to new housing developments in AMAs. Groundwater savings facilities, coupled with an innovative approach to water pricing, have enabled affordable use of CAP water by agriculture. The AWBA was established to put Arizona's entitlement of CAP water to full use and to prepare for anticipated shortage conditions on the Colorado River. Programs use funding sources deemed acceptable in a state known for fiscal conservatism. A temporary tax used to jump-start underground storage provided funding for the AWBA, and already authorized groundwater withdrawal fees were redirected to the AWBA. There is considerable connectivity of functions and expertise among the AWBA, CAP, and CAGRD.

There are outstanding issues, however, associated with these innovative approaches to meeting Arizona's policy goals. In particular, CAGRD membership has grown more rapidly than anticipated, proving that Arizona did indeed create a useful mechanism. To meet its replenishment obligation, the CAGRD has identified the same water supplies that other central Arizona water providers have eyed to meet future demands. Future conflicts may be unavoidable. The AWBA may not have enough excess Colorado River water or funding available to it to meet all of its firming targets. Plans for recovery of water stored by the AWBA are not yet in place. Despite these and other related challenges, Arizona's significant reliance on its underground storage and recovery program can be expected to contribute to meeting state and regional water management and policy objectives for the foreseeable future.

References

Arizona Department of Water Resources (ADWR). 2005. Upper San Pedro Basin Active Management Area Review Report.

Arizona Water Banking Authority (AWBA). 2005. Annual Report for 2004. http://www.awba.state.az.us/pubs/final2004report.doc (accessed November 22, 2005).

Assured and Adequate Water Supply Rules. 1995. Arizona Administrative Code, Rule 12–15–701 et seq.

Central Arizona Groundwater Replenishment District (CAGRD). 2004. Plan of Operation. http://www.cagrd.com/pdfs/submitted_plan.pdf (accessed October 17, 2005).

Central Arizona Project (CAP). 2002–2004. Water Deliveries. http://www.cap-az.com/operations/index.cfm?action=deliveries&subSection=15 (accessed October 17, 2005).

Colby, B.G., S.B. Megdal, D.A. de Kok, K.L. Jacobs, G. Woodard, M.A. Worden, and R.P. Maguire. 2004. Arizona's Water Future: Challenges and Opportunities. Background Report of the Eighty-Fifth Arizona Town Hall. Tucson, AZ: University of Arizona.

Gelt, Joe. 2004. Arizona, Nevada Are Partners in Major Water Banking Deal. *Arizona Water Resource* November–December, 13(3). http://cals.arizona.edu/azwater/awr/novdec04/feature1.html (accessed November 8, 2005).

Groundwater Management Act of 1980. Arizona Revised Statutes, Title 45, Ch. 2, secs. 401, 403, 411, 461, 491, 452, 454, 511, 576, 591.

Pulwarty, R.S, K.L. Jacobs, and R.M. Dole. 2005. The Hardest Working River: Drought and Critical Water Problems in the Colorado River Basin. In *Drought and Water Crises: Science, Technology, and Management Issues,* edited by Don Wilhite. Boca Raton, FL: Taylor & Francis.

14

Tribal Water Claims and Settlements within Regional Water Management

Dana R. Smith and Bonnie G. Colby

The significance of tribal or aboriginal water rights to native tribes and other regional water users cannot be underestimated. All interest groups in regions where tribal water claims exist have a stake in addressing these issues because water claim settlements can play a crucial role in shaping the future of both tribal and non-Indian communities. In the state of Arizona, Indian tribes control large amounts of land and have vast, and often unquantified, entitlements to water resources. Twenty-six Native American reservations account for about 28% of the state's land base (Figure 14-1). According to some people, the water entitlements of Arizona tribes, including those that remain to be quantified, surpass the total surface-water supplies in the state. Arizona Indian tribes also control several senior rights to surface water along the lower Colorado River.

The pressure to resolve tribal water claims in Arizona has resulted from numerous factors, including Arizona's rapid urban population growth, the full appropriation of dependable surface-water supplies, declining groundwater levels, and environmental opposition to new water development projects. Additionally, there is increasing pressure to provide water for environmental restoration and to develop water-based recreation to boost local economies. However, the uncertainty regarding the extent and scope of Native American water rights in Arizona interferes with state and regional water management planning.

Tribal water rights are also relevant in many other areas of the United States and in other countries throughout the world. For example, in New Mexico, the water rights of the Pueblo Indians are protected by the United States' guarantee in the Treaty of Guadalupe Hidalgo that it would recognize and preserve the rights the Pueblo Indians enjoyed under Spanish and Mexican rule (Colby et

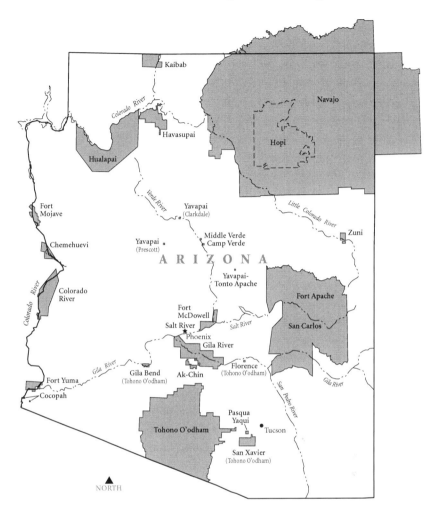

FIGURE 14-1. Arizona Tribal Water Map

al. 2005). Native Hawaiians' traditional and customary water uses are recognized in Hawaii's water code (Hawaii State Water Code 1987). In Australia, aboriginal water rights are protected under the Native Title Act (1993), and in New Zealand, the water rights of the Maori people are based on the doctrine of aboriginal title and the Treaty of Waitangi (1840). In Canada, the water rights of first nations are similarly addressed by the doctrine of aboriginal title or treaty rights (University of Calgary 2006).

For many years, resolving tribal water claims in the United States meant that tribes and other water users were drawn into long and costly court battles. In Arizona, tribal water rights are often discussed in the context of general stream adjudications, in which the water rights of every user in a particular water source are quantified in a single court proceeding. These adjudications often take decades to complete and involve thousands of water users. In fact, no water rights have been completely adjudicated to date in Arizona's two major adjudications (on the Gila and Little Colorado Rivers). Apart from litigation, parties in Arizona have successfully negotiated eight congressionally approved tribal water rights settlements, more than any other state in the United States (Table 14-1). In this chapter, we will discuss the context for Native American water rights and then profile some recent Arizona tribal water rights settlements and tribal water leases.

The Context for Tribal Water Settlements

The settlement of tribal water rights claims in Arizona is important because under U.S. law, Indian tribes have some of the highest priority, and thus most reliable, water rights available. In the western United States, water rights are administered under the prior appropriation system, which awards the most senior and reliable water rights to those who were the first to put the water to use. The priority date of the water right reflects its seniority. In times of drought, the water rights of senior appropriators will be fulfilled first, and those with junior rights may receive no water at all. Thus, under the prior appropriation system, senior water rights are very valuable.

In 1908, the U.S. Supreme Court decided in *Winters v. United States* (1908) that tribes that were moved to reservations were entitled to enough water to make those reservations habitable. The Supreme Court found that when Native American reservations were established, sufficient water to fulfill the purposes of the reservation was implicitly reserved for tribal use. These federally reserved water rights are integrated into the state-law based prior appropriation system by fixing the priority date for tribal water rights as the date the reservation was established. Because the priority date for Indian reserved water rights is the date the reservation was created, and most reservations were established before non-Indian settlers began using water, Indians tend to have superior water rights to most users under the prior appropriation system. This makes tribal water rights some of the most reliable and valuable rights in Arizona.

The 1908 *Winters v. United States* decision established that Native Americans have reserved water rights, but it wasn't until 1963 that the U.S. Supreme Court approved of a standard to measure the exact amount of water to which Indians were entitled. In *Arizona v. California* (1963), the Supreme Court held that Native American reserved water rights were to be quantified based on the number of acres of land on the reservation capable of being irrigated. This method of quantification is known as the practicably irrigable acreage (PIA) standard. In 2001, the Arizona Supreme Court became the first court in the United States to formally reject the PIA standard when it instead created a homeland standard to be used in quantifying Indian water rights in the case known as *Gila River V* (2001). Rather than allocating water to tribes based on whether their reservation is capable of being irrigated, Arizona's homeland standard quantifies Native American water rights based on the tribe's actual and proposed uses for the water, along with the parties' recommendations regarding feasibility, and the amount of water necessary to accomplish the homeland purpose of the Indian reservation.

Though tribal water rights are strong on paper, in reality, these senior water rights are of little value to tribes who have not had their rights quantified. Only in the past three decades have tribes begun to assert and develop their water rights through litigation and negotiation. In the meantime, non-Indians, often with federal assistance in the form of water project financing and dam building, have staked their claim to water that has technically already been reserved for tribes. Thus, settling Indian water rights claims often involves disrupting established non-Indian water uses. Yet the consequences to Native Americans of not having their theoretically formidable "paper" water rights transferred into "wet" water flowing to the reservation are even more profound. For example, on the Navajo reservation (located in parts of Arizona, New Mexico, and Utah), approximately 40% of the population lacks a potable domestic water supply.

In addition to concerns involving possible displacement of non-Indian water uses, developing tribal water rights also may result in environmental concerns. After Congress passed the 1902 Reclamation Act, federally financed water storage and development projects provided an incentive for non-Indians to settle the West and maximize their use of water. Understandably, non-Indians relied on this water to develop farms, businesses, and large urban populations. These massive water development projects often transported water over great distances or between basins but were built with minimal attention to environmental consequences. However, now that Native American tribes are seeking to develop and use their long-ago reserved water rights, tribes can find themselves at odds with environmental advocates who oppose new water development projects. Additionally, because water development has advanced slowly on Indian reservations, the water sources on reservation land may provide the last remaining habitat for aquatic species on the brink of extinction. The Endangered Species Act prohibits any federal agency from engaging in any activity that might jeopardize an endangered species or its habitat. Because federal agencies are involved in Native American water rights settlements, this means that tribes may be limited in the use of their water supplies by the federal Endangered Species Act or other applicable environmental protection laws.

Overview of Recent Arizona Tribal Water Settlements

Arizona now has more than a quarter century of experience in negotiating Indian water rights settlements. The key features of each of these congressionally approved settlements are discussed in Table 14-1, but only the two most recent settlements will be profiled in this chapter. Some generalizations can be

TABLE 14-1. Arizona Tribal Water Rights Settlements in Chronological Order (as of September 2005)

Name of settlement	Indian tribe	Quantity of entitlement (acre-feet annually)	Comments
Ak-Chin Water Rights Settlement Act (1978, 1984, 1992)	Ak-Chin Indian Community	85,000	-Original legislation modified due to impractical water supply plans -Was fully federally funded and required no local cost share
Southern Arizona Water Rights Settlement Act (SAWRSA) (1982, 1992, 2004)	San Xavier and Schuk Toak Districts, Tohono O'odham Nation	66,000	-Allows limited off-reservation leasing -Provides federal project water for tribe -Title III of Arizona Water Settlements Act of 2004 settles litigation concerning implementation of 1982 settlement
Salt River Pima-Maricopa Indian Community Water Rights Settlement Act (1988)	Salt River Pima-Maricopa Indian Community	122,400	-Complex multi-party water exchanges -Significant local cost sharing at insistence of federal government
Fort McDowell Indian Community Water Rights Settlement Act (1990)	Fort McDowell Indian Community	36,350	-Considerable controversy over water supply to be used for the settlement -Secretary of Interior to identify source -Allows limited off-reservation leasing
San Carlos Apache Tribe Water Rights Settlement Act (1992)	San Carlos Apache Tribe (Salt River claims only)	77,435	-Entitlement comprised primarily of CAP water -Allows limited off-reservation leasing -Portion of water source strongly opposed by Arizona's non-Indian agricultural community

Name of settlement	Indian tribe	Quantity of entitlement (acre-feet annually)	Comments
Yavapai Prescott Indian Tribe Water Rights Settlement Act (1994)	Yavapai Prescott Tribe	Up to 16,000	-Tribe has the right to pump groundwater within the boundaries of the reservation -Water contract with the City of Prescott -May divert water from nearby creek currently diverted by local irrigation district
Zuni Indian Tribe Water Rights Settlement Act (2003)	Zuni Pueblo	1,500 afa groundwater; up to 3,500 afa surface water may be purchased	-Settlement addresses Zuni Pueblo's land in Arizona, known as Zuni Heaven -$26.5 million would be used to acquire water and settle claims, implement the agreement, and restore Zuni Reservation land. Of that sum, $19.25 million will come from federal government.
Arizona Water Settlements Act (2004)	Gila River Indian Community	653,500	-Water from CAP, Gila, Salt, and Verde Rivers used for the settlement -Allows off-reservation sale or leasing, but not out of state -Sets Arizona's CAP repayment obligation at $1.65 billion

References: P.L. 102-497, 106 Stat. 3255 (1992) P.L 108-451, 118 Stat. 3478 (2004); P.L. 97-293, 96 Stat. 1274 (1982), P.L. 102-497, 106 Stat. 3255 (1992) P.L 108-451, 118 Stat. 3478 (2004); P.L. 100-512, 102 Stat. 2549 (1988); P.L. 101-602, 104 Stat. 4480 (1990); P.L. 102-575, 106 Stat. 4600 (1992); P.L. 103-434, 108 Stat. 4526 (1994); P.L. 108-34, 117 Stat. 782 (2003); P.L. 108-451, 118 Stat. 3478 (2004) made about the nature of Native American water rights settlements in Arizona. First, these settlements have been shaped by Arizona's comprehensive groundwater management code. The code is designed to eliminate groundwater overdraft in selected areas of the state, which in many instances coincide with Indian reservation boundaries. An important part of settlement negotiations involves constraints imposed on tribal groundwater pumping, so that Native American water settlements are consistent with the goals of the groundwater management code. The constraints imposed by the management code have resulted in increasingly complex settlement provisions. Secondly, most Arizona settlements provide federal project water to tribes through the Central Arizona Project (CAP). Finally, the more recent settlements explicitly authorize the tribe to lease their CAP water to users within designated areas within the state. The more recent settlements also require the tribes to create their own tribal water code to govern water use on the reservation. Keeping these general features in mind, two recent Arizona tribal water rights settlements are discussed next.

Zuni Indian Tribe Water Rights Settlement Act of 2003

The Pueblo of Zuni reservation is located in northwestern New Mexico, near the Four Corners region where the borders of Arizona, New Mexico, Utah, and Colorado meet. For centuries, members of the Zuni tribe have made pilgrimages to land known as Zuni Heaven, a marshy riparian area located near Hunt Valley, Arizona, close to the Little Colorado River. Every four years, members of the tribe have made the almost 110-mile pilgrimage by foot or horseback during the summer solstice to perform religious ceremonies. Though the tribe lost ownership of the Zuni Heaven land by an executive order in 1877, both the tribe and Congress have been working since 1984 to reacquire lands and restore the Zuni Heaven area.

Zuni Heaven was heavily damaged by construction of the Zion Dam in 1920. The outflows from the dam scoured the Little Colorado River channel, and the river's historical flood plain was abandoned. This led to destruction of the lush wetlands that supported watercress, cottonwood, and willow trees. Additionally, extensive groundwater pumping by non-Indians near the Zuni Heaven area dried up the natural artesian springs. Finally, nonnative plants invaded the area, and cattle grazing further damaged the site.

Beginning in 1984, the U.S. Congress and the tribe took steps to remedy the destruction of the Zuni religious site. The first step was to reacquire lands around the site, as well as to give the tribe permanent rights of ingress and egress to the site. Because extensive channel work was needed to facilitate the necessary volume of water delivery to irrigate the restored areas, several large ranches upstream of Zuni Heaven were acquired, and a small corridor of land along the Little Colorado River was given status as trust land held for the benefit of the tribe by the federal government. In conjunction with the Bureau of

Reclamation, the Environmental Protection Agency, and the Arizona Water Protection Fund, Congress also established the Zuni Indian Resource Development Trust Fund to provide money to restore the wetland area. The money contributed to the fund by Congress and the state of Arizona will be used to buy water rights from willing sellers so that the tribe may use the water to restore Zuni Heaven's natural wetland habitat.

After almost four years of negotiations among the tribe, the state of Arizona, local irrigation districts, two utility companies, and a number of towns in the area, Congress passed the Zuni Indian Tribe Water Rights Settlement Act in 2003 (U.S. Statutes at Large 2003). This tribal water rights settlement is unique because of its extensive focus on environmental restoration through a voluntary water rights acquisition program. Implementation of the settlement will result in restoring the Zuni Heaven religious site to the oasis it was before the destruction took place. The cornerstone of the settlement is a voluntary exchange of water rights from willing upstream sellers to the tribe so that the water may be used for irrigation to return the site to its original wetland habitat. The parties to the negotiated settlement agreed to allow the tribe to purchase up to 3,500 acre-feet of water rights from upstream sellers. The newly purchased water rights would retain their early priority date and, once transferred to the tribe, would be free from any state water law restrictions.

Another important aspect of the settlement dealt with groundwater pumping and its effect on the springs that once flowed in the Zuni Heaven area. Two large utilities signed "pumping protection agreements" that limit the utilities' pumping near the Little Colorado River. Other parties to the settlement agreed to limit pumping near the area critical to the restoration habitat to a rate below 500 gallons per minute. These agreements effectively create buffer zones around the tribe's reservation and limit groundwater use by non-Indians in that area. The parties agreed to allow the tribe to pump as much as 1,500 acre-feet of groundwater per year on the reservation to supplement the surface-water irrigation of the restored wetland area in times of drought or shortage.

For its part, the tribe waived any rights or claims it had in the ongoing Little Colorado River general stream adjudication. In the end, the negotiated settlement provides the tribe with the necessary resources to acquire land and water from willing sellers to restore an important religious site.

Arizona Water Settlements Act of 2004

The Arizona Water Settlements Act (U.S. Statues at Large 2004) is actually a comprehensive treatment of three separate settlements and provides an element of finality and certainty to many critical issues facing Arizona. (For a more detailed account of the act, see McGinnis and Alberts 2005.) The three titles of the act represent settlement of three areas of concern for the state. The first title reallocates CAP water among various water users in the state and fixes the amount of debt Arizona must repay to the federal government for construction of the Central Arizona Project. The second title authorizes the Gila River Indian Community Water Rights Settlement, and the third title amends the 1982 water rights settlement with the Tohono O'odham Nation. The act also sets aside money and CAP water for use in future Native American water rights settlements in Arizona. Because the Gila River Indian Community Water Rights Settlement represents the largest Native American water rights settlement in the United States, it will be profiled in this chapter.

Approval of the Gila River Indian Community Water Rights Settlement marks an opportunity for the Pima and Maricopa tribes living on the Gila River reservation to return to their agricultural heritage. Tribal ancestors, whose name translates as "People of the River," had farmed the Gila River Valley since at least 300 B.C., establishing complex irrigation systems to grow crops. However, non-Indian settlement and farming upstream from the reservation began to dry up the Gila River and, as a consequence, tribal farming operations declined. For the almost 20,000 tribal members living on the Gila River reservation, the water settlement means that they will have the opportunity to begin farming land that has been fallow for decades. Though the tribe currently operates a successful casino, the water settlement represents the means for the tribe to continue to develop both economically and culturally.

The settlement resolves all of the community's water rights claims in the Gila River general stream adjudication, which concerns much of the water supply of central Arizona. Under the agreement, the tribes will receive a total water package of around 653,500 acre-feet. This water entitlement includes water from the Central Arizona Project, the Salt River Project, groundwater, and a reclaimed water exchange with the cities of Mesa and Chandler. Under the innovative reclaimed water exchange agreement, the cities will exchange treated effluent for part of the tribe's CAP water, on a 5 to 4 ratio. The cities benefit by securing the rights to potable water for their citizens, and the tribe benefits by getting treated effluent to use for agricultural purposes.

Other provisions of the settlement include $200 million of funding for the tribe to rehabilitate and construct water-delivery facilities, defray operation and maintenance costs associated with CAP water delivery, implement a water quality monitoring program, and rehabilitate subsidence damage caused by groundwater pumping. The tribe also will receive protection from excessive groundwater pumping in areas south of the reservation by changes to Arizona law that will limit pumping in these areas adjacent to the reservation. Another important provision of the settlement is the opportunity for the tribe to lease some of its water to cities in the Phoenix area.

Leasing Tribal Water Rights

Opportunities for leasing tribal water often arise during tribal water right settlement negotiations. Water transactions develop when economic benefits can be realized by transferring water to new locations or uses in which it generates higher economic returns than it did under its previous use patterns. Senior water rights in strategic locations in Arizona are increasing in value. Regional economic growth in the western states exerts upward pressure on water values. Increasing urban populations generate pressure to acquire water for maintaining stream and lake levels for fishing, boating, and other water-related recreation. Private sporting groups and state agencies acquire water for these purposes. There are increasing pressures for water to fulfill environmental needs, as protecting endangered fish species in the Colorado River basin will require additional streamflows to assist in species restoration. Additional water is also needed to meet Environmental Protection Agency water quality standards for surface-water flows. In Arizona, every developer in an active management area is required to demonstrate an assured water supply that will be physically, legally, and continuously available for the next 100 years before the developer can subdivide land in the new development. These multiple demands for water generate increased interest in leasing tribal water.

The tribes' senior water rights are attractive to those seeking additional water to support population growth and to those who seek supplies that are more reliable during drought. Experience with drought has prompted many cities to actively seek water supplies that will protect them from future dry-year shortages. However, surface-water supplies are fully appropriated, and Arizona limits groundwater pumping in active management areas. The costs, both in monetary terms and in environmental terms, of developing new water supplies are high, and leasing water is often the most economical means to obtain additional supplies.

Controversies over Tribal Water Leasing

Though leasing water from tribes may be an attractive way to obtain additional water supplies, off-reservation leasing can be controversial. Some tribal leaders favor leasing their water as a way to raise capital for on-reservation economic development, especially in an era of limited federal budgets to support tribal economic development. Some non-Indian water users maintain that Native American water leasing is an economically efficient and environmentally sensitive way to obtain additional water supplies. Indeed, many Arizona Native American water rights settlements specifically provide for the leasing of tribal water to off-reservation users, and these provisions are seen as important to negotiating water rights settlements with tribes.

On the other hand, there is some opposition to off-reservation leasing from both tribal and non-Indian leaders. Some tribal leaders are concerned that leasing their water to off-reservation users could lead to the loss of their water rights, as non-Indian communities become dependent on tribal water. Others do not feel that it is appropriate to treat water as a commodity for sale. Some non-Indian leaders are opposed to tribal water leasing because they do not want to pay for water that they have historically been using for free, even though tribes have legal claims to it. Non-Indians who have been using Native American water without cost are reluctant to pay for it, unless tribes construct diversion and storage facilities or in some other way withhold tribal water. Other non-Indian leaders are concerned about the effects that tribal water leasing would have on non-Indian water users. In times of drought, non-Indian water users could have their allocations reduced or curtailed completely to fulfill the more senior Native American water rights under the prior appropriation system. Finally, western state governments usually vigorously oppose interstate tribal water leasing because it has the potential to disrupt the carefully balanced interstate apportionments, especially in the Colorado River basin. Despite the controversy, negotiated leases of tribal water can be a mutually beneficial water management arrangement. Tribes benefit from having an ongoing flow of water lease revenues, and non-Indian water users benefit from improved water supply reliability.

The Indian Non-Intercourse Act (1834) prohibited the sale or lease of tribal land and natural resources without federal government approval. Tribes have not been authorized permanently to sell their reserved water rights, but they can get congressional approval to lease their water rights to off-reservation users. A lease between the tribe and a new user would be a negotiated agreement to use a quantity of water over a specific period of time. Leases of tribal water are limited to terms of 99 or 100 years and can usually be renegotiated at the end of the lease term. Water leases are just one type of water transaction into which tribes may enter. They may also sign dry-year option agreements, in which the new water user enters into a contract with a tribe to use tribal water only under specific drought conditions. This type of arrangement provides a valuable source of water for dry years for water users, such as cities, which need highly reliable water supplies. Another option for tribes that have irrigated agriculture operations on their reservations is to make water available for other users by having the new user pay for water conservation improvements in exchange for the use of the water that is conserved.

Tribal Water Leases in Arizona

Off-reservation leasing provisions of tribal water to non-Indian users are included in many of Arizona's negotiated Native American water rights settlements. These leasing provisions generate income for tribes, offset the effect of the settlement on local non-Indian water users, and in some instances, help provide consistency with state water management goals. In most Arizona settlements, tribes may lease only their CAP entitlements, and only within designated portions of the state. Cities in the Phoenix metropolitan area have leased thousands of acre-feet of water from several Arizona tribes, thus providing a long-term water supply for growing cities. An important feature of these leases is that the water retains its Native American priority date, so that in times of shortage the water leased to non-Indian users is a reliable supply. Additionally, when a tribe leases its CAP water to a city and the city orders water pursuant to its tribal lease, it does not have to pay the capital repayment charges it would have to pay if it were ordering the water in its usual capacity as a city. Table 14-2 highlights the features of Arizona tribal water leases.

Reflections and Conclusion

Some lessons can be learned from Arizona's quarter century of experience with negotiating tribal water rights settlements. Many factors can provide the motivation for parties to negotiate and settle Native American water rights claims. One reason many settlements are achieved is because they are part of a larger litigation process, such as a general stream adjudication. Other settlements are reached because of pressure from strong political leaders. Finally, many tribal water claims are settled in Arizona because urban interests have worked toward finalizing tribal claims as a means to enhance long-term municipal supplies by gaining access to Native American water. It takes strong and persevering motivation by the important water interests in a region to bring these negotiations to a successful agreement. Moreover, the prospective settlement must include broad and tangible benefits in the form of reduced uncertainty, new water management tools, enhanced water supplies, improved ecosystems and water quality, enhanced information exchange, and money for water projects and other needs.

Another observation to keep in mind is that just because the parties finally agree on a settlement does not mean that the settlement is final. Once an agreement has been reached, it requires several layers of approval—from Congress, the state court, and the tribe's governing body. Problems may arise in implementing the agreement that may threaten the integrity of the settlement. In Arizona, the Ak-Chin settlement was amended twice to address water supply and delivery problems and to allow off-reservation leasing. The Southern Arizona Water Rights Settlement Act also had to be amended to address problems in delivering water to the Tohono O'odham Nation. These examples raise the question of whether any settlement is ever really final. Quantifying tribal rights, delivering water to the reservation, and managing those water resources once they are delivered is an ongoing process. An ideal tribal water settlement should identify ongoing dispute resolution mechanisms that will be available to address potential conflicts involved in implementing the agreement.

Finally, during seemingly endless water settlement meetings, it is important to remember that the negotiating process itself brings important benefits. Multiple parties have been brought together to work through an uneasy dialogue and have exchanged information and perspectives. Everyone engaged in the process learns more about the physical and social characteristics of the water basin in ways that would not have been possible without the settlement nego-

TABLE 14-2. Arizona Tribal Water Leases (as of September 2005)

Name of settlement	Indian tribe	Quantity of water available for leasing (acre-feet annually)	Comments
Ak-Chin Water Rights Settlement Act (1978, 1984, 1992)	Ak-Chin Indian Community	10,000	-Original settlement was amended to allow leasing in 1992. -The tribe increased their on-reservation irrigation efficiency in order to provide water for leasing. -Water was leased directly to a developer to provide an assured water supply for a planned community of 40,000 people north of Phoenix.
Southern Arizona Water Rights Settlement Act (SAWRSA) (1982, 1992, 2004)	San Xavier and Schuk Toak Districts, Tohono O'odham Nation	10,000 of groundwater; 66,000 of CAP water	-2004 amendments allow the tribe to lease its CAP entitlement within Pima, Pinal, and Maricopa counties. -The tribe may market their groundwater entitlement off-reservation, but only within the Tucson Active Management Area. -No tribal water may be marketed out of state.
Salt River Pima- Maricopa Indian Community Water Rights Settlement Act (1988)	Salt River Pima-Maricopa Indian Community	13,300	-The tribe may lease its entire CAP allocation to local cities. -The City of Phoenix began leasing water from the tribe in 2001, paying a lump sum of approximately $1,200 per acre-foot.
Fort McDowell Indian Community Water Rights Settlement Act (1990)	Fort McDowell Indian Community	18,233	-The tribe's CAP allocation may be leased only within Pinal, Pima, or Maricopa counties. -The City of Phoenix leased 4,300 acre-feet from the tribe.

Name of settlement	Indian tribe	Quantity of water available for leasing (acre-feet annually)	Comments
San Carlos Apache Tribe Water Rights Settlement Act (1992)	San Carlos Apache Tribe (Salt River claims only)	64,135	-Off-reservation leasing of tribe's CAP allocation permissible within Pima, Maricopa, Pinal, Yavapai, Graham, and Greenlee counties. -City of Scottsdale is leasing tribal water.
Arizona Water Settlements Act (2004)	Gila River Indian Community	41,000	-Allows off-reservation leasing in Maricopa, Pinal, Pima, La Paz, Yavapai, Gila, Graham, Greenlee, Santa Cruz, or Coconino Counties. -No tribal water may be marketed out of state. -Water will be leased to Phoenix-area cities for $1,500 to $1,800 per acre-foot. -The tribe may also trade part of its CAP water for a city's treated effluent water to be used for tribal irrigation operations.

*acre-feet annually

References: P.L. 95-328, 92 Stat. 409 (1978) P.L. 95-530, 98 Stat. 2698 (1984) P.L. 102-497, 106 Stat. 3255 (1992); P.L. 97-293, 96 Stat. 1274 (1982); P.L. 102-497, 106 Stat. 3255 (1992) P.L 108-451, 118 Stat. 3478 (2004); P.L. 100-512, 102 Stat. 2549 (1988); P.L. 101-602, 104 Stat. 4480 (1990); P.L. 102-575, 106 Stat. 4600 (1992); P.L. 108-451, 118 Stat. 3478 (2004) tiation process. In the end, the enduring value of a settlement agreement may be the ongoing relationships that have been forged among communities that inevitably will need to address future water management challenges in their regions on an ongoing basis.

References

Arizona v. California. 1963. 373 U.S. 546.

Australia Native Title Act. 1993. Act Compilation—C2004C00803.

Colby, Bonnie G., John E. Thorson, and Sarah Britton. 2005. *Negotiating Tribal Water Rights: Fulfilling Promises in the Arid West.* Tucson, AZ: University of Arizona Press.

Endangered Species Act. 1973. 16 U.S.C. Sec. 1531–1544.

Gila River V. 2001. In re *All Rights to Water in the Gila River*, 35 P.3d 68.

Hawaii State Water Code. 1987. Chapter 174C, Hawaii Revised Statutes.

Indian Non-Intercourse Act. 1834. U.S. Code. Vol. 25, sec. 177.

McGinnis, Mark A., and Jason P. Alberts. 2005. Southwest Water Decisions. *The Water Report* 20 (October 15): 1–15.

Reclamation Act. 1902. 32 Stat. 388, 43 U.S. Code, 391.

Treaty of Waitangi. 1840. New Zealand, February 6.

U.S. Statutes at Large. 2003. Zuni Indian Tribe Water Rights Settlement Act of 2003. Vol. 117, 782.

———. 2004. Arizona Water Settlements Act of 2004. Vol. 118, 3478.

University of Calgary. 2006. Canada's First Nations: Treaty Evolution. http://www.ucalgary.ca/applied_history/tutor/firstnations/terms.html (accessed on July 5, 2006).

Winters v. United States. 1908. 207 U.S. 564.

15

Lessons for Semiarid Regions Facing Growth and Competition for Water

Bonnie G. Colby, Katharine L. Jacobs,
and Dana R. Smith

Water policy in Arizona has many innovative features that are likely to prove valuable if adopted in other semiarid regions facing rapid population growth, high agricultural use, and water supplies that are both limited and variable. In this concluding chapter, we highlight both those aspects of Arizona water policy that are highly successful and those that have proven problematic. Our intention is to assist other regions in considering water management strategies likely to be valuable while avoiding the pitfalls encountered in Arizona.

Multiple features of Arizona's groundwater code deserve consideration by regions wishing to develop groundwater management policies. Among those emphasized in Chapter 3 are the following:

- the prohibition of new irrigation within active management areas (AMAs) with any type of water, so that water use by agricultural land that goes out of production (usually for housing developments) cannot be replaced by bringing new land under irrigation;
- a requirement that only state-licensed drillers may construct wells so that construction standards can be established and valuable data can be collected from drillers on hydrogeology and water levels; and
- the assured water supply requirements, which have markedly reduced the use of groundwater for new urban growth.

Other important contributions include

- the development of new approaches to water conservation;

- the development of a sophisticated understanding of water-use patterns that has resulted from data collected from all large water users through annual reports; and
- the grandfathered rights system that protected existing users when the Groundwater Management Act was first adopted, thereby ensuring their support for the significant legal changes involved.

Other innovations are discussed below.

Arizona's careful attention to Colorado River politics and policymaking illustrates the importance of integrating water management across regional and national layers of regulation. The various policies that encourage underground storage and aquifer replenishment also represent an important innovation for arid regions, especially in the context of increasing uncertainty about changing climate conditions. Arizona has successfully incorporated effluent as a critical resource for water managers in arid regions. Moreover, the establishment of a system of groundwater pumping permits and the move from little regulation of pumping to a focus on long-term management of groundwater use in selected areas of the state is a major accomplishment.

There are, however, a few significant problems with Arizona's current legal framework. The scientific recognition of the connectivity between groundwater and surface water has not been integrated in Arizona water law, which remains bifurcated. Litigation over wells near streams in the adjudication courts has the potential of causing widespread disruption, to either the groundwater or surface-water users. Despite a quarter century of active groundwater policymaking, Arizona is still experiencing overdraft throughout the state. Given continued rapid growth in rural and urban areas and limited new water sources, all water-using sectors are under pressure to become more efficient. The legal framework for water transfers could use further refinement to bring water supplies more cost-effectively to new development.

In Chapter 2, August and Gammage remind us that human societies need only land, air, sunshine, and water. Of these four, water alone is easily transported, and so the ability to capture, store, and move water defines the history of Arizona and other arid regions. Designing policies to govern access to water has proved complex. Sometimes water is viewed as a private-use good (for example, when it is beneath private land and landowners have the right to pump and use it), and sometimes it is something closer to a common-use good (for example, when it is in a free-flowing river available for recreation). This sorting out of the private-good vs. public-good nature of water has involved complex institutions and laws. Arizona's history illustrates the challenges of shaping a harsh and arid environment to make it habitable for large numbers of people. The population influx into Phoenix and the Salt River Valley depended on political, legal, and financial ingenuity to bring reliable water supplies to fertile desert soils and to begin the infrastructure necessary for urban growth. Arizona water history also highlights the shift over time from accommodating large agricultural acreage to the hydropolitics of accommodating urban growth, recreation, and the environment.

The Central Arizona Project (CAP) was first envisioned as an agricultural rescue project in the face of dwindling local water supplies, but it is now a lifeline to Arizona's growing cities and an important component of tribal water settlements. The CAP illustrates the virtues of building flexibility into water projects that may end up serving different purposes than originally intended. Arizona's tribes, cities, and farmers quickly learned that they could play a major role in the distribution of the benefits of the CAP if they developed constructive and open relationships with one another and a unified approach to negotiating with the federal government.

In Arizona, water is the "consummate shared enterprise," shared across layers of federal, tribal, state, and local jurisdictions and across urban, rural, and tribal constituencies. Arizona has created institutions to obtain and protect its supplies, has built vast public plumbing systems with public monies, and has crafted laws, contracts, decrees, and decisions to give order to water management. The state celebrates as its greatest statespersons those who have focused on the collective water endeavor.

Arizona's water supplies come from groundwater formations lying within the state and surface-water and groundwater inflow from adjacent states and Mexico (described in Chapter 4). Arizona annually consumes more water than is available from its renewable sources. This imbalance is buffered by groundwater aquifers capable of storing vast quantities of water from past eras, recent precipitation, and artificial recharge. Arizona's aquifers constitute its largest reservoir of freshwater, and groundwater is sustaining much of the state's population. The surface-water supplies of Arizona are monitored by a network of streamflow gages and flood warning or special-purpose gages operated by a variety of public agencies.

As discussed in Chapter 4, consistent long-term monitoring of aquifer conditions is critical to sustainable management of aquifers. In contrast to surface water, the systematic monitoring of groundwater availability is far more challenging. Changes in groundwater discharge to streams and springs can be a useful method of monitoring changes in groundwater storage, where the streams and springs are the primary modes of groundwater discharge. Streamflow gaging methods can be used to monitor variations in winter base flow, which is the groundwater contribution to streamflow after the transient effects of runoff events and riparian vegetation discharge during the growing season have dissipated.

Chapter 5 points out that Arizona's major renewable water supply, the Colorado River, is affected by climate conditions occurring months earlier and at distant locations in upstream states. More than 70% of this river's annual runoff is from winter snowpack in high-elevation areas outside Arizona. The climate of this distant region is of paramount importance to water users in Arizona.

Whereas the Colorado River reservoir system stores several times the annual mean inflow, systemwide water uses approximately equal mean inflows, so reservoir deficits accumulate rapidly during multiyear drought. These deficits in stored water are not rapidly compensated by years with average precipitation, leading to concerns about surface-water shortages during long-term drought. However, groundwater reservoirs in much of Arizona are large enough that short-term climate variability does not have an immediate effect on groundwater users.

Like many regions, Arizona has climatically unrelated precipitation seasons: summer monsoon and winter storms. As described in Chapter 5, this multi-peaked precipitation seasonality presents challenges for water managers, who must store winter precipitation for summer peak demand while also balancing seasonal and interannual drought and flood control. Peak water use occurs in summer, accompanied by intense heat, high summer evaporation rates, and high demand for water to irrigate crops and landscape. Winter precipitation stored as snow is released gradually and is subject to lower evaporation rates. Summer precipitation contributes to reservoir and groundwater recharge, but it falls in spatially discontinuous downpours and is subject to extremely high evaporation rates. High interannual precipitation variability adds to the challenge of assuring water supply reliability for cities and farms.

Climate change models predict higher minimum and maximum temperatures, increased precipitation intensity, enhanced rates of evaporation, and increased precipitation variability for Arizona. Enhanced evaporation rates, combined with earlier snowmelt in the regions that provide most of Arizona's surface water, likely will increase water supply vulnerability. Moreover, global warming is likely to increase the risk of extreme droughts and floods.

Arid and semiarid regions worldwide are subject to periodic drought. In response to recent severe drought conditions in the state, multiple public agencies and stakeholders collaborated to produce Arizona's first drought plan. The plan seeks to limit drought impacts through specified drought responses across four stages of drought severity. Response activities are triggered by drought status reports submitted by a multiagency monitoring committee that assesses drought severity through a science-based system of drought indicators. Short- and long-term drought status is currently calculated separately for each of the seven Arizona climate divisions, using a combination of drought indicators.

The greatest challenges for drought monitoring are improving the density and variety of indicator measurements and effectively communicating drought status when it appears inconsistent with observed conditions, such as during seasonally heavy precipitation. Arizona's current distribution of precipitation observations is heavily weighted toward populated areas, with relatively little coverage in rural or wilderness areas. A supplementary volunteer observer network is being implemented to monitor precipitation and other drought-related variables, bringing the benefits of both citizen participation and improved density of observations.

Although improved technical information is essential, climate forecasts often are conveyed in ways not easily grasped by nonexpert users. Online forecast evaluation tools have been developed and are being applied in Arizona and elsewhere. Outreach efforts by forecast science agencies are proving among the best means available to develop well-informed forecast users.

Lack of institutional flexibility to respond to new sources of knowledge can be another limiting factor in responding to drought and climate change. Water managers typically are constrained by operating procedures and may not have the flexibility to respond to new information even when the benefits of a different operating regime are clear. This is a policy challenge faced in Arizona and many other regions, and solutions must include dialogue among climate scientists, water managers, and policymakers.

Voluntary water transactions between economic sectors and between locations of use (discussed in Chapter 6) are an important water management tool for achieving cost-effective response to drought and for supplying new development. They are a valuable tool, but transfers can create unintended social and environmental problems and may require complex negotiations among multiple interests. Transactions can be both a stimulus for conflict and a means of accommodating new demands and resolving conflict. Rural communities consider themselves especially at risk from transfers. In Arizona, "water farm" purchases in the late 1980s triggered intense controversy because of the large scale of the land purchases and the potential economic, social, and environmental costs. Water farming in western Arizona became possible because the CAP canal provides a means of transporting the "farmed" water to Phoenix during dry years if space is available, but farming was subsequently restricted by limitations on cross-watershed groundwater transfers.

Most of Arizona's surface water is delivered by large water districts such as the Salt River Project and irrigation districts located in western Arizona that use Colorado River water. The use of this water has shifted over time within each district, but surface water generally has not been transferred out of these districts, and changes in the location and purpose of use are handled as matters internal to the district.

Another important source of water transactions in Arizona has been effluent transfers. Pima County, for instance, sells treated sewage effluent to farmers, and the city of Tucson requires all new golf courses to irrigate with effluent. Treated effluent from Phoenix area municipalities is sold to a nearby nuclear power station for use in cooling the nuclear plant's reactors. Effluent transfers have also been used as part of tribal water settlement packages. Arizona tribal governments have been involved in water transactions both as acquirers of water through water settlement processes and as lessors of water to others.

The Arizona Water Banking Authority (AWBA) plays an important role in Arizona's plan for using water transfers to prepare for drought. Though the water bank doesn't facilitate water marketing in the traditional sense of buying and selling water, it does facilitate water transfers in the sense that it substitutes the use of one type of water for another in times of drought or shortage.

Dry-year only water transfers have not been implemented in Arizona but are actively under consideration. If a shortage were declared in the lower Colorado River basin, CAP water users would be among the first to experience reduced deliveries. Recent proposals to address this risk point to irrigation forbearance in Arizona and the lower Colorado River basin as a drought coping mechanism. The proposed dry-year fallowing strategies are triggered by reservoir levels, such that when Lake Mead is drawn down to specific elevations, conservation through predictable, small-scale reductions in use by lower basin users is activated. Such transactions will be temporary and will leave irrigated farming intact in normal water supply years.

Preparing for and responding to drought is not only a concern for the human population, but it is also an important issue for the natural environment as a whole. As Chapter 7 relates, Arizona is a treasure trove of biological diversity, the most diverse state in the United States without a coastline. This diversity is due to Arizona's unique location at the intersection of two ecologically rich and distinct desert ecosystems (to the west and east) and two large mountain ecosystems (to the north and south). Riparian habitat is essential to the many bird species that use Arizona in migration between North America and tropical Central and South America, and loss of habitat for these species is an international concern. Streamflows are central to this rich diversity of life, but the majority of Arizona's free-flowing stream miles have been lost or altered.

The loser in competition over water in Arizona is the natural environment. Dams and groundwater pumping have severely disrupted streamflow regimes. Groundwater pumping creates cones of depression that can dry up entire river reaches. Even though modern hydrology teaches that groundwater and surface water are intimately connected, Arizona water law treats them separately, and policies fail to consider the effect of groundwater pumping on streamflows. Land development, overgrazing, and fire suppression contribute to flash floods, erosion, and invasion of nonnative species such as tamarisk.

Arizona water policy has not yet given adequate recognition to the connection between human water uses and environmental impacts or to the benefits provided by healthy watersheds. Among these benefits are water supplies, flood control, water filtration, and recreation. As described in Chapter 7, there are serious efforts under way in several watersheds to address water-related concerns regarding the natural environment. The multijurisdictional effort to mitigate the effects of reservoir operations on threatened and endangered species along the lower Colorado River has committed significant resources to species and habitat restoration over the next decades. A diverse group of stakeholders has devised recommendations to resolve controversies over operating the Yuma Desalting Plant in Arizona and the consequent impacts to the Cienega de Santa Clara, a 40,000-acre wetland in Mexico essential to many bird species of the Americas. Another option discussed in Chapter 6 is an innovative conservation before shortage strategy that has been proposed to address both water supply and environmental concerns through dry-year leasing of irrigation water.

Chapter 8 discusses efforts to protect a regionally vital riparian habitat. The Upper San Pedro Partnership (USPP), a consortium of federal, state, county, and local public agencies and environmental groups has received substantial federal funding to address the progressive decline of the riparian habitat of the San Pedro River. The USPP hopes to achieve widespread local water conservation, recharge of municipal effluent, and capture of storm-water runoff. However, local conservation projects alone cannot compensate for ongoing overdraft of the aquifer. The pessimistic outlook for this rare desert ecosystem rests squarely on the failure of Arizona to integrate its groundwater and surface-water polices and to prevent groundwater pumping from reducing surface-water flows. Elsewhere in Arizona, there are numerous examples of other river ecosystems threatened by the effects of groundwater pumping on streamflows.

Population growth worldwide is concentrated in semiarid areas, so much can be learned from Arizona's experience with water management and its ecological implications. Additional authorities would empower counties and jurisdictions to connect land use policy with water supply planning. However, state and local agencies are reluctant to use the tools they already have at their disposal to regulate land use with water and environmental concerns in mind. Primary lessons from Arizona's experience include the following:

- protect ecologically important lands, wetlands, and rivers before population pressure makes it too expensive or politically difficult;
- use landowner incentives to spur conservation programs;
- when planning to protect species and habitat, involve nearby landowners and water users in crafting solutions in which they will feel "ownership";
- provide for water supplies to support important habitats during drought conditions; and
- regulatory hammers like the federal Endangered Species Act are often necessary to bring diverse local interests together.

Policymakers in other regions would do well to integrate groundwater and surface-water law and management, avoiding some of the difficulties currently encountered in Arizona. Finally, it is important to educate the public about the connection between a healthy environment and the corresponding tangible benefits to people and communities, thus encouraging willingness to protect water supplies, property values, and quality of life.

Another aspect of environmental protection in Arizona is its water quality programs. When the U.S. Congress passed the Clean Water Act in 1972, it provided a regulatory framework to ensure that surface water was clean enough to drink, good enough for recreation, and safe for fish and wildlife. As Chapter 9 explains, before the Clean Water Act, Arizona's water quality programs focused primarily on public health in drinking water and wastewater treatment. Little data existed to evaluate water quality, and Arizona had no comprehensive program to monitor its surface-water or groundwater quality. When Arizona completed its first assessment of surface waters in 1976, the primary problems revolved around wastewater. In the 20 years since, the state has faced a complex array of water quality concerns.

Salinity, perhaps Arizona's largest water quality issue, is not well addressed by any one regulatory program. As salinity levels increase above 500 milligrams per liter, people find the taste objectionable and do not drink water from the tap. Higher levels of salinity harm crop yields, as it affects water uptake by the plants and will build up in the soil, resulting in soil toxicity. Flushing salt from soil uses a substantial amount of water, which runs counter to the need to reduce water use. Furthermore, there are increased costs to industry and to households, as salinity causes increased corrosion and early failure of pipes and appliances. When saline Colorado River water is recycled through municipal water and wastewater systems, salinity levels further increase. A coalition of water users and public agencies is evaluating salinity threats affecting central Arizona and seeking reliable and cost-effective alternatives to deal with the more than 1 million tons of salt that are added to the region each year.

Overall, Arizona has made substantial gains in developing regulatory programs and setting water quality and performance standards for water and wastewater facilities. The water quality problems of the 1970s, such as pathogens in wastewater, pesticide concentrations, and disposal of industrial solvents, have largely been solved. New concerns focus on perchlorate, newer pathogens, and endocrine-disrupting compounds. These are the subject of considerable attention because of potential adverse effects on human and ecosystem health. Arizona's water quality policies combine traditional permitting approaches (numeric limits and established water quality standards) and less traditional performance-based approaches. Nonregulatory programs, such as those for nonpoint source pollution and for salinity, rely on performance-based best management practices. The water quality policy framework involves federal, tribal, state, and municipal water managers and seeks to manage the risks to humans and to fish and wildlife and the associated costs to mitigate these risks.

As Chapter 10 observes, Arizona provides a valuable example of a water management setting in which agriculture is the primary water user. Although crop irrigation accounts for 80% of Arizona's freshwater withdrawals, agriculture faces growing competition for water from other sectors. Its use defines the remaining supplies available for all other purposes. This phenomenon is found in arid regions worldwide where irrigated crops are produced. Arizona's growing demand for water will be met primarily by shifting water from agriculture to other uses. Small changes in irrigation withdrawals translate into large percentage changes in water available for other uses.

Overall agricultural water use depends on scale effects (total acreage), crop-mix effects (which crops are grown), location effects (where they are grown), and technology effects. Water use by Arizona agriculture depends on farm production decisions, which are heavily influenced by federal farm programs. U.S. farm policy includes a complex array of programs intended to support farm income or reduce agricultural pollution. Studies of the effects of farm programs found important scale effects, suggesting that the programs of the 1980s led to significant additional acreage planted. However, Chapter 10 points out that it is difficult to move from acreage effects to overall effects on water use. Federal programs change relative profitability among crops and can encourage shifts to either more or less water-intensive crops. Moreover, the cost to farmers of surface water provided under some federal water projects is so low that water demand is unlikely to be influenced by changes in crop profitability.

Disputes in the World Trade Organization (WTO) call into question the entire structure of U.S. farm policy and could significantly affect water use in Arizona agriculture. The WTO dispute may also cause conservation programs to play a more prominent role in the 2007 farm bill. Environmental groups have already begun to press for a shift in emphasis from traditional farm payments to conservation payments. Because agriculture accounts for such a large share of Arizona's overall water consumption, changes in national agricultural policy have profound implications for the task of balancing water supply and demand.

Moving from agricultural to urban demands, Chapter 11 focuses on Arizona's municipal water supply and management techniques. The Groundwater Management Act (GMA) established a regulatory water management and conservation program that currently applies within five active management areas (AMAs), which are centered mainly in the urban areas of the state. The GMA includes four broad areas of state authority and tools to regulate municipal water management: groundwater withdrawal authorities, water measurement and reporting, demand management programs, and supply management programs.

Chapter 11 points out that an important feature of the AMAs is the flexibility to legislatively establish unique management objectives for each area that relate to their particular water supply and demand situations. The three safe-yield AMAs face a different array of challenges than the Pinal and Santa Cruz AMAs. The 1999 determination that the Prescott AMA was no longer at safe yield was a highly contentious issue and generated a rush of development applications, a legislative effort to halt them, and preparation of an alternative groundwater model to dispute the findings that the AMA was not at safe yield. The Santa Cruz AMA has the unique goal of preventing local water table declines and needs to facilitate the conjunctive management of surface water, effluent, and groundwater. The other safe-yield AMAs require only basinwide accounting and management, but the Santa Cruz AMA's programs require water tables to be stabilized throughout the AMA. In the Pinal AMA, goals include preserving water supplies for future municipal use as well as protecting the agricultural economy, so that new subdivisions are allocated a relatively large quantity of allowable groundwater use. However, the Pinal AMA is now experiencing rapid population growth, and some local water interests are seeking to reduce the groundwater allowance for new development so that renewable or imported supplies must be acquired and that future groundwater overdraft will not be exacerbated.

The state of Arizona and federal agencies invest significant resources in tracking groundwater levels, monitoring surface-water flows, measuring snowpack in the watersheds, and monitoring land subsidence. Water-level information is used for basin characterizations, as input for groundwater modeling efforts, and for administering the assured and adequate water supply programs and well impact regulations. The Arizona Department of Water Resources monitors land subsidence, earth fissure zones, and changes in water storage. Numerical computer models of the aquifers in the AMAs were developed initially to improve understanding of hydrologic conditions and available supplies. Now, these models are being used for Assured Water Supply Rule implementation and to facilitate regional planning.

Arizona innovations to ensure sustainable water supplies sufficient for continued urban growth include the following:

- adoption of mandatory conservation programs and investments in use of renewable supplies;
- the assured water supply provisions of the Groundwater Management Act discussed in Chapters 3 and 11;
- recharge and recovery programs, along with the water banking and replenishment programs discussed in Chapter 13;
- water rights settlements with Native American communities discussed in Chapter 14; and
- water supply, drought, and conservation planning by water providers throughout the state.

Arizona is in a strong position to address linkages between water and growth within the AMAs where new development is subject to the assured water supply requirements. However, as discussed in Chapter 12, in the rural non-AMA areas, Arizona has among the weaker programs in the country.

Adoption elsewhere of Arizona's assured water supply approach will be feasible only where alternative water supplies are available to meet the requirements. However, requiring investments in renewable supplies for new growth is much more likely to be accepted than is halting growth altogether. Placing the authority for requiring adequate water supplies at a level of government higher than that responsible for approving new growth is critical to a successful program.

The sustainability of urban growth in central Arizona is an important issue for Arizona's future. Central Arizona has been one of the fastest growing areas of the country since the 1970s and is projected to continue growing rapidly well into the future. Huge investments have been made in water management, particularly in the development of renewable supplies. Arizona, as it grows, will have to continue to address challenges to the availability and management of long-term supplies.

The architects of the 1980 Groundwater Management Act believed that water supplies for new growth would come in part from urbanization of previously irrigated agricultural lands. However, new development is generally not allowed to use mined groundwater, so there is no particular incentive to develop over irrigated land and retire the grandfathered irrigation rights. Urban development primarily relies on renewable or imported water supplies to meet the requirements of Arizona's assured water supply program. The assured water supply requirement for renewable water supplies as a condition of new municipal growth is arguably the most stringent program linking available water supplies to urban growth in the United States. Water-use efficiency is also an important component of Arizona's strategy for achieving safe yield and ensuring a sustainable water supply, and it may become more important in the future as supply availability becomes more limited.

From a water management, supply, and data availability perspective, there are two Arizonas: the central metropolitan areas and irrigation districts, with multiple sources of water, including Colorado River supplies, and the rest of the state, which has limited water supply alternatives and planning information. Outside the AMAs, Chapter 12 notes, the regulations of the Groundwater Management Act have minimal impact, and there is less information about water availability, less water supply planning, and fewer alternative water supplies. The effects of drought are felt most strongly in these areas, and the implications of continued growth are of great concern.

Arizona's Rural Watershed Initiative (1999) assists watershed groups outside AMAs to develop information to support water resource planning in their areas, focusing on locally initiated efforts to manage water supplies. This approach empowers local citizens to explore solutions that match the specific problems in their own regions. Several rural partnerships in Arizona are involved with water management or planning, including the Upper San Pedro Partnership, discussed in Chapters 7 and 8. However, the accomplishments of local watershed groups are limited by lack of paid staff, inadequate hydrologic data, little incentive or ability by diverse water interests to forge regional cooperative efforts, and a strong private property rights sentiment suspicious of regulatory approaches. The Arizona Drought Preparedness Plan (2004) emphasizes the importance of drought planning within rural communities and depends on local area impact assessment groups to assist with monitoring drought conditions. These groups, composed of local governments and resource managers, will assist with assessing local drought vulnerabilities and developing mitigation strategies.

Although the bulk of efforts to promote water conservation in Arizona have occurred within AMAs, there are numerous conservation opportunities in the rural non-AMA portions of the state. These opportunities include system improvements to reduce leaks; expanded metering of deliveries; producing price-related conservation signals; writing ordinances limiting high-water-use landscaping; and encouraging water harvesting, conservation-oriented hookup policies, and stringent building code provisions.

Implementing a more rigorous water adequacy program and enforcing subdivision laws would assist non-AMA areas in addressing growth. Establishing new AMAs with management goals tailored to local conditions is an option. These AMAs could implement many of the existing AMA programs such as metering, annual reporting, groundwater pumping limits, and mandatory conservation. Although support for new AMAs in rural Arizona is limited, some residents of these areas are concerned about effects of growth on their quality of life and their water supplies. Nevertheless, Arizona's outlying areas eschew a "one size fits all" regulatory structure and seek local solutions. Only time will tell whether local solutions can be effective in the face of growth pressures and limited information, water, and money.

As an arid region with high year-to-year variability in surface-water supplies, Arizona has given considerable effort to groundwater recharge and recovery as a management tool. The state's groundwater storage and recovery programs (described in Chapter 13) allow for the replenishment of groundwater with surface water or effluent and provide a flexible, cost-effective approach to renewable water supply use. The Arizona Department of Water Resources administers storage and recovery activities through a system of permits and accounts. Permits are required at all stages of the recharge and recovery process. More than 4 million acre-feet of water have been recharged in Arizona, and the amount of water in storage is growing.

Underground storage and recovery can reduce treatment costs. Municipal use of surface water typically involves treating the water at a centralized treatment facility before delivery into the potable water system. Some water suppliers find storage and recovery of CAP water an attractive alternative to operation of a treatment plant at a centralized point of delivery. Tucson Water, for instance, relies on recharge of CAP water and then recovery through a series of groundwater wells to meet system demands. This process makes its system less vulnerable to outages, an advantage given its location at the end of several hundred miles of conveyance infrastructure and the absence of surface-water storage reservoirs. To the extent that this approach continues to meet water quality goals, the system also is less vulnerable to the problems of operating a large treatment plant.

Regional recharge programs can address the problems of communities located further from surface-water canals. In central Arizona, not all water providers with legal entitlements to use CAP water are located near the delivery canals. This lack of proximity could require expensive infrastructure to deliver CAP water to the suppliers' service areas. However, recharge and recovery in large regional aquifers allows the surface water to be stored underground close to the canal and an equivalent amount to be extracted at a more cost-effective location. If a water provider or developer is a member of the Central

Arizona Groundwater Replenishment District (CAGRD) and certain conditions are met, groundwater can be used to meet the needs of municipal growth. The CAGRD must replenish its members' "excess groundwater use" (the use in excess of allowable amounts under the rules). The replenishment may occur at any location within the AMA in which the groundwater is pumped. To date, surplus CAP water has been used for replenishment, although the CAGRD must identify a firm, long-term source of water supply.

Like the CAGRD, the Arizona Water Banking Authority (AWBA) is a legislatively created government entity that uses Arizona's storage and recovery program to meet important water policy and management objectives. The AWBA relies on multiple sources of funding and stores water on behalf of cities along the Colorado River and in the central part of Arizona to ensure that their future water deliveries are secure in the context of shortages on the Colorado River. This storage process is also called "firming" the supply. During future dry periods, the Colorado River cities will take water from the Colorado River that otherwise would have flowed into central Arizona. The central Arizona users will then recover and use water that was stored underground. This process is also how the AWBA accomplishes interstate banking, particularly on behalf of Nevada. The AWBA stored more than 2.2 million acre-feet of water in 2004.

Although most storage and recovery in Arizona involves the three-county CAP service area, water storage also occurs elsewhere to meet specific needs. In the Upper San Pedro watershed, local efforts to recharge water aim to reduce groundwater overdraft and negative impacts on riparian habitat. A large facility to store CAP water has been constructed by a private company west of the Phoenix AMA, and another private company operates a recharge project in western Arizona closer to the Colorado River. This latter facility is permitted to store 100,000 acre-feet of water annually. This water may be transported into central Arizona through the CAP canal. As other parts of Arizona actively seek more (and more reliable) supplies, additional storage and recovery projects are likely.

As Chapter 14 explains, tribal or aboriginal water rights are important to all regional water users because water settlements can play a crucial role in shaping the future of both tribal and non-Indian communities. The pressure to resolve tribal water claims in Arizona has resulted from the uncertainties that these unquantified claims create for regional water management and planning. As described in Chapter 14, provisions for off-reservation leasing of tribal water to non-Indian users are included in many of Arizona's negotiated Native American water rights settlements. These leasing provisions generate income for tribes, offset the effects of the settlement on local non-Indian water users, and help provide consistency with state water management goals. An important feature of these leases is that the water retains its original priority date, so that in times of shortage the water leased to non-Indian users is a reliable supply.

One reason so many Native American water rights settlements have been achieved in Arizona is because settlements are viewed as an improvement over continuing to participate in a larger litigation process, such as a general stream adjudication. Settlements also require leadership from strong political leaders. Powerful urban interests work toward finalizing tribal claims to gain access to Indian water. It takes strong and persevering motivation by the important water interests in a region to bring these negotiations to a successful agreement. Settlements must include broad and tangible benefits in the form of reduced uncertainty, new water management tools, enhanced water supplies, improved ecosystems and water quality, enhanced information exchange, and money for water projects and other needs.

Arizona's experience with tribal water settlements illustrates that just because the parties finally agree on a settlement does not mean that the settlement is final. In the United States, settlements require several layers of approval—from the national Congress, the state court, and the tribe's governing body. Problems can arise in implementing the agreement that may threaten the integrity of the settlement. For example, several of Arizona's settlements have been amended to address water supply and delivery problems. Quantifying tribal rights, delivering water to the reservation, and managing those water resources once they are delivered are ongoing processes. Consequently, settlements need to identify ongoing dispute resolution mechanisms to address potential conflicts involved in implementing the agreement. In the end, the multistakeholder negotiating process itself brings important benefits. The enduring value of a settlement agreement may be the ongoing relationships that have been forged among communities that inevitably will need to address future water management challenges in their regions on an ongoing basis.

In closing, we briefly return to the seven cross-cutting issues introduced in Chapter 1. The first issue, growing demand and finite supplies, is a challenge worldwide, arising wherever growing populations, irrigated agriculture, industry, and environmental water needs run headlong into limited regional water supplies. In past eras, this problem was addressed by developing or importing new water supplies. However, Arizona's current conservation, assured supply and recharge and recovery policies illustrate an approach necessary when the era of large developed water projects is over.

Arizona water managers have confronted many implications of the second issue, changing social values. Arizona has relatively successfully addressed injustices involving Native Americans, whose water needs were overlooked for almost a century. With respect to providing for environmental and recreational streamflows and lake levels, Arizona's record is more mixed, with progress hindered by the disconnect in state law between groundwater and surface-water regulations. Addressing the third issue of safe yield versus sustainability also continues to prove elusive as the groundwater management goals of basinwide safe yield do not cover localized effects of groundwater pumping on habitat and surface flows.

The fourth issue, connecting land use and water supply planning, is a politically divisive issue whenever and wherever it arises. Arizona has tackled this issue directly within its active management areas through the assured water supply program. However, regions not included within active management areas are facing rapid population growth, yet are not included in the assured water supply program rules. Progress on the fifth issue, connecting water's value and users' costs, has been gradual and mixed. Some cities have adopted water rate structures designed to encourage conservation through pricing signals, but rate-setting policies focus on delivery cost recovery and make it difficult to charge customers a scarcity value for the raw water supply. Moreover, many agricultural water users enjoy below-cost access to surface water and to electricity for groundwater pumping and water conveyance. Thus, many agricultural water users face water-pricing systems that do not link water's value with its costs.

The sixth issue, climate change and supply variability, raises the question confronted worldwide: how do water managers and policymakers incorporate sophisticated new scientific information into their own operational and policy decisions? The need in Arizona is crucial, given the state's surface-water dependence on snowpack in latitudes vulnerable to increased temperatures. To address this issue, a valuable dialogue is under way among climate scientists and water managers. The seventh issue, framing issues and making choices, focuses on public input, consultation with stakeholders, and the ways in which resource managers from federal, tribal, state, and municipal governments interact and make choices. Arizona has successfully crafted specialized water districts and agency task forces to address its changing decisionmaking needs.

Across many decades and complex issues, we note that Arizona's water managers have an excellent track record for working together and developing innovative programs to address the state's water management challenges. Recent examples include establishing the recharge and recovery programs to store Central Arizona Project water to offset expected shortages in Colorado River supplies, negotiating tribal water settlements, and discussions with other Colorado River basin states to develop shortage-sharing criteria. Nevertheless, numerous ongoing challenges remain:

- working throughout the state and the Colorado River basin to secure supplies for urban growth;
- forging partnerships to address both water quantity and water quality needs;
- remedying the disconnect between surface-water and groundwater policy;
- facilitating an appropriate balance between direct delivery and groundwater pumping and replenishment;
- incorporating understanding of climatic variability and future global climate change into water management;
- looking beyond the legislative safe-yield goals to longer term sustainability; and finally,
- addressing environmental quality and ecosystem health as they relate to water management.

The continued rapid growth of Arizona's urban areas requires that it build on past water management successes and further invest in infrastructure and water management capacity to ensure long-term sustainability. Many aspects of Arizona water policy will prove valuable if adopted in other regions struggling with similar issues, and we trust that the difficulties and policy gaps we have experienced will prove instructive to other regions as well.

References

Arizona Drought Preparedness Plan. 2004. Governor's Drought Task Force, October.
Arizona Rural Watershed Initiative. 1999.
Clean Water Act of 1972. U.S. Code. Vol. 33, sec. 1251 et seq.
Groundwater Management Act. 1980. Arizona Revised Statutes, Title 45.

Index

For Product Safety Concerns and Information please contact our EU
representative GPSR@taylorandfrancis.com Taylor & Francis Verlag GmbH,
Kaufingerstraße 24, 80331 München, Germany

Printed and bound by CPI Group (UK) Ltd, Croydon, CR0 4YY
12/05/2025
01867467-0001